GROWING
Sustainable
TOGETHER

PRACTICAL RESOURCES
FOR RAISING KIND, ENGAGED,
RESILIENT CHILDREN

SHANNON BRESCHER SHEA

North Atlantic Books
Berkeley, California

Published by   Cover art © gettyimages.com/invincible_bulldog
North Atlantic Books   Cover design by Jasmine Hromjak
Berkeley, California   Book design by Happenstance Type-O-Rama

Printed in the United States of America

Growing Sustainable Together: Practical Resources for Raising Kind, Engaged, Resilient Children is sponsored and published by the Society for the Study of Native Arts and Sciences (dba North Atlantic Books), an educational nonprofit based in Berkeley, California, that collaborates with partners to develop cross-cultural perspectives, nurture holistic views of art, science, the humanities, and healing, and seed personal and global transformation by publishing work on the relationship of body, spirit, and nature.

North Atlantic Books' publications are available through most bookstores. For further information, visit our website at www.northatlanticbooks.com or call 800-733-3000.

Library of Congress Cataloging-in-Publication Data
Names: Shea, Shannon Brescher, 1983- author.
Title: Growing sustainable together : practical resources for raising kind,
   engaged, resilient children / Shannon Brescher Shea.
Description: Berkeley : North Atlantic Books, 2020. | Includes
   bibliographical references and index. | Summary: "Drawing from
   cutting-edge social science research, parent interviews, and
   experiential wisdom, science writer and parenting blogger Shannon
   Brescher Shea shows how green living and great parenting go hand in hand
   to teach kids kindness, compassion, resilience, and grit...all while
   giving them the lifelong tools they need to be successful, engaged, and
   independent"— Provided by publisher.
Identifiers: LCCN 2020003928 (print) | LCCN 2020003929 (ebook) | ISBN
   9781623174712 (trade paperback) | ISBN 9781623174729 (ebook)
Subjects: LCSH: Child rearing. | Resilience (Personality trait) in
   children. | Kindness.
Classification: LCC HQ769 .S494 2020 (print) | LCC HQ769 (ebook) | DDC
   649/.1—dc23
LC record available at https://lccn.loc.gov/2020003928
LC ebook record available at https://lccn.loc.gov/2020003929

1 2 3 4 5 6 7 8 9 KPC 24 23 22 21 20

To Dylan
and Ethan

CONTENTS

INTRODUCTION

Taking stock of my backyard garden, I wondered what happened to my dreams of an oasis brimming with fresh produce. The leaves on the zucchini plant were shades of gray. Some of their stalks were broken, the result of large and small feet stomping on them. Several of the tomato plant's branches were yellow, while others' ragged ends bore the toothmarks of a local deer. The weeds ran rampant. While the mess was frustrating, its wildness did have a vibrant beauty. In fact, it reminded me of the challenges and rewards of being a parent.

I glanced over to the corner of the garden at Ethan, my younger son. He's three now but has been "helping" me in the garden since he was one. He had dirt in his hair, all over his shirt, and probably up his nose. At least it wasn't in his mouth.

Under a mess of foliage, I spotted red on a pepper. Peering under the leaves, I saw some insect had colonized it.

"Ick," I muttered, twisting off the offending vegetable.

"What did you say?" asked Dylan, my older son. He's gone from swinging around his little blue metal watering can to commanding the actual hose these days at six years old.

"I found a pepper, but it's probably got a bug in it. So we can't eat it." I frowned. Looking up at him, I smiled a bit. "That would be pretty gross, wouldn't it?"

He eyed the pepper. "Yeah."

Looking around the garden, he noticed another splash of red. "Look, a red tomato! I'm gonna eat it," he exclaimed as his eyes went wide and his mouth expanded into a smile. He ran over and plucked off the tomato.

I started to tell him that he couldn't eat it until I washed it. Then I paused. I didn't want to ruin the moment. The fact that he helped grow it sparked his enthusiasm. So many values were wrapped up in this tomato: hard work in preparing the garden, precision in planting seeds, patience in waiting for those seeds to sprout, and responsibility in watering. He popped the tomato in his mouth and chewed. "Mmmm. I love our tomatoes."

Watching his expression reminded me of how the chaos of gardening with little kids is worth it. While some days it feels like there's a conflict between sustainability and parenting, moments like that make it worthwhile. What's good for Earth is good for my kids—and yours too.

★ ★ ★

Like many of us who care for the environment, my love for nature harkens back to childhood. I spent hours in our backyard digging and dreaming. My love for the environment and "living green" followed not long after.

When I was in third grade, my family visited Homosassa Springs State Park in Florida, a protected manatee habitat. As soon as I saw those large, awkward marine mammals, I fell in love. While the ranger chatted about the animals, I leaned forward and listened as if I was going to take a pop quiz afterwards. I could have stayed there for hours.

Reading every sign, I learned that my new favorite creatures were endangered. For nine-year-old me, the idea that they might not exist was too much to bear. When I got back to school, I launched a "Save the Manatees" campaign. As I held the photo of the manatee my class adopted, I felt I had done something important.

So I kept going. After building a "lemonade stand" out of PVC piping, I opened a store on our lawn called "Planet in Peril." I donated every cent earned (all of which came from my mom) to environmental groups. I read and reread my copy of *50 Simple Things Kids Can Do to Save the Earth* until the pages fell out.

As I grew into adulthood, my passion for the environment strengthened. Sunny days in college were devoted to convincing my fellow students to buy organic food. Graduate school involved organizing bike rides and poetry slams to raise money for climate change advocacy. Once I was in the working world, I planted community gardens and taught composting workshops. I even froze my butt off marching against the Keystone XL pipeline while I was five months pregnant.

When my children were born, all of this came into question. Raising kids takes time and makes you rethink your priorities. Some activities I ramped down. Attending weekly community meetings seemed less important than putting my kids to bed. Weekends became sacred family time. Any parent with a passion knows the struggle.

But most things I turned into family affairs, with all of the ups, downs, and altered expectations anything with small children involves. Learning from others who had come before me and my own experience, I found out it was possible to adapt most of my environmental activities into kid-friendly ones.

Gardening became a balancing act of keeping my kids and plants safe. When he was a toddler, Ethan often evaded my supervision to eat dirt. To keep from having panic attacks, I reassured myself that it was building his immune system. Dylan took great pride in watering the blueberry bushes and has since expanded to the entire garden. While he uses the hose these days, he used to fill his watering can from the rain barrel. He often sprayed water all over himself. One time, after the fifth incident that month, he yelled, "I'm all wet!" I was so over him insisting he could control the hose that I just responded, "Yeah. I see that." Natural consequences for the win. But despite many incidents of dripping sneakers, he still comes out to water the garden. His loyalty isn't unusual—a number of studies show children often find great fulfillment in participating in school, home, and community gardens.

Transportation became even more of a challenge. But I was determined to remain a one-car family. To walk long distances, we purchased a stroller designed to handle city streets and bumpy sidewalks. When Dylan was born, I managed my postpartum anxiety by taking daily walks, pushing him all over the neighborhood.

When our family expanded to two kids, Dylan started using his own feet. While walking to the grocery store with a preschooler tests your patience, by age four he had the stamina and attention to walk more than a mile. While there are plenty of days I want to hurry, the times spent picking dandelions in abandoned lots, saying hello to the neighbor's dog, peering at spiderwebs, and watching for trains have been some of my favorites. Observing my child's thoughtfulness toward the world, I see a kid who knows how to spot beautiful things. Since then, I've learned that other families who walk for transportation find the slower pace connects them more to their neighborhood and each other as well.

To supplement walking, we bought a fancy trailer to turn my bicycle into a kid-hauling machine. In the beginning, Dylan hated the trailer. Over time, he grew to look forward to it, hopping right in after I attached it to my bike.

Once Ethan was old enough to ride in it too, I was excited to get both of them in there. But squishing both of them in a tight space with few windows was asking for trouble. The first time, they didn't seem to mind. Although I scrambled to keep them from fussing with my brakes or licking bike grease, everyone got home safe and calm. But the second time, Ethan had other plans. As I tried to strap him into the trailer for our trip home, he screamed like he was being murdered. My eyes darting around the strip mall parking lot, I hoped no one thought I was kidnapping him in the slowest and most awkward way possible.

Sadly, not long after Ethan finally started enjoying the bike trailer, it bit the dust. Through time, it had suffered flat tires, rainstorms, a mouse moving in, and an ant infestation. Each time I took it out, I had to steel myself against whatever weird thing might have happened since our last ride. When the shoulder straps literally fell apart, we knew it was time to move on.

Thankfully, my love of biking has rubbed off on my kids. On his sixth birthday, Dylan graduated from a pedal bike to one with gears. As he's gone from tooling around the local park to riding on the street, he's learned hard work and responsibility. Ethan has seen the independence Dylan has gained with his bike. When I asked him if he wanted a bike for his second birthday, his little blond head bobbed up and down.

My love of family biking has rubbed off on my neighbors as well. For several years, I led family bike rides in my town, with Dylan behind me in the trailer. A group of parents and kids would ride a short distance to a fun destination, like a playground or ice cream shop. It was like being the Pied Piper on a bike except without the creepiness. I loved chatting to the parents about family biking setups, from trailers to bike seats to cargo bikes, and watching the kids learn confidence on the road. Building those community connections brought a whole new aspect to riding together as a family. Other cyclists who run family rides have shared similar stories with me.

While our house had always provided opportunities to tackle sustainability, it became even more important when we had kids. Installing solar panels provided us with clean energy. As the installers climbed on the roof, it also provided Dylan with an afternoon's worth of entertainment. Since my kids were toddlers, I've taught them to turn off the lights when they leave a room. (Even if they usually forget.) Inside the house, we've tried to minimize our toy purchases. Being thoughtful about what we buy has allowed us to spend less time cleaning and more time playing together. Taking advantage of the many free activities in our area always felt to me like it created more memories than a pile of toys could. My intuition on that turns out to be backed by research—social scientists have found that experiential gifts build relationships far better than material ones.

The one thing that seemed to be missing in my life after having kids burst back onto the scene in the spring of 2017. While I had put activism to the side for the first years of my children's lives, it sparked my passion too much to give it up. The People's Climate March presented a perfect opportunity to embrace it. Plus, I wanted to show my children that their voices matter. We attended the march as a family, appreciating the opportunity to speak up collectively for our future.

But despite our efforts, the excesses of modern parenting kept catching up with us.

Well-meaning relatives bestowed loads of toys upon my kids, including electronics that broke far before their time. The floor of our finished basement is constantly covered with stuff, from little plastic animals to puzzle pieces. When I told Dylan, "I think experiences are better than things," he replied, "Well, I like things." Our garbage overflows with disposable diapers because cloth diapers overwhelmed our ability to keep up with the laundry.

More significantly, I worried about my children's future. I wondered, will the rushed, materialistic world squash my older son's love of simple things? Will the fast-paced nature of our schools allow my younger son enough time to play or move his body? Will society convince them of the need to always have more, more, more? I also knew that I wasn't the only one with these concerns. As I heard on social media and in talks with friends, so many of us parents share the same concerns about the world's effects on our kids.

Outside of our family, I worried about the big picture of climate change. An iceberg the size of Delaware broke away from Antarctica. Asia had its highest temperatures ever. People in India died from a heat wave made worse by climate change. Mosquitoes that spread the Zika virus had larger ranges because of higher temperatures. Some of the most intense hurricanes in history pounded Puerto Rico, Texas, and Florida. California and the Pacific Northwest burned. The headlines just kept popping up day after day. While my kids were too little to notice the news, older children did—concerns about climate change started rising among teenagers over the past few years. Although I didn't know it yet, the youth climate movement was about to explode.

I started to feel torn between my responsibilities to my kids and the environmental and social justice movements. My email inbox overfilled with demands to sign this petition or call that senator. Organizers announced new marches nearly every day. Town halls sprouted like flowers, promising the chance of having your voice heard. I tried to sign petitions in the passenger's seat of the car and call my senators on the walk to the train.

But no matter how much I did, each one instilled more guilt for what I wasn't doing. The announcements reminded me, "Look at how much more there is to do!"

When I took time away from my kids, the mom guilt piled on. Ethan clung to me as soon as I got home from work and cried at the bathroom door when I took a shower. As I tried to put Dylan to bed, he'd whine, "But I just want to play with youuuuuu."

Was that because I wasn't giving them enough time? Was I doing the right thing organizing community bike rides and going to marches? Was I doing them a disservice by losing a little time with them now in hopes of making their future brighter?

It seemed as if there was no right choice. Anything I did was less time for something else that seemed equally important. There was an endless number of activities I could take on, but never any more of me to do it.

Between my full-time job, family, volunteering, and writing, I was pushing the boundaries of what could be accomplished in a twenty-four-hour day. While my husband supported my efforts, he never felt the toxic combination of "mom guilt" and "green guilt" that plagued me. My anxiety ratcheted up a little every time I looked at my to-do list. My lack of sleep started making me dizzy. Unfortunately, I know that many of us involved with environmental and social justice movements feel this sense of overwhelm and burnout.

I wanted to be everything to everyone all the time: a super mom, green goddess, and eco-warrior. But I was exhausted, worn-out, and a little cynical. There were beautiful, moving moments like our experience at the Climate March. But too much of the time, I was overwhelmed and under-resourced. No one—including my husband—could provide the extra time and sleep I wanted so badly. Instead of being a world-changer, I was becoming an eco-grump.

Frustrated with my situation, I talked to a number of other parents trying to live more sustainably. I asked all of them the same question: "What conflict do you face between being green and raising your kids?"

And almost all of them had the same answer: nothing. Absolutely nothing.

This answer baffled me. No one else found themselves torn like I was? I wrestled with this for months. What were they doing right that I wasn't?

One day as I read a parenting book, it hit me. I closed the book and blinked. Those other parents were right. As I've talked to more experts and read more studies since then, I've realized it wasn't just them.

While there are conflicts between having kids and being sustainable, they aren't all that different from the conflicts anyone in America or even other industrialized countries faces. Food, transportation, energy usage—they're all issues we struggle with, no matter if we have kids or not.

As for the effects on my kids? Despite the little guilt-tripping voice in the back of my head, I realized green living was good for them all along. They were learning to see beyond their little piece of the world. They were coming to appreciate how their actions impact other people. Getting them outside calmed their minds and squirmy bodies. Biking gave them a sense of independence. Saving energy helped them develop responsibility. In fact, green living was protecting them against many of the risks of modern society I worried so much about.

My light-bulb moment was realizing that my priorities of living green and teaching my kids to be kind, engaged, and resilient weren't in conflict at all. In fact, they were one and the same.

But perhaps I was being overly optimistic without any proof. Can green living really be better for your family, society, and Earth at the same time?

CULTIVATING KINDNESS

"**G**uys, stop," I said, dragging out the second word as I walked up to the couch. My kids were sitting not just on the couch but practically on each other. My older son was flailing his legs in the direction of his younger brother's head. "You, stop kicking your brother," I said, pointing at Dylan, then turned to his brother. "You, don't punch back! Just walk away." I would let them work it out, but Ethan is half Dylan's size. Even roughhousing can turn painful quickly.

They calmed down, even if momentarily. I sighed and let them go back to messing around. "Am I raising them to be good kids? Why are they so disrespectful toward each other?" I wondered. Then I reminded myself, "Nope, this is normal behavior between siblings. They love each other very much."

Despite my reminder to myself about developmental stages, I was also right to be concerned about bringing up my kids to be kind, moral people. Don't we all want our kids to be happy and good people?

Bizarrely, society often sets up these goals as polar opposites. It dangles the promise that our children will be happy if we do everything we can to get them "the best," whether that's the "best" kindergarten teacher or college. But when people who already have much more than others fight for "the best" for their kids, people with less privilege end up with even fewer opportunities. There's only so much room at the top, especially if some people are shoving others out of the way. As an article titled "Ethical Parenting" from *New York* magazine stated so bluntly: "Protecting and privileging one's own kids at the expense of other people has been the name of the game. . . . Every hour, it seems, a parent is given the opportunity to choose between her child and a greater good, and in those moments the primal parental impulse can be overpowering." While this attitude isn't specifically anti-environmental, it doesn't provide much room for caring about your carbon footprint or pushing for societal change.

Unfortunately, kids are getting the message that they matter more than anyone else. A 2014 survey of 10,000 middle and high school students by Harvard University's Making Caring Common project found that more than 75 percent of teenagers said that personal success or happiness was more important than caring about others. This wasn't just a small subset of spoiled brats. They interviewed kids in diverse schools; the results were true across classes and races. This lack of kindness played out in actions too. Other studies found that half of high school students reported cheating on a test at some point; nearly 30 percent reported being bullied during a particular year.

These attitudes and actions were a direct response to what students saw modeled by their parents. More than 80 percent of the students said that they thought their parents judged achievement and happiness as more important than caring for others, while only 19 percent said they thought caring for others was their parents' top priority for them. The more parents emphasized individual achievement and happiness, the less likely kids were to do altruistic acts. Even if their parents were telling them they cared about kindness, that message was getting drowned out by more self-centered ones.

Ouch.

If these are the messages we as parents are sending—even inadvertently—how do we send the right ones?

To start with, we can reject the idea that the most prestigious, expensive, or "impressive" option is actually the best. Wealth and achievement aren't linked to happiness. Psychology consistently shows that lives based on meeting external standards make kids less happy, less able to learn life skills, and less likely to form healthy relationships. In fact young people from upper-middle-class and upper-class families have similar rates of behavioral and emotional problems as low-income youth, even though they should face a lot less stress. A 2019 National Academies study listed students in "high-achieving schools" as a major "at-risk" group due to the constant pressure to be perfect. In contrast, children who are engaged in activities that involve them in a bigger cause have more life satisfaction and well-being later as adults. People in places with the world's longest life expectancies actually don't have the most achievement. People in these places instead emphasize having a purpose, simplifying, reducing stress, and having strong relationships with others.

Instead of the competitive attitude of our kids versus everyone else, our families can embrace ways of living that are simultaneously fulfilling and moral. By satisfying children's core psychological needs while also teaching them to be socially and environmentally sustainable, we can make a better world for everyone.

WHAT WE ALL NEED AS PEOPLE

Everyone has basic needs, both physical and emotional. Some of those are physical needs—no one is at their best when they're hungry. Others are related to the basic need to feel safe. And sometimes it's a bit more complicated.

According to self-determination theory—a psychological theory that attempts to explain what motivates people—there are three major psychological needs: relatedness, competence, and autonomy. Relatedness is wanting to feel connected and like you belong. It includes a desire to have relationships with others, both in your family and out-side of it. Competence is feeling like you and your actions can influence your environment. It includes a desire to be useful and valuable as well as the belief that you can accomplish your goals. Autonomy is feeling like you can be true to your values and free to be yourself. It's a desire to take actions that fit "who you are" and use your personal strengths.

Everyone—kids included—tries to get these psychological needs met. But sometimes how they do it is immoral or self-destructive. Meeting these needs internally through self-growth is better for every-one. As children grow up, parents can help meet those needs in healthy ways as well as teach their children how to fulfill those needs when they become adults.

WHAT MAKES SOMEONE A GOOD PERSON?

While various political and philosophical viewpoints define morality differently, most of them focus on "prosocial" attitudes and behaviors. Prosocial means doing things that benefit other people, even if they bring no benefit or even a loss to yourself. Children as young as two years old start showing the desire to help. While this is a trait that emerges early, it needs support from parents to fully develop.

Morality involves knowing the right thing to do, caring about doing it, and then actually doing it. Having all three qualities requires chil-dren be aware of others and their needs, be able to respond to others' needs, and have the self-control and ability to take care of themselves without hurting others.

A number of different characteristics are part of being a proso-cial or moral person. These include kindness/compassion, empathy, conscience, a sense of fairness, respect for self and others, integrity, and gratitude. It also includes humility, which allows us to recognize our faults, take responsibility, and work to be better people. On the societal level, being moral involves kinship, the ability to appreciate differences and desire social justice. It involves working to reduce priv-ilege and create a more egalitarian society for all, including through anti-racism, economic equality, environmental justice, feminism, and other types of civil rights work. These characteristics are all much bigger and more complex than merely "being nice" or following rules set by society.

In addition, there are a number of skills children need to develop so they can act morally. Self-discipline or control helps people manage their emotional responses, delay gratification, and make choices in line with their morals and long-term goals. Wisdom and moral judgment allow children to make decisions that benefit others. Social orientation enables us to form relationships with other people; collaboration helps us work with them. Resilience makes it possible for people to deal with problems, overcome barriers, and see problems as opportunities for growth instead of blame. People with resilience can take stress that would otherwise be toxic and make it tolerable. Optimism enables us to encourage ourselves and others when things don't go the way we expect. Problem-solving skills help children work out issues through communication rather than force.

Looking at life from other people's perspectives allows us to build empathy, minimize hurting people with backgrounds different from ours, and work effectively with others. The skill of "zooming in" allows children to pay attention to other people's feelings. "Zooming out" allows them to expand the people they care about beyond their family and friends.

The theory of positive youth development summarizes all these characteristics and skills in its "5 Cs": competence, confidence, connection, character, and caring. Once adolescents gain these, they're ready to take care of both themselves and others.

HELPING CHILDREN BUILD MORAL CHARACTERISTICS AND SKILLS

As parents, one of our roles is to be "character coaches," teaching our children both the values and skills needed to be moral people. We must also offer them opportunities to practice these skills as they gain them.

One of the best ways to be a character coach is to be an "authoritative" parent. An authoritarian parent tries to control their children as much as possible, while a permissive parent allows them to do anything. In contrast, authoritative parents are warm and caring while also holding high but reasonable expectations. They are sensitive and responsive caregivers, show affection, and spend time with their children. Authoritative parents love their children for who they are, helping them embrace their strengths while learning from their mistakes. Achieving this balance may seem like a high bar—it always feels that way to me—but it's a goal to work toward more than anything else.

This warmth and responsiveness are associated with children developing moral reasoning, a conscience, and self-esteem. As parents actively listen and appreciate their children's point of view, children learn empathy. Having a stable, committed, and close relationship with an adult is key to developing personal resilience. Caring relationships can counterbalance stressful situations and help children learn how to manage stress.

As children get older, authoritative parents say no when appropriate, provide a safe environment with limits, and set boundaries. Instead of relying on fear, they earn their children's respect and teach rather than humiliate. They use natural and logical consequences to help children learn. These actions build self-control, executive functioning, problem solving, and other skills that help children adapt to changing circumstances.

In addition to the general approach of authoritative parenting, there are a number of actions parents can take to encourage prosocial behavior.

Explaining the reasoning behind your own behaviors and talking through ethical issues are two of the biggest things that parents can do to teach empathy, moral reasoning, and altruism. Connecting your values to your actions helps children understand how their actions affect other people, which helps them judge moral decisions for themselves. Talking through real-life situations shows children that being kind requires courage and may require going against societal norms. Back-and-forth conversations where both sides ask questions and share perspectives build a level of mutual respect between parents and children. Parents admitting and talking through their mistakes model personal growth. Discussions about prejudice and other difficult issues help children gain new perspectives and demonstrate that they can come to adults with hard questions. In these conversations, children grow to understand the bigger picture.

Part of these conversations can involve teaching children to resolve conflicts and think through problems. For children to develop this skill, parents can't jump in and solve problems for them. Instead, adults can work together with children to solve problems by brainstorming choices, thinking about consequences, and weighing possible decisions.

Part of this problem-solving ability is developing a growth mindset, where children see challenges as opportunities to learn from rather than as failures. A study of nearly 400 seventh graders found that students who believed their skills were inherent and unchangeable had their math grades decline over the next two years. In contrast, the students with a growth mindset actually had their grades improve over the same period of time. Similarly children who received coaching about a growth mindset improved their test scores and motivation, no matter what kind of mindset they started with.

Dealing with challenging issues often involves intense and heated feelings. It's essential to help children learn to label their emotions, calm themselves, tune into positive emotions, and demonstrate their feelings in healthy, kind ways. Talking through what you're grateful for individually and as a family helps children recognize good things even during bad times. Discussing how other people think and feel in situations, in both fiction and real life, helps children develop empathy. Teaching children how to make amends for the ways they've hurt others helps them carry out those skills later as adults.

Thankfully parents don't have to teach these lessons alone. Building relationships with neighbors and other community members can provide a wider variety of role models. These relationships help children build social capital, the network of relationships you have within your larger community. Stronger social networks are associated with better physical and emotional health as well as moral development. Interacting with others gives parents chances to model generosity, gratitude, cooperation, and kindness. Being in community with people who are different from your family helps children embrace differences. These relationships also give children the opportunity to regularly help others, which builds confidence, competence, and feeling like part of a community.

Developing competence also comes from having real household responsibilities. Asking for children's perspectives and taking them into account when making household decisions create a democratic environment and teach critical thinking. Collectively working to take care of the house builds cooperation, the ability to recognize others' needs, and responsibility.

CONNECTING KINDNESS AND SUSTAINABILITY OF ALL KINDS

Just like being happy and being a good person aren't a zero-sum game, neither is being happy and environmentally sustainable. They're actually all tied together, although not always with a nice, neat bow.

Parents can teach most of these skills without a hint of environmental concern. But many actions that are environmentally sustainable also fulfill children's psychological needs or teach them the skills and values needed to be a moral person. While the follow-on effects of growing your own food, walking places, saving energy, picking up garbage, or attending a protest may not be obvious immediately, they add up over time. Even when it seems like our children aren't listening to us, they're definitely seeing what we do as a family.

Many environmental issues also tie directly to human rights. Polar bears are cute, but environmental issues are about so much more. Heat waves, natural disasters, and flooding exacerbated by climate change most affect people who are already oppressed, including Indigenous, Black, and other people of color. Air pollution disproportionately causes asthma and other breathing problems in children in poor communities. Coal plants tend to be located in low-income neighborhoods and are disproportionately located in communities of color. Purchasing items just to throw them and their packaging away reinforces abusive global supply chains and burdens people in other countries that must deal with what we've disposed of. Taking environmental action is in and of itself kind to other people, not just Earth.

Each of the following chapters will address an area of environmental sustainability. It will explain this activity's benefits to your family, backed by expert perspectives, academic literature, and my own experiences. At the end of each chapter, you'll find tips to carry out these actions, a family activity, recommended books, and resources to follow up with for more information.

At the same time, I won't guarantee any of this will lead to a particular outcome. I hate parenting books that promise results, as if children are video game characters that behave the way you want them to if you push the right buttons in the right order. The bond between parents and children (as well as other caregivers or responsible adults) is a relationship, not a formula. We're also not the only influence on our children's lives—friends, community members, and media will all affect them. We can't determine exactly who our child will be, nor should we.

Instead, parenting is like gardening. We can't make plants grow, but we can provide them with the right environment to do so. While plants need soil, air, water, and sun, children need a loving home, good role models, and opportunities to learn these skills and values.

For the sake of ourselves and our families, we need to remember that there's no such thing as a perfect parent or perfectly sustainable person. Everyone is human; everyone makes an impact, both good and bad. No one can do every single thing in this book to its maximum extent—even me. We all have restrictions. Some of them are individual, like disabilities, income, or strict work schedules. Others are because of societal limits, like a lack of sidewalks, minimal green space, or high cost of living. As I tell my kids, everyone has strengths as well as struggles. What may seem like small steps for some people, like buying more in bulk or calling a member of Congress, may be huge wins for others. In addition, those strengths and struggles may shift over time, as health, children's ages, geographic locations, and economic situations change. What seemed simple before may be hard later and vice versa. It's all a process and a journey.

What we can do is try to be "good enough" parents and people in the world. Psychologist D. W. Winnicott proposed the idea of the "good enough mother" back in 1971 in his book *Playing and Reality*. It's the idea that while a mother (of course it was a mother) starts off by adapting completely to her baby's needs, she slowly backs off as the child becomes older and more independent. Reducing that dependency teaches the baby that the parent is a separate person. While much of Winnicott's work draws on Freudian psychology, there's a lot we can learn from the concept. We can't be all things to our children, nor should we. Even if we could, it wouldn't be good for them. If we devoted everything to them, they would never gain independence or understand anyone outside of themselves. Similarly we can't be perfectly environmentally sustainable. It's not physically possible and would quickly lead to burnout. Collaborating with and relying on others teach us new perspectives and interdependence. It's good enough to be "good enough."

We all maintain a balancing act through life. We're all trying to do the best we can with the resources we have available to us. This book isn't meant to set up unattainable ideals or shame anyone for their challenges.

This book is instead meant to inspire and empower you. It's a toolkit for you to work toward the changes that you want to make in your life. As you read it, look for the things that truly appeal to your family and would make a difference. They're usually the things that grab your heart and make you say, "I want to do that!" Embrace those and expand on them as it makes sense to you. Think about how small steps can build to become big ones. If a baby step doesn't work for you, try something else. No one can do everything, but everyone can do something.

CONNECTING
WITH OUR FOOD

66 I love my mom because she plants things in her garden and I can help," read my three-year-old's preschool teacher off the back of a laminated flower. She handed the flower to my son, Ethan, who ambled over to me in the back of the classroom. He handed it to me, saying, "Here, Mommy."

Standing up from my tiny chair, I took the flower and smiled. "Thanks, honey." I looked at the text, written in the preschool teacher's neat handwriting. That's what he loves about me? I thought. Not what I would have expected. I kept chewing it over in my mind as I broke off and ate pieces of a giant chocolate chip muffin. I would have thought it would have been my hugs, sitting with him at bedtime, or playing with him. But nope, it's gardening. I think that's a good thing? Yes, it's definitely a good thing.

I shouldn't be surprised by my kids' love of gardening. Since the days I wore them in the baby carrier, I've included them as I've worked in the garden. In fact, they always liked sitting in the dirt a lot more than being in the carrier. As I weeded and watered, I'd glance over to make sure they weren't stuffing rocks in their mouths. Fortunately that only happened once; I scooped the rocks out before my older son tried to swallow them. The kids have since moved on to starting seeds, watering the garden (and each other) with the hose, and weeding. At their current ages of three and six, they aren't the world's most precise gardeners, but their enthusiasm makes up for it. Even though the main garden is only eight by fifteen feet, it's a center of our family's activity.

Gardening is a holdover from my own childhood, when I spent hours upon hours messing around in the dirt. While my mom tended to her flowers, I gathered weeds to make magical potions. Entire worlds existed only in my head and backyard.

As an adult I moved onto growing my own food. I learned that carrots actually have a smell and how cherry tomatoes taste straight off the vine. I found it so rewarding that I wanted to pass that appreciation and those skills on to my kids. We don't grow much, but it's enough to learn something and start a conversation about the broader food system.

When we can't get produce from our garden (which is the vast majority of the time), we try to get as much of it as possible from local farms. Depending on the week, that could mean a trip to the farmers market, picking up a box from a local farm, or picking our own fruit from a nearby orchard. Even though my kids hide behind me when I talk to the farmers, they still like mooching samples off of me or selecting the vegetables they want that week. When I say that something is from the garden, farm box, or farmers market, my kids are more willing to try it. While there are never any guarantees, it at least gives us an "in" to a new food.

Local food can also be more socially and environmentally sustainable than food from the grocery store. When you grow your own food or buy from local farmers, you have more knowledge of and control over how that food is grown. At the grocery store, all the information comes from labels alone. While the U.S. Department of Agriculture "Organic" label provides useful information—such as that farm doesn't use synthetic pesticides, herbicides, or fungicides—it only tells part of the story. Organic certification is expensive, can take time to earn, and is lost if farmers use any techniques that aren't allowed. In addition, it doesn't describe how the farm is treating its workers. Farmworker organizations have criticized some very large, well-known organic companies for underpaying and abusing their workers. Buying from local farmers allows you to ask those questions and make better decisions for yourself. Even when local farmers aren't following full organic regulations, they often use integrated pest management or other techniques that limit the application of pesticides and herbicides. Buying from nearby farms also cuts down on the carbon footprint of transporting the food around the country and sometimes the world to you.

Increasing the number of fruits and vegetables my kids are willing to eat also makes it possible to eat less meat, dairy, and processed foods. Vegetarian and even vegan meals make appearances at our dinner table on a regular basis. Even if a meal has meat or dairy in it, it can be more of a flavoring with vegetables taking a starring role. My husband's excellent cooking certainly helps, but if the kids weren't willing to eat vegetables, minimizing meat would be a much harder sell.

But could being closer to the food system benefit all kids, even if they don't have access to a backyard garden?

TO THE YOUTH GARDEN!

If anyone knows the answer to this question, it's the folks at the Washington Youth Garden at the National Arboretum. They run one of the country's longest running gardens dedicated to teaching children. In 1971 the Youth Garden opened in Washington, DC, to teach horticultural skills, raise environmental awareness, provide team-building opportunities, and build responsibility in participants.

While most of the gardens established back then have since come and gone, the Washington Youth Garden is one of only three from that time period still running. In the nearly half a century that it's existed, it's gone from a small garden space to a presence across the city. Now the staff members work with low-income DC public schools through the Garden Science program. They help schools start, maintain, and run gardens to supplement the schools' science, technology, mathematics, and engineering activities. Students visit the Youth Garden's space in the National Arboretum to learn about basic gardening skills, soil, pollinators, nutrition, water, and the larger food system. It's not just elementary school kids either. Their Green Ambassadors Program brings in high school students through paid summer internships. The teens learn to garden, cook, connect with other environmental organizations, lead field trips for younger kids, and get communications training.

All of this sounded pretty damn amazing to me.

Fortunately the Washington Youth Garden offers weekend workshops to local families. My kids got psyched for the workshop on pollinators. Our garden is fine, but someone else's garden with games and activities? Awesome. As Slimey the worm from *Sesame Street* is three-year-old Ethan's favorite stuffed animal, he was excited to see their worm composting.

Thunderstorms threatened all week. But the morning of the workshop, the sun was shining, the sky was blue, and the temperature hovered right around 75 degrees. We were dressed and about ten minutes from running out the door.

Then Ethan puked. While I ran to get a towel, my husband comforted him. Wiping puke off of our very well-worn couch, I sighed. Poor kid. There was no way we could bring him somewhere with other children. Unfortunately, I had played it up so much with Dylan that I didn't want to disappoint him.

"Honey, I promise that we'll bring you next time," I said, kissing Ethan on the top of the head. Dylan and I headed out the door.

GROWING ENGAGING EDUCATION

Following the winding road through the Arboretum, I pulled the car into a small parking lot. As we walked to the main green space, Dylan spotted an arch. It marked the entrance to a small maze of paths.

"Can we do a race?" he asked. Already, the space was engaging! But we had a workshop to get to.

"Not right now—afterwards, I promise," I said, hoping that I'd remember to follow up. He ran through the paths ahead of me. We passed by a huge painted monarch butterfly, groups of green plants, and a wooden insect hotel.

The main gathering space centered around a huge wooden, hand-painted statue of carrots and celery rising out of a stump. Carved earthworms circled around the bottom. There were already a few kids from three to nine years old running around.

Two young women greeted us and gave us nametags. After letting the group of eight or so kids play for a bit, they gathered everyone up. In an engaging conversation, they provided a brief introduction to pollinators. They explained how three-quarters of food crops rely on them, including apples, tomatoes, and peppers.

Just before the kids' attention started to drift, the instructors brought in the first activity. Setting up wooden baskets in rows, they shuffled the kids into two lines and placed a set of Wiffle balls at the front.

"Now, we're going to act as pollinators!" one staff member said. "First, we're going to be bees and carry the pollen with our knees to the flowers." She held up the Wiffle balls. "Hold the ball between your knees and try to get it to the basket on the opposite side."

The kids all shuffled across the grass, their legs wobbling. As balls fell and others made it into the basket, they giggled and cheered. Wanting to join in the fun, I tried it as well; I dropped the ball far more than the kids did.

After we mostly accomplished our task, the teachers gathered us up again. "We know that bees can pollinate. What else can help pollinate?" one asked.

Kids shouted out various answers, including other insects and animals. Eventually, one landed on the answer the teacher was looking for—the wind. "We're going to pretend to be the wind," she said. "Can the wind see?"

"No!" yelled the kids.

"So we're not going to see either. I need you to turn around." After directing them back into lines, she once again handed out balls. "Now, try to throw it in the basket—without looking."

If the first activity was humorous, this was hilarious. Balls went every which way except into the baskets. Mine was nowhere near anything resembling a basket.

As it started devolving, the instructor asked, "Did we get a lot in?"

"Yes!" shouted the single kid who landed a ball in a basket.

The instructor shook her head. "Not really. But what could we have done to get more in?" The kids contributed various answers: have more baskets, put the baskets closer together, and have more balls. Nodding, the teacher responded, "These are all things that plants that use wind for pollination do. Farmers plant corn close together. Trees produce a lot of pollen, which is why we sneeze in the springtime."

Throughout the activity, the kids were totally engaged. They definitely learned more about pollination techniques than they would have from a textbook. While they could have done this activity without a garden, being in the outdoor space gave it extra significance.

Gardens can play a major role in increasing children's engagement in education, especially science and mathematics.

John Fisher, the director of programs and partnerships at Life Lab, a garden-based educational program in Santa Cruz and Watsonville, California, started working as an environmental educator in 1996. "[I] started realizing that farm- and garden-based education was the most potent form of environmental education," he said. "Gardens are elementary to everybody's life. They are a microcosm of the world in terms of how natural systems work. . . . Everything we eat, everything we wear, it's all there in the garden."

One study out of Texas A&M looked at the effects of a gardening curriculum on a group of almost 650 third, fourth, and fifth graders. The teachers in the experimental group taught in school gardens and worked to incorporate gardening into their curriculum. When children in both the group that gardened and a control group that didn't took a science achievement test at the end of the program, students in the experimental group scored 5.6 points higher on average than the control group.

Similar studies with smaller amounts of time in the garden have also had good results. A project run by Louisiana State University in urban schools used a similar curriculum. Small groups of fifth graders visited the garden once a week to take care of herbs and cooler-weather plants including mint, rosemary, basil, and broccoli. Kids who participated in the program had a significant increase between their pre-test and post-test scores, whereas kids in the control group didn't. A study done by Portland State University researchers observed 113 students in low-income schools in Portland, Oregon, following them from sixth to seventh grade. The students came into the school garden once a week, where they'd discuss curriculum-based science topics. They also talked about how they could use their skills to solve issues in their own neighborhoods. The researchers reported that the garden program seemed to help students feel more in control of their learning, particularly those who may have been told in the past that they weren't good at science or math.

Many garden educators see gardening as a key tool for engaging students who may struggle in a traditional classroom.

"Often we hear from teachers that the student who is much more challenging inside really thrives in an outdoors setting," said Brianne Studer, the Washington Youth Garden's education manager. Between in-school programs and class field trips, the Youth Garden staff get to interact with students regularly. She said, "It really allows a different subset of students [to] show off their talents and their interests."

While the Youth Garden hosts students from Washington, DC, this benefit goes far beyond city borders.

"It allows us to access different learners, different types of learning," said Amani Olugbala, a community educator at Soul Fire Farm in Petersburg, New York. Soul Fire Farm is a community farm specifically devoted to ending racism and injustice in the food system. Olugbala said, "Some folks are going to be really excited about the colors, other folks are going to be about the texture, other folks are going to be like, 'How can I bring this flavor in?' It offers us more for the people whose brains work differently."

One of the most empowering aspects of garden-based teaching is the opportunity for children to guide their own learning.

"So often as adults, we want to be like, 'I know all of these things, let me tell you them,'" said Studer. She explained that the Youth Garden staff instead encourage students to explore, especially with their senses. The garden has signs that say "taste this" and "smell this." She said the staff members tell the kids, "In this space, you have a little more freedom."

TEACHING RESPECT AND RESPONSIBILITY FOR LIVING THINGS

Wrapping up the activity, one instructor gathered us in a circle with our hands in the middle. "Let's cheer the bees!" she said. In response, we yelled, "Thank you, bees!"

It was finally time to enter the garden. Although it was surrounded by a tall chain-link fence to keep deer out, a wide gate beckoned us in. A hand-painted sign next to the door said:

WELCOME TO THE WASHINGTON YOUTH GARDEN:

1) Pick with permission

2) Walk on the woodchips

3) Respect all living things

4) Close gates

5) Have fun!

Before entering, the teacher gave us a refresher on what is and isn't proper garden behavior. She emphasized the need to act gently toward all living creatures, both plants and animals. While kids liked the idea of cheering for bees, the particulars of interacting with insects seemed a bit more difficult. Not everyone was completely enthusiastic.

Of course, the kids in our class aren't unusual in their hesitancy. While Ethan, my three-year-old, declares that all worms are Slimey's friends, many kids aren't comfortable around crawling critters.

"They freak out and they smash the spider," said Fisher, talking about how some students who visit Life Lab aren't used to the animals that live there. "They don't quite understand that a spider serves a purpose, that this is the spider's home." Fortunately experience in the garden can build that comfort. "You can use those teachable moments of seeing the gopher, seeing the spider, seeing the hawk," he said, "talking about how they are part of this microcosm of life."

Olugbala said at Soul Fire Farm they try to move beyond fear of other living things to true understanding and appreciation. They recalled a time when a set of kids hurt a small frog by mistake. One of the other students was distraught. Although the school teachers accompanying the student minimized her distress, the farm instructors tried to respect and support her and her emotions. Olugbala views gardening as providing opportunities to fulfill the "watering of the empathy seed that a lot of young folks already have." They told the girl that "the way that you're tending to this frog is the same way that we tend to the Earth, the same way that we tend to this land."

Taking care of living things further builds this sense of respect and responsibility. With a parent or teacher's guidance, children who care for plants quickly learn what they need to do to keep them alive. If they don't water the plant, it will wilt. If they don't protect it from frost, it will die.

Unfortunately that love can come with disappointment. Studer talked about how in the Washington Youth Garden's Garden Science partnership schools, elementary school students started seeds and couldn't take care of them over a school break. No one came in to water the plants and almost all of them died.

The kids were heartbroken. She recalled them asking, "My plant, what happened to my plant?" The Youth Garden staff used the experience as an opportunity to discuss what the plants needed—sunlight, air, and water—and how to do better next time. Many parenting experts recommend using natural consequences—which gardening has in droves—to teach responsibility.

Even if you do all the right things, gardening never quite goes the way you expect it to. Insects, diseases, droughts, and other natural phenomena are unavoidable. Fortunately these disappointments can build resiliency. "Failure is part of this experience," said Studer. "You can learn things from those opportunities honestly more than you can if something grows really well the first time."

This sense of urgency can also be motivating.

"With the garden, you have to pay attention to it daily. You see results in a way that you don't necessarily see with the house," said Natasha Nicholes, who gardens with her four kids in Chicago. Nicholes also founded the We Sow, We Grow community farm, which grows food locally and serves as an educational resource for people in the community.

BUILDING A RELATIONSHIP WITH NATURE AND THE ENVIRONMENT

With the rules thoroughly established, we got the chance to explore the garden. As per the Youth Garden's philosophy of giving control to kids, the instructor gave them an exploratory activity—a scavenger hunt.

Handing each kid an empty egg carton, the instructor said, "Find up to twelve different colors of flowers. And go!"

Roaming the space, the kids kept a look out for a variety of colors. Among the green leaves, picking out purple, red, yellow, and white flowers took a keen eye and close attention to detail. "There's a purple one!" declared Dylan, running up to a plant.

Along the way, they observed a lot more than just flowers. "Look, a ladybug!" exclaimed one kid, pointing to said bug sitting on a leaf. A few other kids rushed over to see. Other children noticed the strawberry vines snaking along the ground and the white cabbage moths fluttering in the air. The staff didn't redirect the kids back toward the task, allowing them to guide themselves.

Left to their own devices, the kids made the activity collaborative rather than competitive. When one kid had finished, they helped other kids find flowers they were missing. Coming back together, we sorted the flowers by color and put some aside for our salad.

Next were the stars of the show—the bees. The Youth Garden raises their bees in simple, old-fashioned beehives. Some were white-washed, while others were painted in pastels. The bees buzzed in and out of the narrow holes, flying back and forth between the boxes and flowers.

While giving the bees plenty of space, one instructor retrieved a fake section of beehive filled with photos and diagrams. She explained that just as people have jobs, bees do too. Close-up photos of the hive and honeycomb familiarized the kids with bees in a nonthreatening way.

Then it was the moment of truth. "Now, we're going to walk past the beehives. We don't want to scare them, so we need quiet hands and mouths," the instructor said.

In a single-file line, kids and adults crept around the back of the beehives. We whispered, "Hi, bees," as we went by. Just after walking around the hives, Dylan and I stopped to watch the insects. He focused his gaze on them in wonder.

Even the kids who experienced a bit of hesitation came out on the other side enthusiastic about their buzzy friends. It helped that every-one got a tasty treat afterward—a stick dipped in honey. By the end, there wasn't a bit left.

Gathering the flowers and interacting with the bees—and their honey—gave the kids a sensory experience they never would have had indoors.

"Gardening is very unique in that it's a very tangible way for chil-dren to experience life," said Lisa Whittlesey, Junior Master Gardener program coordinator at Texas A&M University. Run through univer-sity agricultural extension programs, the Junior Master Gardener program uses gardening to encourage learning and service in children around the world.

This experience can be particularly powerful for kids who haven't had much of a connection to nature before. Olugbala described a young man who visited Soul Fire Farm. Although he arrived thoroughly unin-terested in getting dirty, by the end of the day, he chose to put his feet in the mud. "He said that his grandmother's speaking to him through the Earth. It just opened him up," they said. For many children coming to Soul Fire Farm's program, it offers them an opportunity to find rest in nature, especially when they may have faced prejudice in the past. "I feel like [gardening] is a direct interruption of that trend of more and more young folks not having an understanding . . . that they have a home on the land," Olugbala said. "Feeling like it's a place for them no matter what their identities are."

Often, lessons learned in the garden can extrapolate to the bigger picture of the ecosystem. Alethea Jo Mshar gardens with her three kids in rural Michigan. She said that gardening helps her children see the effects that people have on the natural world. Whether it's the dog digging up plants or ensuring rabbits are both safe and away from their produce, the garden exposes the complexity of humans' role in natural systems. "It's a very hands-on way for them to understand how nature does work," she said.

Building these connections flows down to children's attitudes toward the environment. A study by Texas A&M researchers with more than 230 second and fourth graders looked at kids' attitudes toward nature. The students who participated in a school gardening program had significantly more positive environmental attitudes than those who didn't. In particular they were more concerned about people's negative impacts on the environment. A Washington State University study that surveyed adults showed how far this influence can extend. Participants who lived near gardens or actively cared for plants as children were more likely as adults to find trees calming, appreciate them on a personal level, and participate in a gardening class.

We can gain some insight into how those values develop from a project in Vancouver studied by researchers from the University of British Columbia. The project teamed former farmers and older, experienced gardeners with students. Teams of older and younger gardeners worked together to plan, plant, and harvest vegetables while also learning about the larger food system. Throughout the year, student participants began seeing "nature" as less of a place they go to and more of a system they're personally part of.

While "the environment" can be a broad concept, gardening makes it more concrete and relatable. Even Dylan didn't know what to say in kindergarten when his teacher asked what they could do to help Earth. It was just too abstract. But he can rattle off why he loves to garden.

CULTIVATING EMOTIONAL AND SOCIAL SKILLS

Having searched for flowers, it was time for us to plant our own. Gathering the kids around an empty patch of dirt, the instructor knelt down with a trowel.

"Just dig up a little bit of dirt," she said as she pushed some soil aside. "Take a few flower seeds and spread them around. Then put some dirt on top."

She plucked a few seeds from her hand and dropped them in each child's open palm. Just like the instructor, the kids knelt down and dropped their seeds in the dirt. While some moved just a bit of dirt aside, some dug holes as if they were trying to reach China. Similarly, some put a few seeds down at a time, while others dumped their entire batch in one go. A few parents tried to help, saying, "Maybe you should spread them out," while others stood back and watched. I tried to be in the latter group, although I was often in the former.

As we planted, the instructor told us about how some of the flowers they had already planted were important to pollinators. Describing how eating milkweed makes monarch butterflies poisonous to predators, she declared, "It's like a superpower!" The kids nodded in agreement.

Finally, it was time to harvest.

The kids gathered around a raised bed full of spinach and lettuce. Leaning down and taking a spinach leaf in her hand, the instructor said, "Pinch the spinach and pick it with two fingers." Spaced out along the long narrow box, each kid pinched off two spinach leaves—or at least two parts of spinach leaves.

Moving on, the instructor produced a pair of garden scissors from her apron and snipped a bit of lettuce. She then passed out blunt scissors to each kid. Empowered by having real tools, the kids went to town.

We next moved on to kale, the much-maligned hipster green. But we were going to do something a little different here. "Do we eat flowers?" the instructor asked the group. When the kids looked confused, she said, "We can eat these! Pick two yellow kale flowers and put them in the bucket." They smiled—they definitely knew how to pick flowers.

We weren't going to pass by the strawberry patch without stopping. Each kid plucked a strawberry and put it in the group basket. While most of the kids weren't tempted by the spinach or lettuce, the prospect of fresh-picked strawberries was alluring. A few, including Dylan, almost had the fruit go in their mouths before the instructor said we were collecting them for the group. While we would be eating them eventually, the kids would have to wait.

Last were the peas. The children had to show self-control here too. The instructor gave them permission to eat one single pea pod—no more.

Throughout the process, I saw the kids demonstrating many of the emotional and social skills that can be gained in the garden, from cooperation to independence.

"Gardens always provide a new and novel way for children to work together," said Studer, referring to the students visiting the Youth Garden. "There's always this informal negotiation that happens because this is a novel space to them." Cooperation made picking greens for the entire group take much less time than if one person did it alone.

Taking only what they needed that day, not eating the peas, and even staying on the paths required a level of serious self-control from such young children. In a long-term garden project, there's even less immediate gratification.

"There's also something nice about gardening that it's kind of time released in terms of your experience of it," said Fisher, talking about his experience at Life Lab and his son's school garden. "It's a different way to experience things, [not] how we're used to seeing everything now in a two-minute YouTube video."

That long-term commitment combined with independence leads to children feeling invested in their work. At his son's school garden, Fisher said, they set up "caretaker stations." Each student has a specific job to do when they arrive at the garden, whether that's taking care of the compost, checking the weather station, or monitoring the greenhouse.

"There's pride associated with what you're caring for," he said. Unlike other parts of the school run by adults, students feel ownership over the garden.

"There's a lot of life lessons that go along with it as far as a kind of a loyalty, a kind of discipline," said Mshar. In addition to growing food, Mshar's children also help her can tomatoes and peas at harvest time. She said, "They understand that we have a lot of vested work in it and it's important to keep investing [in] the work until it's all the way completed."

In addition to learning skills, this cooperation and independence can build children's feelings of accomplishment. They see that they can set and achieve personal goals, have control over their learning, and contribute to the greater good.

In one study from researchers at Sam Houston State University and Texas A&M, nearly 200 third, fourth, and fifth graders in Fort Worth and Temple, Texas, participated in a school gardening program. Another 90 students were in a control group that didn't do the program. Children in the gardening group had a significant improvement in life skills after the program, while the control group didn't. The researchers saw improvements in how the kids worked with their peers and understood their own emotional needs. Similarly, a study of more than 300 sixth and seventh graders in the Pacific Northwest found that students who were the most engaged in a gardening program also felt the most control over their ability to learn.

Beyond measurable characteristics, a lot of people find deep emotional resonance in the garden. The Junior Master Gardener program grew out of Whittlesey's work twenty-five years ago as an instructor in a federal prison for women. She saw the effects gardening had on the women: it helped them reduce their stress levels, develop more empathy, and manage their anger.

"A lot of them saw significant changes in themselves as a result of participating in the gardening project," she said. Many of the women applied the ideas they saw in the garden to themselves. Whittlesey said, "There was something about being a part of regeneration and growth and taking something that others were throwing away and creating something that our seeds could grow into."

While a number of inmates wanted to work with their children during visits, there were few resources available for gardening with children at the time. To meet that need, Whittlesey collaborated with others to develop the Junior Master Gardener program. Although she no longer works with inmates, she sees similar growth in some students. She said, "You're using [gardening] as a vehicle to really help that person to be able to be more resilient or confident, more able to cope, more able to realize they can be an active part of solutions in their community."

BECOMING EMPOWERED AROUND FOOD

As we finished picking peas, one kid exclaimed: "This is a yummy garden!" He didn't know the half of it yet.

The instructors moved us over to picnic tables under a pavilion, where a water jug and cooking tools awaited us. After each kid scrubbed and rinsed their hands, they sat down at the table behind a plastic cutting board.

Soon the instructors were passing around the food we had picked. Before each ingredient, they demonstrated to the kids how they would prepare it. First lettuce and spinach, which the kids tore with their hands into bits and spun in the salad spinner. Then they used scissors to cut chives and peas. Finally each kid had a chance to shake a giant glass jar full of homemade salad dressing. The kids could do all of it independently with minimal adult intervention or assistance.

They relished the tasks. I've never seen spinach or lettuce ripped so thoroughly. Each time the salad spinner or glass jar came around, they put some serious muscle into it.

As the kids prepped each ingredient, they tossed it into a big bowl, combining it into one giant salad. As we finished, the instructors doled it out into small metal bowls, passing it around for the kids to eat.

The meal being salad, there wasn't universal enthusiasm. A few kids said, "I don't want it," and refused to try anything. Most picked at it, tasting some things and not others. A few ate all of it and asked for seconds. Even though most of the kids didn't gobble it down, it was a much warmer reception to a salad with spinach, kale, and turnip than you'd ever see in a restaurant or at most people's dinner tables. Even my vegetable-loving kids make faces when I try to serve them salad. The fact that most of the kids tried it at all was a kind of miracle!

"There's excitement about eating the food you grow," said Fisher. He sees this same result in his son's school in Davenport, California. The school's cafeteria not only gets a large amount of its produce from the school garden but heavily involves students in preparing and cooking the food. While the kindergarteners through second graders don't eat a lot of salad, most of the third through sixth graders eat the greens right up. At that point, they've been working in the school garden for years. He said, "You can say, 'All of the lettuce from today's salad came from the garden! Raise your hands if you helped harvest that!'" One day his son picked out and ate only the red-skinned potatoes in his potato salad because he knew he had helped grow them.

Nicholes reports she's seen similar things at the We Sow, We Grow community farm. "The children who worked with us . . . are more adventurous with eating and that makes me happy," she said. The kids are interested in different varieties of tomatoes and ask questions about whether they're heat resistant or not—an essential characteristic during hot Chicago summers. She said, "I'm loving the fact that the kids are thinking about their food in a different way. But also learning to love what they grow."

These experiences are backed by data. An academic review looking at fourteen different studies found that in ten of the studies, students had notable increases in the number of fruits and vegetables they ate after participating in a gardening program. Although many studies had significant limitations, the review's authors said the results suggest that gardening has a positive influence on children's consumption of fruits and vegetables. Even in studies that didn't result in behavioral change, students who gardened said they were more interested in eating vegetables after the program than before.

As Mshar said about her own children, "It's exciting to see broccoli on your plate when you planted the seed and watched it grow and watered it and had to put on manure and worms and compost and everything else around it. It really opens up their whole world."

Even when kids aren't a fan of a specific vegetable, growing and preparing them gives children more of a sense of control over their diet. It helps them figure out what they actually like or not. At the Youth Garden's school programs, they offer students the chance to try sauces with different flavor profiles: salty, sweet, and sour. Then students pick if they loved the sauce, liked it, or "just tried it." Studer said, "You have to be willing to try things, but the more you can learn about what you genuinely like, the more power it gives you to figure out how to make healthy food for yourself that tastes good to you."

Olugbala said they cook with students at Soul Fire Farm for similar reasons. "I feel like that just ties right into their own health, understanding the different things that they're putting into their bodies," they said. In addition, cooking gives children a chance to develop life skills. Just as we saw at the Youth Garden, there are plenty of things kids can do to help prepare food. At home, my kids add ingredients, stir, and chop with kid-friendly plastic knives. The possibilities expand even more as children get older. In the Youth Garden's Green Ambassadors program for high school students, participants cook a meal each Friday for the entire staff with produce from the garden.

BUILDING RELATIONSHIPS AND SERVICE TO OTHERS

With the food eaten and the program over, it was time to go home. But I still had a promise to fulfill. On our way out, we stopped by the maze of paths we spotted walking in. "It's a Mario level!" Dylan proclaimed, talking about his favorite set of video games. "You stand there and I'll stand here. Whoever gets to the end first wins!"

Taking off running, I wove back and forth along the garden path. I held back the first time, letting him win. "Let's do it again!" he yelled. Okay then. "And go!" I sprinted hard back to where we started, barely beating him. "One more time?" he asked and I acquiesced. This time, despite running as hard as I could, he beat me. One more sign of him growing up.

On our way home, I reflected on how great our time at the workshop was. Thankfully, that bonding time doesn't need to be limited to workshops. Gardens can be important meeting spaces for families, schoolkids, and even entire neighborhoods.

"The family engagement piece is really important," said Whittlesey, talking about the Junior Master Gardener program. "Children and families are more connected and are working together."

Similarly, Nicholes said that both her home garden and the We Sow, We Grow community farm are places her family can spend time together without planned activities. "I do think that in society, we're losing that ability to have togetherness without having something scheduled," she said. Time in the garden is "just without any type of expectation at all."

The public nature of community gardens provides that space for entire neighborhoods. Nicholes established We Sow, We Grow specifically to build relationships with her neighbors. "What better way to connect with people than food?" she said.

A study of students in southwest Detroit found that after participating in a community garden program twice a week, children had more positive attitudes about their neighborhood than before. They built relationships with adult neighbors and friendships with other kids. As Kameshwari Pothukuchi, author and a researcher from Wayne State University, summarized: "Community gardens also foster contacts between people from diverse cultural, ethnic, and class backgrounds in non-threatening environments in which they may communicate about common interests or shared concerns."

Even though we don't have a community garden in my neighborhood, I've seen similar things working in my own garden. It's right next to the bus stop and near the community center, so we always have folks walking by. A number of neighbors have stopped to chat with me as I work in the garden, whether to discuss their own gardening ambitions or just admire the amount of produce we get from our scraggly mess. (Early on, one neighbor had a bet with another about whether our garden would produce tomatoes or not. She proudly informed me that she lost.) Dylan frequently spots friends walking to the park and joins them after he finishes his gardening tasks. In addition he's become a walking, talking neighborhood ambassador for youth gardening. After playing at a local park one summer afternoon, he invited our neighbor and kids over to our garden to check it out on their way home. As the sun set, they stood in our backyard chomping on fresh green beans and cherry tomatoes.

From building community it's a natural step to serve others.

Sharing knowledge can be one form of service. Nicholes continues to build connections by welcoming questions and requests for advice. "Folks now realize that our space is a safe place for them to come and talk and be curious without feeling like they're being a burden on anyone," she said. "For people to see folks smack-dab in the middle of the city, growing food, their curiosity gets the better of them and then they want to know more about it." When she teaches people, she often finds that they pass the knowledge on to others.

The service piece can also be more formal. To get the Junior Master Gardener certification, students must participate in a service project. These projects can include growing vegetables to donate to a food bank, teaching younger children how to garden, or working with senior citizens. "We use gardening as a vehicle by which to grow kids," Whittlesey said. "When children are given the opportunity to really look and evaluate what the needs are for their community and realize that they can be part of making a difference in a positive way, that can be really empowering for young people."

Similarly a garden project in Flint, Michigan, that partnered students with adult mentors focused on serving the community. They turned abandoned lots into spaces that grew food, donated the produce to homeless shelters, and helped elderly neighbors with their yardwork. The students appreciated feeling like they were contributing to a greater good, especially in a neighborhood with limited access to fresh vegetables.

Starting down the path of service via gardening can lead to kids finding new ways to help others. After Hurricane Harvey destroyed a number of school gardens in Houston, the kids were distraught. While so much had been lost in the hurricane, the gardens held a special place in their hearts. Fellow Junior Master Gardeners in Michigan heard about the problem and their leader reached out to Whittlesey in Texas. The leader's students wanted to donate their seeds to the Houston schools to help them re-establish their gardens. By Whittlesey connecting the Michigan group with contacts in the Houston Independent School District, some of the schools were able to replant their gardens. As Whittlesey said, "Children really saw a need and they wanted to do their part to help others be successful."

UNDERSTANDING THE BIG PICTURE OF THE FOOD SYSTEM

Participating in the local food system opens up opportunities to talk about the bigger picture in a way that can be difficult when you're looking at cereal in the grocery aisle.

Just participating in the process of growing helps kids realize how much work goes into producing their fruits and vegetables. "They understand how hard it is to go from farm to plate," said Fisher. "To see that food takes time, tending, sun, soil, water, and air is a pretty refreshing experience."

The work provides a little bit of insight into the people and systems behind what we eat. The Youth Garden makes these connections explicit with their Food Systems trip for schools. This workshop acknowledges that while growing our own food is great, most of us can't depend on it. We're all still part of this larger system. Soul Fire Farm focuses on this in their curriculum as well. "People talk a lot about how young folks just think that food comes from the grocery store and not understand there's a whole system connected to it," said Olugbala.

In particular it's essential to understand who grows produce, who benefits from it, and who has access to it—or doesn't. When students arrive on the farm, Olugbala said they greet them by saying, "Hey, welcome to Soul Fire Farm, we're committed to ending racism in the food system." Students talk about how injustice permeates the food system, from how fast-food advertisements target children of color to how farmworkers are vastly undercompensated. "People want to gloss over things and make things pretty," Olugbala said. "No, keep it real."

While the staff of Soul Fire Farm definitely discusses problems, they also talk about essential roles that Black, Indigenous, and other marginalized people have played in agriculture throughout history. Walking through growing spaces, they describe how George Washington Carver—famous for his many uses of the peanut—also established the field of regenerative agriculture to restore the soil. By teaching Black farmers how to use techniques like planting legumes that add nitrogen, adding compost, and growing a variety of crops, Carver helped empower them. Plantings of corn, beans, and squash together—called the Three Sisters crops because of their ability to support each other—generates discussion on how the Muscogee Native American tribe established this growing strategy. The educators especially focus on aspects of Black history that students don't cover in school, such as the fact that the Black Panthers ran the first free urban school breakfast program. "Knowing that Black folks have history with farming that isn't only enslavement is really powerful for them," Olugbala said.

Talking about both resistance and resilience inspires young people. "There are a lot of things wrong with the food system," Olugbala said. "This is evidence that you don't have to just take it. We're in a space that is an actual point of resistance."

ALTERNATIVES TO HOME AND SCHOOL GARDENS

While home and school gardens can be incredibly valuable places, not everyone has access to them. One alternative may be to have a small container garden on your windowsill or deck. Many herbs, such as mint, basil, and thyme, can thrive in containers as long as you give them enough sun and water. "Start with a planter box in your window and see what you can grow in there," said Studer. "Herbs are fantastic." Just planting seeds or raising seedlings can help children build responsibility and cope with delayed gratification.

Many areas also have community gardens or after-school programs that include gardening. Junior Master Gardener and 4-H programs exist across the country, even in major cities. Googling "community garden [city]" will often come up with a map of nearby gardens that you can join.

Even if you never grow anything yourself, the nearly 9,000 farmers markets across the country allow you to talk to and buy from local farmers. The community atmosphere offers children more opportunities to interact with food and farmers than they would have at a grocery store. In addition, sellers at many farmers markets accept payment via the Supplemental Nutrition Assistance Program (SNAP), for those who get federal nutrition assistance. A study of farmers markets in upstate New York that followed twenty-two families with young children through a visit found that about a third of the interactions at the market were sensory. Both kids and parents picked up food, smelled the food, tried samples, and ate food immediately after purchasing it. Buying directly from farmers can help start conversations about the larger food system similar to how gardening does. While farmers markets are far from perfect, they're still a solid alternative to growing your own food.

Purchasing a farm share in a community supported agriculture (CSA) program provides even more direct support to farmers. The CSA we participated in allowed us to choose which fruits and vegetables we wanted for the week. Buying a share for the entire year was also far cheaper for us than buying the same amount of produce from the farmers market and less expensive than shopping at certain grocery stores.

Even if you can't buy local, eating less meat and dairy can substantially lower your carbon footprint that contributes to climate change. Agriculture makes up 9 percent of U.S. greenhouse gas emissions, with a good deal of that from meat and dairy production. While it may seem tough, there's a lot of vegetarian and vegan meal options available for families. Personally, I find that combining vegetables with dipping sauces, trying out a variety of protein sources (especially beans), and cooking one-pot stews and soups make vegetable-based dishes more appealing to kids. Talking about why your family eats less meat than others can stimulate conversations about climate change and animal welfare.

For all of the benefits of local and sustainable food, one thing it doesn't do is teach your children to listen to you. One evening, we were getting out of the car when Ethan was struck with the intense urge to garden. Or at least his version of gardening, which involved poking the ground with a bamboo pole used for staking peas. "I want to garden. Pleeeeeeeeeeease," he begged. Then he whined. Then he screamed.

As much as I loved his enthusiasm, it was way past his bedtime. Giving in to his demands wasn't going to result in anything good. To bring him inside, I ended up picking him up surfboard style. I hated tamping down his enthusiasm, but there's a time and place for everything.

You can't win them all, I suppose.

What to Know

Start Small and Relatively Simple

Over-ambition is one of the biggest killers of gardens. Whether it's a home, school, or community garden plot, start small.

"Sometimes what we see is that there's a lot of fear with people not knowing how to get started with gardening," said Whittlesey.

Begin with plants that are relatively easy and fun to grow, including lettuce, basil, peas, beans, tomatoes, and sunflowers.

Starting plants from seed is a great way to introduce kids to the beauty of growing. "All of the sudden, you look one day and it's green and it's growing," said Mshar. Pick bigger seeds that are more likely to be successful, like beans and peas.

However, don't put the expectation on yourself to start everything from seed. There's nothing wrong with buying seedlings.

Involve Kids from the Beginning and Respect Their Knowledge

My first time working with kids in the garden was humbling. Long before I had my own kids, I volunteered with a group running a series of workshops for elementary school students. Talking to my fellow volunteer, Zachari, I was listing off all of the things we needed to teach the kids. Since the children lived in downtown Washington, DC, I assumed they knew little about nature. Midway through my rambling, Zachari gave me a severe look and said, "Shannon, they know much more than you're giving them credit for." Zachari was right; a number of the students had already gardened at school before the workshop. That lesson stuck with me.

Since my own kids have been big enough to have opinions, I've worked with them to plan our garden. In the winter, we look at the seed catalog together and they make suggestions about what types of seeds to buy.

Asking kids for their ideas and listening to their perspectives are essential to building trust. "Don't insult children thinking that they don't know what's happening at all," said Nicholes. "Talk them through the entire experience and you'll find out that they know more than what they let on."

In many cases, your kids may know more about the outdoors than you do, especially if they already spend time digging in the dirt. Olugbala recommends "letting their own expertise shine. Let them be a teacher."

Give Kids Real Responsibility

Your staying as hands-off as possible allows children to develop a sense of responsibility and independence. The garden may not come out the way you think it "should," but that doesn't mean that it's bad either. "Don't think that everything's going to be orderly. Gardening isn't orderly for us," said Nicholes. "We should expect stuff to happen and make it a huge experiment."

Even younger children can have jobs that are both truly useful and won't destroy the plants. My three-year-old does a great job pulling weeds creeping in from the edge of the garden. If children know that they're truly helping, they'll take pride in their contribution.

To support those efforts, buy your kids their own garden tools. Be suspicious of tools labeled "kids' tools"—they're often junk that don't hold up to real gardening. Instead buy appropriately-sized gloves, shovels, and if they're old enough, hand shears. They may still swipe your tools, but at least you'll have extras.

It's great if you can set aside a space for kids to do whatever they want. In our yard, we have a small raised bed that our kids plant and dig in. We've planted giant sunflowers with enough space for our three-year-old to still fuss around in the dirt.

"There's a huge sense of pride from children when they can tell people, 'We grew that,'" said Nicholes.

Next Steps

Choose Plants That Are "Kid-Friendly"

Think about the multiple ways your children will interact with the garden throughout the year. "The kids need to be able to touch and smell and feel those things in their hand," said Whittlesey. "They're all really tactile." Lemon balm, mint, and oregano all have very distinctive scents in addition to their taste. Sorrel is interestingly sour.

Plants that are physically accessible to kids are particularly good. Children should be able to reach and pick things themselves with minimal help. Cherry tomatoes, beans, and strawberries can all be harvested through the summer and fall. Once these "snacking" or "crunch and munch" gardens start producing, kids can grab veggies from them over and over again.

Figure Out the Needs of Your Space and Family

One of the great things about gardening is that it forces you to learn about the nature around you. Whether it's a backyard plot, a community garden space, or even just your windowsill, explore the space you have available with your children. If it's outside, note how much sun it gets throughout the day, where the water flows, and what the soil is like. Does it rain much? How hot does it get at the peak of summer? When does the frost end in the spring and begin in the winter?

If you live in an urban area and plan to plant straight into the soil, you should test your soil for lead before planting. The Soil and Plant Tissue Testing Laboratory at the University of Massachusetts Amherst does it for a small fee. If lead levels are too high, you will need to garden in pots or raised beds that are blocked off from the original soil and filled with new soil.

In addition think about your own needs. Are you away for long periods of time during the year? Do you have neighbors who will be willing to care for your garden while you're gone? Where do you walk most often? If you put your garden in the backyard but you're hardly ever there, you probably won't remember to water it. If you want to build those bonds with your neighbors, a garden that's visible from the sidewalk is a better bet.

It can be useful to set a time of day to care for the garden. Raising kids is hectic; it's easy to let a garden fall through the scheduling cracks. Whether it's in the morning, after lunch, or when the kids come home from school, having a consistent time makes it more likely you'll remember to do necessary maintenance.

Share Your Joy for Gardening, Vegetables, and Learning

Enthusiasm can be contagious, especially among small children. "What excites you is going to excite them. They will follow your passion," said Studer. She recommends discussing what you like about eating and growing different vegetables.

Mshar said that one of her favorite activities in the garden is digging up potatoes. She particularly enjoys pretending that she and her children are going on a scavenger hunt. When her children were younger, she would use chalk to draw Xs where she expected potatoes to be and let her kids loose as they hunted for treasure. "Every year, it never gets old. It's always exciting; it's always an adventure," she said.

To demonstrate your commitment to learning, keep a gardening notebook or journal. Chronicling what you did, what challenges you ran into, and what solutions you came up with can help you and your kids learn from year to year. It also allows your family to run mini-experiments, such as which plants grow the best together or need more or less sun.

FAMILY ACTIVITY: *Starting Seeds*

CHOOSE YOUR SEEDS

Our family has had the most success starting tomatoes, basil, and peppers. When picking seeds, consider what vegetables you want to grow and what varieties. Some varieties may be bred for your region or to be resistant to certain problems like fungus.

FIGURE OUT YOUR TIMING

If you plan to transplant your seedlings outside, you need to consider timing. (If you plan to grow them on a windowsill, timing is less of a concern.) The timing of seed starting depends on both your area's last average frost date and what types of seeds you're planting. Cold-tolerant plants like broccoli can go in early while more sensitive plants like tomatoes will die if there's a frost.

PREPARE YOUR CONTAINERS

Terra cotta or plastic containers from the garden store will work just fine. If you want to use recycled containers, quart-sized yogurt containers with holes punched in the bottom are perfect. Before planting, clean dirt or other contaminants out of the containers. A natural and effective way to sanitize them is to spray them with vinegar, let them dry, and rinse them in water.

PREPARE YOUR SOIL

If possible, don't use garden dirt for your seeds. Instead, buy seed starting mix, which has the right mix of nutrients and water-absorbing materials. Before planting the seeds, combine the water and seed starting mix in a large bowl. Allow your kids to mix it together to the texture of thick mud.

PLANT YOUR SEEDS

Have your kids scoop up handfuls of mud and move it into the flowerpots. Then, have each child stick their finger in and brush a little bit of mud to the side. Give each child a few seeds and direct them to put them in the tiny hole. Then have them brush a very small amount of dirt back on top of the seeds.

SPROUT YOUR SEEDS

If you have a very sunny windowsill, place your seeds there to get light. If it is warm enough during the day, put the plants outside on a deck, balcony, or patio. Once you get serious, you may want to consider purchasing a cold frame (which acts like a mini-greenhouse) or using a grow light. Have your children water the plants whenever they are dry, usually once a day. You may want to use a tiny watering can or spray bottle to prevent overwatering. Children can also gently "pet" the seedlings, which makes them stronger.

TRANSPLANT YOUR SEEDS

At some point the seedlings will get too big for their original pot. If you're growing your plants inside or on a porch, just transplant them to a larger pot. If you're transplanting them to an outdoor garden, you'll need to get them ready for being outside. Over the course of a week, bring them outside for a few hours a day. Transplant them when you expect to have warm, mild weather. Water them immediately after transplanting.

Books

PICTURE BOOKS

Up in the Garden, Down in the Dirt, by Kate Messner and Christopher Silas Neal: This lyrical, beautiful book follows both what's happening above the ground with a girl and her grandmother as well as below the earth with the plants and animals. Our family often pulls out this book in late winter as we're getting jazzed for gardening season.

Growing Vegetable Soup, by Lois Ehlert: This simple book does a lovely job introducing the steps and tools of gardening with bright, colorful illustrations. As a board book, it's excellent for the youngest gardeners.

The Thank You Dish, by Trace Balla: This sweet and clever book shows how many people really are involved in getting our food to us and how we can show them appreciation.

How a Seed Grows, by Helene J. Jordan and Loretta Krupinski: With a science-based approach to understanding seeds, this book walks children through planting their own bean seeds and watching them grow.

From Seed to Plant, by Gail Gibbons: This book provides a nice introduction to the more in-depth science vocabulary involved in planting, including pollination and germination.

Pizza at Sally's, by Monica Wellington: Not only does Sally source her tomatoes from the local community garden, but this charming book also illustrates the many steps needed to make a favorite food.

Old Manhattan Has Some Farms, by Susan Lendroth and Kate Endle: To the tune of "Old MacDonald," this adorable book talks about urban gardens in cities across America.

ACTIVITY BOOKS

Gardening Projects for Kids, by Jenny Hendy: This book of more than sixty step-by-step projects has a lot of options for potted and indoor plants, in addition to some fun craft activities related to gardens.

The Book of Gardening Projects for Kids, by Whitney Cohen and John Fisher (Life Lab): With a huge, lovely variety of activities ranging from initially setting up a garden to cooking the harvest along with lots of explanatory context, this is a comprehensive introduction to family gardening.

Resources

Soul Fire Farm Youth Program (if you are going to use any of their materials in a formal program, make sure to read and agree to their integrity guidelines): www.soulfirefarm.org/food-sovereignty-education/youth -program/

Life Lab, especially the school garden resource section under For Educators: www.lifelab.org

Washington Youth Garden, especially the Curriculum section: www .washingtonyouthgarden.org/curriculum

Junior Master Gardener Program: www.jmgkids.us

Farmer's Almanac List of Frost Dates: www.almanac.com/gardening /frostdates

U.S. Department of Agriculture Farmers Market Directory: www.ams. usda.gov/local-food-directories/farmersmarkets

Local Harvest Directory of Community Supported Agriculture, Farms, and Farmers Markets: www.localharvest.org

How to Create the Best Low-Maintenance Garden with Kids: https:// welleatyouupweloveyouso.com/2016/11/29/green-kids-building -a-lasagna-garden/

WHAT DO YOU DO WITHOUT A MINIVAN?

WALKING, BIKING, AND PUBLIC TRANSIT

"What was your favorite thing today?" I asked Ethan, my younger son, as I tucked him into bed. I ask him this question every night as part of our bedtime routine.

I wondered what his response was going to be. That day, we had eaten cupcakes, visited a massive indoor play space with a pretend mountain, and hung out at our neighborhood park. There was no lack of options.

"Riding the bus," he said immediately. I chuckled. Then there was that possibility.

Although the play space was far enough away that we would normally drive, my husband and older son had taken the car to a classmate's birthday party. As I wanted to get out of the house, I looked up the best route via public transit. While catching a bus, hopping on the subway, and then catching another bus was complicated, it seemed like it wasn't going to be all that time-consuming.

While we had ridden the first bus and train route many times, the second bus ride was all new. As we waited for the bus, Ethan and I pointed out items of interest to each other: a newspaper on a bench, words on the side of a bus, and gum stuck to the ground. (Admittedly, most of these items were more interesting to him than to me.) Once we got on, he noticed there was an upper floor, so of course we went up those few steps to sit in the back. Walking by fellow passengers, we smiled and nodded. As we drove, he looked out the window and provided a running commentary of his observations. Trucks, stores, and stoplights went by, much easier to see than it would be if he was looking out the window from his car seat.

Apparently all of that was more fun than the pricey play space.

Yep, he's my kid all right.

While we didn't have any public transit where I grew up, many of my fondest memories as a child were biking places with my parents. We regularly cycled over to the local pie shop or through the foothills of the Adirondack Mountains to get ice cream and play mini-golf. In college, I walked everywhere, even when it was frigid out. Even though it was tough at times—especially when it was icy—walking kept me sane under stress. Moving to Washington, DC, I was thrilled to find a house in a neighborhood with good walking and biking infrastructure and a bus stop steps from my property line.

When I became a parent, I wanted to share the benefits of active transportation with my own kids. I'm the person who wants to take the bus when there's no reason we can't take the car. Who encourages my family to walk to a restaurant even when it's 90 degrees out. (It's a hard sell.) Who loves biking to get ice cream across town, the cool treat making the pedaling even more rewarding.

Among the many benefits of not taking the car is the fact that walking, biking, and public transit produce far less pollution than driving. According to the U.S. Environmental Protection Agency, 29 percent of U.S. greenhouse gas emissions are from transportation. It's the sector that makes the biggest contribution to climate change. Passenger vehicles make up half that slice of the pie. (The other half is mainly freight and aircraft.) In addition to carbon dioxide, a whole host of pollutants that contribute to smog come from cars. Smog exacerbates cardiovascular and respiratory diseases, especially asthma among kids in urban areas. Although our hybrid car is better than most, all motor vehicles produce some pollution.

I also try to leverage the fact that I'm privileged enough to have a variety of transportation options so that I can help others. While our family is "car-light" by choice, being forced into that position by finances, disabilities, or other barriers can be very limiting. This is especially true in the many places where there are very few non-car options. Public transit isn't reliable or available in many suburban and rural areas, including my hometown. Walking and biking for transportation are unsafe in many places, especially at night. In the town I grew up in, I never biked at night despite being an experienced cyclist. The roads were too dark and drivers weren't aware enough of cyclists for me to take that risk. Similarly, the lack of decent sidewalks in many places minimizes walking as an option.

But if you have that biking, walking, and public transportation infrastructure, taking advantage of it can encourage local governments to make it available to more people in the future. Similarly, seeing the success of walkable and bikeable neighborhoods in other cities can persuade policymakers that it's a strategy to emulate. By using and showing support for transit, sidewalks, and bikeways, I try to improve these resources for everyone.

A TRUE LIFE SKILL

But the greater good isn't the only reason to ride a bike or walk. Teachers in the Washington, DC, Public Schools (DCPS) see bike riding as a lifelong skill they can pass along to children. These days, the schools are teaching every second grader to ride a bike as part of their Physical Education core curriculum. As a result, kids are experiencing all kinds of benefits, from learning independence to gaining resilience.

The program started when DCPS launched its "Cornerstones" effort. Through this program, every grade has at least one real-world, in-depth core project in common per subject area. Administrators focused on learning to ride a bike for physical education in second grade because they saw an increasing number of students not knowing how to ride a bike. While parents wanted their children to learn how to ride, many did not have the time, ability, or space to teach them. As bike infrastructure in Washington, DC, continues to expand, the administration wanted to ensure all children could take advantage of it as much as possible. School officials also recognized that riding to school for transportation could increase physical activity and reduce traffic congestion near schools.

As the country's first large-scale elementary school program with this goal, DCPS was blazing new (bike) trails. Collaborating with the Washington Area Bicyclist Association, a local bike advocacy group, DCPS launched the program at the beginning of the 2015 school year.

These days, all DCPS elementary schools run the program for six weeks, one lesson a week. A set of about 1,000 bikes cycle through 78 elementary schools, with 4,000 students participating per year. In addition, the school makes almost 600 balance bikes available to children in younger grades so that they can be better prepared to start the second-grade program.

At the beginning of the program, physical education teachers assess each child, deciding if they're total beginners, advanced beginners, or already know how to ride. By the end of six weeks, almost all the students—even those who started with zero skills—participate in a bike ride through the city.

JUST PLAIN FUN—AND RELAXING TOO

The anticipation starts way before the bikes arrive at a school. Incoming second graders have often heard about the biking program ahead of time from older siblings or classmates. "Students have overwhelmingly enjoyed the program," said Miriam Kenyon, DCPS's director of health and physical education. "They ask their teachers all of the time, 'When are the bikes coming?'"

This sense of excitement continues throughout the program. The school picked second grade because at that age, students would gain skills quickly. While they've developed enough balance that learning feels natural, they're also light enough that falling doesn't hurt too much. In addition, they're excited to learn how to ride a bike instead of embarrassed that they don't know how. As a result, students truly appreciate their progress.

"They enjoy that sense of accomplishment when they realize that they're a lot better," said Kenyon. As described in a 2017 report detailing the success of the program's first year, teachers, principals, and parents throughout the district all reported that students had very positive experiences.

Other families who regularly forgo driving for transportation report their kids have similar feelings about traveling by bike, foot, or transit. Shane Rhodes rides regularly with his eight-year-old twin sons and his ten-year-old daughter. Along with his day job as the transportation options coordinator for the City of Eugene, Oregon, he's also started an international family biking movement called Kidical Mass. This is a man who knows about the ups and downs of family biking.

"Every trip becomes an adventure," he said. In fact, he thinks that the toughest mornings are when it's the most important to get on the bike. Whether it's seeing a chicken rambling down the road or a ridiculous sign on someone's lawn, there are always things that make his family smile. He said, "There's some joy that comes out of those moments."

As I saw with my son, that sense of adventure can make riding the bus an exciting experience. Carla Saulter, known for her *Bus Chick* blog, hasn't owned a car for more than a decade. Instead, she walks and takes transit everywhere in Seattle with her nine- and eleven-year-old children. When her children were younger, they especially loved pointing out the various landmarks and ringing the bell to tell the bus driver to stop.

"They were part of the adventure, not just put in the back and driven somewhere," she said. "They got to participate in going somewhere via the excitement of being on the bus."

While most adults aren't as enthusiastic as kids about transit, walking and biking are associated with higher rates of life satisfaction. Both are related to lower levels of stress, better mental well-being, and overall higher quality of life. An international team of researchers surveyed 3,500 commuters in seven European cities and found that driving places more was associated with lower levels of energy. In contrast, people who biked and walked for transportation were more likely to say they had more energy. Biking specifically was associated with less stress and better mental health. Similarly a study in Barcelona, Spain, of nearly 800 adults found that people who commuted by bike were significantly less likely to be stressed than non-bike commuters.

In my personal experience, my bike or walk home from the Metro is often one of my favorite parts of the day. For both kids and adults, having that transition time spent doing a physical activity outdoors can provide a mental and emotional break between school/work and home.

TAKING RESPONSIBILITY ON THE ROAD AND IN THE CLASSROOM

Wanting to see the DCPS program in action, I was lucky enough to observe a class during their second bike lesson of the year. Waiting for students to arrive, I noticed the gym had plastic half-domes laid out in lines on the floor. Bikes were lined up in neat rows at the back, while bulletin boards extolled the virtues of wearing a helmet. As I chatted to Pam Parker, the physical education teacher in charge of the class, I learned that she's a huge fan of the program.

"This Cornerstone has been amazing," said Parker. "This is an opportunity."

As the kids walked in, clad in sweatpants, leggings, and T-shirts, she led them between the rows of half domes. After an enthused "Morning, Ms. Parker!" they walked around the gym to warm up. As they walked, Parker asked, "Why is it important to ride a bicycle? Tell your partner." The kids chatted as they made circles around the gym.

Following the warm-up, the students split into three groups: beginners, advanced beginners, and bike riders. Each group grabbed helmets and different color vests. As the kids put on helmets, a few struggled to buckle them. Almost immediately, their classmates stepped in to help.

Once they all had helmets on, they gathered around Parker in the middle of the room. She asked, "I need someone to tell me, using proper terms, how do you tell if your helmet is on correctly?"

A kid called out, "Doesn't move!" Parker affirmed, "It doesn't move—that's right." She asked them to check each other's helmets to ensure that they could fit two fingers—no more, no less—near the ears and under the chin.

Once the helmets were settled, Parker asked, "What are some of the benefits of bicycling?"

Another kid piped up: "Because it's good exercise." With encouragement, another responded, "It's something you can do with your family."

Parker then shifted gears, asking, "How many of you like to ride a bike?" Almost all of the kids raised their hands. "How many of you have a bike?" About half to three-quarters raised their hands again. "How many of you have training wheels?" About half the kids who had bikes kept their hands raised—most of them in the beginner group. She followed up: "How many of you are going to get rid of those training wheels after six weeks?" The kids jumped up and down in anticipation.

Looking at the class with a gleam in her eye, Parker asked another question: "Is there anything else we need to do before we get started?"

One student suggested, "We have to do the ABCs."

Parker grinned and responded, "So we need to sing the song?" She started mock-singing the alphabet song.

"No!" the students responded. With a bit of back-and-forth, she coaxed the ABCs of cycling out of them: check the air, brakes, and chain every time you bike. A brave kid volunteered to come in front of the class to demonstrate. Parker gave him a high-five. He then flipped the bike over to squeeze the tires and brakes as well as check the chain.

In an authoritative tone, he informed the class about the chain, "You have to see if it's clean and in the gears."

Teaching how to take care of each other and the bike is a core part of the program. A bike with a flat tire is frustrating at best and dangerous at worst. Kenyon said that a story from her childhood made teaching these skills particularly important to her. When she was in second grade, her family biked from Washington, DC, to Harpers Ferry, West Virginia, and back—a sixty-mile trip each way. That's a heck of a lot for an adult who has trained for that distance, much less a kid. Even though she was rarely tired, she had tremendous difficulty riding up one hill on the way back. When they got home, the family discovered the issue—Kenyon had two flat tires. These days, she wants to make sure that kids know the basics so they don't have to go through the same frustration she did.

The program also teaches children how to be responsible and predictable on the road. "To be safe is to be predictable," said Kenyon. While helmets and bright clothing are helpful, she emphasized, "You are the most important component of making you safe." In the program, children learn how to look out for drivers, signal which direction they're going, and follow the rules of the road—all essential skills for riding for transportation.

That familiarity with how to handle yourself on the road and around other people is also essential to walking. Heather Svanidze is a mom of four kids who lives in Claremont, California, an outer suburb of Los Angeles. She's been car-free her entire adult life. Because her kids hardly ever ride in a car, they're intimately familiar with the responsibility required as a pedestrian. "They have a very early sense of 'You have to look both ways before you have to cross the road,'" she said. The constant activity also helps her kids find an outlet for their energy, which helps them handle being around and respecting others as well.

The physical activity involved in biking and walking often translates to better focus and self-control in the classroom. "Any time you're engaging in physical activity, the endorphins in the body, the hormones that fight depression . . . kick in," said Cass Isidro, the executive director for the Safe Routes Partnership. The partnership works to make walking and biking to school safe for kids of all races, income levels, and abilities. Isidro said, "We know when the bodies are active, the brains are more active." In general, kids who come to school having engaged in physical activity beforehand are more likely to be ready to learn and able to focus.

Medical studies looking at the effects of physical activity on children provide some explanation as to why biking and walking can support students' success in the classroom. In the short term, exercising is associated with temporary improvements in concentration and self-control. Over the long term, studies have shown a relationship in children between physical fitness, memory, and the size of the hippocampus—an area of the brain associated with memory and learning. A variety of other studies with children have found positive relationships between physical fitness and memory, attention, executive function, and other forms of cognitive control (which includes impulse control and switching between tasks). In fact, researchers at the University of Illinois scanned children's brains with MRIs to examine this relationship. In one study, they showed that children with higher levels of fitness actually had their brains "light up" differently on the same task compared to children who were less fit. These differences suggested that the more fit children were, the more their brains functioned like adults' brains. Physical activities that involve complex movement—including biking on the road—may also build mental flexibility and the ability to adapt to new situations.

While there isn't a straight line between these differences in the brain and academic performance, there appears to be a relationship. A review paper of studies that looked at children participating in randomized control trials found that although some of the effects were minimal, all of the studies found physical activity had a positive effect on thinking and academic achievement. None of them found a negative relationship.

These effects may be even stronger for students who face challenges in the classroom. After a bout of moderate exercise, students both with and without attention deficit hyperactivity disorder (ADHD) did substantially better on a test of cognitive control in one study from researchers at the University of Illinois. A study—albeit sponsored by the bicycle company Specialized—looked specifically at the relationship between ADHD and bicycling in fifty-four children. Examining two before-school biking programs in Massachusetts, the study found that children both with and without ADHD had improvements in the ability to pay attention immediately after cycling, as well as in the long term after the program ended.

While my older son doesn't currently bike to school—he takes the school bus—I definitely see an increase in attention span and calm after he bikes. Doing giant circles around our local park or pedaling to a nearby destination is like moving meditation for him.

BUILDING RESILIENCE THROUGH HARD CHALLENGES

One thing I've forgotten as an experienced cyclist is how hard it is to learn to ride a bike. Even though the second-grade students in the PE class learn quickly, it still requires a lot of patience and repetition. As the students biked down the rows of domes serving as indoor bike lanes, the variation in skills quickly became evident.

The beginners were the closest to me. Wobbling on their balance bikes without pedals, they pushed their feet and attempted to coast without falling over. As they went off one at a time, Parker said, "There you go, there you go! Beginners, instead of a push, give yourself a good running start and lift," referring to lifting their feet off the ground. While none of them seemed frustrated, all of the children seemed intensely focused. These kids meant business and that business was riding a bike.

In the next row over, the advanced beginners were working on riding pedal bikes. They had progressed past mere balance into more coordinated motion. A number were still wobbly—adding pedals isn't simple—but they looked more confident than their beginner counterparts.

The furthest away were the actual bicyclists. But even they had plenty to learn. For the kids who already knew how to ride, the class taught them the skills to ride in the street. These include following street signs, being able to brake quickly, and turning. The children were also learning fine control over their bikes. In addition to adjusting quickly when riding in the road for transportation, this control also helps them tackle riding up and down hills. DC has some doozies.

The scaling to different levels of expertise was purposeful. The team who designed the curriculum wanted all students to face a challenge, not just the beginners.

"One of the pieces that we really wanted to see from kids is this idea of perseverance through a challenge," said Kenyon. "You want to enjoy learning, but you also want to be challenged. It's the component of being challenged that really makes it more fun." The children being able to see how they progressed over time plays a major role in that accomplishment. "By the end, they want to show you everything they can do. Now, 'Look at me, can't you see, watch me!'" she said, recalling what kids have said to her.

For most kids in the DC program, their efforts pay off. At the beginning of the first year DCPS ran the program, most kids were either beginners or intermediate riders. By the end of the first year, four out of five students were either advanced or expert riders. At the time, the program was only four weeks of lessons. To keep the learning going even further, DCPS has since expanded the lessons to six weeks.

Building resilience goes beyond the learning process. Just incorporating active transportation into daily activities can help kids build the mental and emotional skills to deal with everyday setbacks.

Saulter, who walks with her kids when they aren't on the bus, said her children are used to dealing with Seattle's notoriously gloomy weather. "I know people have kids and they have to walk a little ways and they just complain," she said. "Whereas my kids don't . . . even think about it. It's just part of their lives." Practice has helped them build up physical and mental stamina.

The Dutch also credit the fact that their children bike everywhere as a major factor in their culture's legendary steadiness. In fact, a popular Dutch parenting book encourages parents to never drive their children to school, even if it's raining. Instead, they should embrace biking because biking in the rain builds character. As Dutch kids are considered some of the happiest and most well-adjusted children in the world, there's likely some truth in it.

FINDING YOUR WAY AROUND LIFE

While riding a bike may seem old-fashioned to parents used to the drop-off car line, one of the goals of the DCPS program was to offer kids another way to get to school. Forty years ago, 50 percent of children walked or biked to school. Today less than 15 percent do.

Although the first few lessons are in the gymnasium, later lessons move outside to help students gain real-world skills. The school district is working to develop "traffic gardens," pretend roadways where students can practice their on-road skills without the risks involved in city streets. Different sections of the traffic garden mimic real obstacles, such as potholes.

As the class wrapped up and the students started leaving, one child lingered by a bulletin board with a photo of one of the traffic gardens. Parker encouraged him: "You like that obstacle course, Zeke? You'll be ready for that in about three weeks. That's lesson five."

Riding on the road comes with both responsibility and opportunity. It enables children to bike places by themselves, which opens up a whole new set of possibilities for learning. Even among the youngest children, getting themselves around teaches a sense of independence.

"It's much more child-scale, walking and biking. It's as small as they are," said Svanidze, whose family of six is car-free. She said her children take pride in "the feeling that I get to get myself somewhere, I don't just have to be pushed in a stroller or strapped in a car."

Once children begin to get around without their parents, that sense of independence grows exponentially. In places where people must rely on cars, children can't travel anywhere by themselves until they're at least sixteen. In contrast Saulter started taking the bus when she was eight years old. Although her dad accompanied her for part of the trip to school, she returned home by herself. "I got to be in control. I got to be responsible," she recalled. "I found that extremely empowering and exciting. Even though I wasn't a very bold kid, that set the foundation for the rest of my childhood."

For her, figuring out what to do when something went wrong in the days before cell phones led to personal growth. Typically her parents only gave her the bus tickets she needed for the day. Although that was usually fine, she lost her bus ticket one day. The bus driver made her ride past her usual stop to get to the bus line's "free" zone. From there, she had to find her way home by herself. Another time, the Queen of England visited the city, causing all of the buses to be rerouted. Saulter waited an hour and a half at one stop before realizing she needed to walk to a different stop. "Those are the kinds of things that kids have to go through to get the independence and the confidence," she said. "I learned that I could apply [this] to other parts of my life. I could figure this out, it's not just something for adults. I don't need someone to lead me around."

Part of problem solving involves figuring out different ways to get to the same place. Speaking of her own children, Saulter said, "They have a really robust range of options in their brain."

To tap into those options, children have to be able to navigate their way around their communities. Walking and biking play a role here too. Learning to travel independently helps children develop spatial knowledge, which is important to feeling comfortable in a place. In a study of twenty-six nine- and ten-year-olds in the San Francisco suburbs, a researcher at San Diego State University asked the children to draw maps of the route from their home to school. The children whose neighborhoods had minimal traffic, which made it easier to bike and walk places, had more detailed, complex, and concrete maps than the kids who lived in the neighborhoods with heavier traffic. The contrast was even higher for children whose parents drove them everywhere. In general the children from the low-traffic neighborhoods showed a much better sense of understanding where locations were related in space to each other. A similar study in Israel also found that fifth and sixth graders from more walkable neighborhoods could draw more accurate maps of their home-to-school routes compared to children from less walkable suburban neighborhoods.

"Kids gain confidence when they gain control of their surroundings," said Isidro, the Safe Routes director. "They successfully set out on an endeavor; they accomplish that by themselves. Therefore, their confidence in that path and their surroundings and their environment and ultimately their world increases."

Gaining this independence early can provide relief to stressed parents. Rather than spending time and energy ferrying children to activities, parents can allow them to transport themselves. While Shane Rhodes's kids are a little too young to get themselves to sports practices or dance classes yet, he expects that day will come soon. "That is childhood independence for them and it's independence for me," he said. "It's a reclaiming of childhood to allow your kids to walk and bike."

BUILDING RELATIONSHIPS WITH FAMILIES AND COMMUNITY

The grand finale to the DCPS program is a huge community bike ride. Each school does a ride of five to seven miles that uses bike lanes and trails in the surrounding neighborhoods. "They have to learn to be safe in the places they have," said Parker, the PE teacher.

Parents often volunteer on the ride to provide additional support. For many of them, it's their first time volunteering at the school. "It's a positive way for them to be part of their student's school experience," said Kenyon.

Many of the rides visit local parks, including Rock Creek Park, a huge greenway that winds through the heart of the city. "Students see a great place that they can ride that's within their community that they can take their family to," said Kenyon. "That was really important to me because this was a really big part of growing up [for me]." In many cases, the rides go places blocks from their schools that students didn't even realize existed. During breaks, they stop and take in the view.

Building these connections with family, neighbors, and the local environment is common to families who regularly rely on active and public transportation to get around.

"The biggest one for me is the togetherness," said Saulter. When her kids were babies, they always wanted to be held. Riding the bus, she could wear them in a baby carrier and comfort them if they got upset. As the children got older, she was able to use the time spent en route to bond by reading books or talking. She said, "There was just always our time."

The slower pace of walking or biking also lends itself to conversation. Isidro, the Safe Routes director, has both professional and personal knowledge on this topic. She said walking with her teenage son is one of the best ways to start up a conversation with him. "You're just next to each other, it's not confrontational," she said. That's a rare thing when talking to a teenager! In the book *Tell Me a Story*, author Elaine Reese points out that walking is one of the best times to share family stories, which she sees as key to emotional development.

With younger children, a slow pace allows parents to stop and pay attention to items that would be impossible to look at if you were driving a car. If you have preschoolers, that's a lot of things. "I love that when we're walking, we can stop and look at something. Especially small things that you wouldn't notice," said Svanidze, who has an eight-year-old, six-year-old, four-year-old, and two-year-old. Her family's walks through an outer suburb of Los Angeles often reveal tiny surprises: lizards, snails, butterflies, and even non-native parrots. Saulter said that her kids notice little details that adults so often miss, like cracks in the sidewalk and figurines in neighbors' windows.

Paying attention to what children point out can open up new worlds to you as an adult. When we walk to the grocery store, Dylan loves to stop and pretend that a vacant but well-kept lot is a restaurant. I've eaten many a pretend meal on the way to shop for groceries. Engaging with my children over these observations sparks conversation and connects them to their surrounding environment.

That awareness lends itself to connecting to your neighbors as well. Each walk, bike ride, or bus ride provides opportunities to meet and interact with people you wouldn't see in a car. When Dylan was much younger, every day we would walk to the pedestrian bridge in our neighborhood to watch the trains go by. As we walked, we'd say hello to our neighbors on their porches and wave to their dogs outside. Just from seeing us on those trips, one of our neighbors invited us to a Labor Day cookout. Similarly Saulter said they moved to a new house several years ago, and within the first month, they knew everyone as a result of their daily walks. "Saying hi to people makes them feel really connected to the place where they live. I think that's not very common these days," she said.

Saulter has found similar fulfillment in being in close proximity to others on the bus. Taking transit, her family regularly runs into many different community members, from the assistant at the doctor's office to people from church. "The beauty of being on the bus is being in solidarity with the community," she said. "It just constantly reinforces our connections and makes us feel more a part of our place."

Transit also tends to expose children to a wider variety of people than they might see at home or school. "There are people of all different abilities, religions, colors, shapes, sizes," Saulter said. "I want them to feel and understand what that means—that everyone belongs. You're going to sit right next to whoever that person is."

Seeing the same people over and over again brings them into your child's view of the world, expanding the idea of who is part of their community. Even though America is becoming ever more diverse, neighborhoods and schools are becoming more racially and economically segregated compared to the recent past. According to one study in Chicago by researchers at the University of Illinois, even though people of all races said they wanted to live in diverse neighborhoods, most White residents chose to live in areas with minimal diversity. (Black and Latino residents, however, were much more likely to move to diverse neighborhoods.) Situations that expose children to diversity day after day can familiarize them with a variety of people, reduce their formation of stereotypes, and demonstrate how to live out your values. "They piece it together and put it into their little vision of the world," said Svanidze. "Their vision of the world has all of these different kinds of people in it."

The slower pace of biking and walking also may reduce snap judgments that often reflect racism and classism. The fast pace of driving enables people to get less information about a person, which can lead to more reliance on stereotypes and judgment of a situation as dangerous. A study from the University of Surrey in the United Kingdom looked at how transportation mode affected people's tendency to stereotype others. In a survey, they found that people who lived in a richer neighborhood and drove were more likely to have a negative attitude toward people in the poorer neighborhood. But people from the more expensive neighborhood who walked through the poorer neighborhood were more likely to have a positive attitude toward it. (Transportation mode didn't influence the attitudes of people who lived in the less expensive neighborhood either way.)

An experiment in the same study showed people videos of the same ambiguous situation of teenagers play-fighting from four different perspectives: in a car, on a bus, on a bike, and walking. The people in the car mode felt more threatened by the young people than those in the bus or walking modes. They also had more negative perceptions overall of the people and situation than any of the other modes.

This lack of connection can lead to building less social capital. Social capital is the value of your social network—the people you can reach out to when you want to solve a problem. It's essential for both individuals and entire societies. Building social capital requires building trust through everyday interactions. A survey of more than 20,000 commuters in Sweden found that people who commuted by car had less social interaction and were less likely to say they trusted people in general than those who rode other modes of transport.

Interacting with people more also provides opportunities for children to show respect and establish boundaries with people who aren't friends or family. While a child kicking the back of a parent's seat might be okay in the car, it's not in the bus.

On the flip side, this exposure also helps children know how to deal with people who might have erratic behaviors. Rhodes, who bikes with his children in Eugene, Oregon, said that they sometimes see homeless people camping out along one of their favorite paths. Rather than pretend he doesn't see these folks, he addresses their presence with his children in a straightforward way. "They're healthy conversations that allow us to talk about it and then not have it be a big deal," Rhodes said. "It allows us to connect more and have sympathy and empathy for other people who are in our community."

That familiarity and connection build a sense of place in children, a key aspect of feeling secure. In the study asking children in the San Francisco suburbs to map their neighborhoods, not only did the children in the heavier-traffic neighborhood have less detailed maps, they also listed more places they disliked and felt were dangerous than the children in low-traffic neighborhoods. That lack of familiarity with the neighborhood translated into a lack of fondness. In contrast, children in the low-traffic neighborhoods were more likely to list places they enjoyed. As the study says, "Without pedestrian and bicycle facilities to provide sanctuary for a child from automobile traffic, the negative senses of danger and dislike appear to limit children's ability to identify the qualities of their neighborhood that are memorable, special, or even positive." Ouch.

Similarly a study of nine- to eleven-year-old children in Birmingham in the United Kingdom by researchers by the University of Birmingham found that children who walked the least in the group were the least likely to say there were parks or other places to play near them. They were also more worried about strangers compared to children who walked more often. While being worried about strangers isn't a bad thing, excess worry can block the formation of community ties. After all, everyone is a stranger until you meet them.

CREATING NEW PATHS FOR TRANSPORTATION

So far, more than 15,000 DCPS students have learned to ride a bike through the second-grade program. The school district wants this program to be a highlight of the children's school experience. From seeing it firsthand, I bet it will be for many kids. The students', parents', and teachers' enthusiasm show how much biking can mean to children if they have the opportunity to embrace it.

Personally, a key part of my children's childhood memories has already been walking, biking, and taking transit. The slow summer afternoons wandering through our neighborhood have been key bonding times for our family.

But I felt the biggest connection to my own childhood when my older son, Dylan, and I biked somewhere together for the first time. While he's been able to ride a pedal bike since he was three, I wasn't confident enough in his judgment to let him ride on the road for several more years. But just before he turned six, we signed up for a community bike ride that had a brief section on the road. To prepare, I bit the bullet and taught him some urban riding skills. With him ahead and me behind, I yelled at him to stop for stop signs, use his brakes going downhill, and watch for cars. My heart beating, I tried to breathe and not let him see my anxiety. While I offered guidance, he was ultimately in control of his bike. We pedaled through our narrow neighborhood streets, next to parked cars, and on the bike lanes in our city's downtown area. Knowing how to ride on the road opened up a new way for him to get around.

A few weeks after the community ride, he was invited to a friend's birthday party. On a whim I suggested, "Do you want to ride our bikes there?" His response was immediate: "Yes!" Winding our way through town, he used all of his newfound skills, from following traffic signals to being visible and predictable. We stored our bikes in the family's backyard while he climbed up and slid down a giant blow-up water slide. On the way back, he spotted the sign with our neighborhood's name on it. He declared, "I know where we are!" and navigated back without needing any directions from me. I smiled and followed him home.

What to Know

Just like most families put a lot of thought into what car to buy, it's important to put thought into the gear necessary for your non-car transportation.

For the most part, transit doesn't require a lot of specific stuff. However, it's very helpful to travel light but effectively. Because you can't store things in your car, you must efficiently carry everything you need for a trip. Paring it down to the essentials—water, snacks, a plastic bag for emergencies, a few things to do while waiting, and diapers if necessary—will make your trip much more fun. It also makes you less likely to leave something essential on the bus. You will never get it back—I've learned from personal experience.

If you have younger children and plan to walk for transportation, investing in a sturdy stroller is a must. We have a stroller designed for heavy city use that's lasted us through hundreds of miles. Its fabric is faded and stained with tea, but it just keeps on chugging. We take its ability to easily roll over sidewalk cracks and bumps for granted. Last year we used a cheap umbrella stroller for a family trip—by the end, our backs were killing us. If your kids are older, the only necessary tools are good pairs of shoes for you and them, plus rain or winter gear for crummy weather.

On the other hand, biking with children requires a lot of thought about appropriate and useful gear. In fact it's easy to get overwhelmed by the number of options. Before you buy any family bike gear, consider how far you'll be riding, how often you'll be riding, and if you'll be carrying children on your bike or if they'll be riding their own bikes. If you plan to carry your children on your own bike for short distances and not very often, a children's bike seat (front or back, depending on your child's age and your skill level) or a trailer may be the best bet. Both are often available secondhand for reasonable prices. If biking becomes a daily lifestyle, you may want to consider a cargo bike built for hauling people and goods. Some parents who carry multiple children or have hilly commutes find that it's extremely helpful to add a battery-powered motor to provide electric assist. That extra boost is especially important if you have knee problems. Whatever you ride, a kickstand, lights, and fenders and chain guards to protect your clothing are essential.

Next Steps

Start with a Trial Run

Walking, biking, or taking transit can be a great experience, but over-ambition can kill future enthusiasm. According to the U.S. Department of Transportation's latest national household travel survey, more than 20 percent of vehicle trips are less than a mile. In addition, 34 percent of trips come in at about two miles.

To get used to walking, start by parking farther away from locations you drive to, or try driving to a single location and then walking to others nearby. If there aren't many destinations within walking distance of your home, take walks around the neighborhood for fun. Just taking an evening stroll can bring you many of the same benefits as walking for transportation.

For biking, start with a quick cycle around the neighborhood. Finding an appointment or errand you can run by bike, walking, or transit is a good option. If you don't want to walk or bike to school, kids' sports can offer another possibility. In a study of families participating in youth soccer in Davis, California, researchers found that of the families who lived less than 1.5 miles from the game, half of them drove. If roads are too crowded or you're in too much of a time crunch to bike to school or daycare in the mornings, roads may be less busy and easier to maneuver on weekends. Taking a bike ride is a great form of recreation.

Another opportunity may be a community event that's difficult to drive to. Our city has a huge multiday celebration for Memorial Day where they close off the streets. It makes it almost impossible to park. As it's about a mile away from our house, we usually walk, bike, or take the bus that stops near our house.

If your location lacks any infrastructure to walk, drive, or take transit, you may be able to test out these transportation modes in a nearby city or on vacation. Park the car for the day and find your way around without having to deal with traffic. Walking is often the best way to see a city. To get around more quickly, an increasing number of places have either bikeshare systems or all-day bike rental shops.

Subway systems in major cities tend to be simpler to understand and less intimidating than bus routes, allowing you to try out a new mode. I remember visiting Washington, DC, as a ten-year-old and being in awe of the Metro. While I'm significantly less impressed by it now that I ride it every day to work, that first impression has stuck with me.

Adjust Your Pace

Even if you're used to walking or biking as an adult, doing it with small children can try your patience. But it's also an opportunity to embrace the newfound pace. Many families struggle with being hectic and over-scheduled—active transportation or taking transit can force you to slow down and be with each other. As Svanidze said, "It created this slowness to our days in a good way. We have time to stop." This slow pace allowed her family to stop and watch a lunar eclipse that they would have missed if they were in the car. She said, "We might not have noticed [it] if we had not been walking that night."

Connect with Other Families for Support

Choosing to not to drive places can feel countercultural. When you're walking home from somewhere, people in some communities may assume that there's something wrong with your car or ask if you want a ride. My suburban hometown had very few places within walking distance of my house, but we occasionally walked the mile or so to church. People were always baffled when they saw us walking home. Finding other families who are car-free or car-light can help provide needed support.

Meeting up in person allows you a chance to build community. Walking school buses, where an adult leads a group of children to school, takes some of the stress off of a parent getting children to school. Kidical Mass and other family bike rides help families discover new routes and have fun together.

Online communities can help too. Local family biking groups on Facebook can help parents learn about the best routes in their area, places to buy gear, and opportunities to improve cycling infrastructure.

FAMILY ACTIVITY: Planning a Car-Free Trip

PICK YOUR DESTINATION

Select somewhere that seems reasonable to walk, bike, or take transit to. Try to choose somewhere that is already a regular destination or that you would want to visit regularly. It's especially helpful to make it somewhere fun. Riding or walking to get food is always a winner. My kids' favorite rides are always to get ice cream. The library, community center, a park, or a playground are all good options.

PLAN YOUR ROUTE

The way you drive to a location may not be the best way to walk, bike, or take transit there. For transit, look up maps and schedules online before going. There have been a number of times when I assumed I knew where the bus was going or how long it was going to take and realized far too late that I was wrong. While bus schedules aren't always the most accurate, an increasing number of buses are equipped with GPS systems that allow you to track the bus's location in real time. For walking and biking, look up directions on Google Maps and choose biking or walking. The directions aren't always perfect, but they can provide a start. If it's a route that you're familiar with, think about where the heaviest traffic tends to be and try to plan around those spots. Also, search online to see if your city or county has a bike map. These are often more comprehensive and useful than Google Maps alone.

SET EXPECTATIONS FOR YOUR KIDS

Get your kids hyped up beforehand for what you're doing and frame it as an adventure. If you're taking transit, remind them of appropriate and safe behavior, such as not standing up while the vehicle is moving. If you're walking or biking, give them an idea of how long it will take. You may want to walk them through a preview of the route. If they're biking on their own (and not riding on your bike), remind them of the rules of the road as necessary. No matter what, make sure they go to the bathroom ahead of time!

PACK YOUR GEAR

Remembering something you absolutely need to have right as you're ready to go is a pain. Getting all of your gear together, whether that's preparing the diaper bag or filling the tires on your bike, before you get the kids out the door is really helpful.

PLAN THE NEXT TRIP

When it's over, evaluate what went right and wrong. While my kids loved getting ice cream at a specific ice cream store, we realized that the one hill was too steep to tackle just yet. If the bus route took too long or the bus was exceptionally late, check to see if there's a similar one that's faster, or consider a different mode for the future. If you tried out a walk or bike ride on vacation, think about if there's any way to apply what you learned to getting around at home.

Books

PICTURE BOOKS

B Is for Bicycles, by Scott and Jannine Fitzgerald: A cute and bicycle-geeky alphabet book featuring a couple of cycle-happy dogs.

Sidewalk Flowers, by JonArno Lawson and Sydney Smith: This gorgeous wordless book follows a little girl and her dad as they walk home.

Even though he's a bit distracted, she notices everything going on around her.

Mike and the Bike, by Michael Ward, Bob Thomson, and Phil Liggett: While the text describing a boy's intense love of his bike is kind of goofy, kids who really love their bikes will enjoy the illustrations and words.

A Good Night Walk, by Elisha Cooper: A lovely ramble with a family through their neighborhood as the sun sets.

Maisy Drives the Bus, by Lucy Cousins: A cute book for the youngest of kids; Maisy drives from stop to stop picking up various animals along the way.

Wherever You Go, by Pat Zietlow Miller and Eliza Wheeler: A lovely poem about travel featuring beautiful illustrations of a bunny on a bicycle with an owl companion.

The Wheels on the Bus, by various illustrators: Everyone knows this classic kids' song. There are a number of books with great illustrations to accompany the lyrics.

Resources

Bus Chick blog by Carla Saulter: www.buschick.com

A Walking Mama blog by Heather Svanidze: http://awalkingmama .blogspot.com

Safe Routes Partnership: www.saferoutespartnership.org

Two-Wheeling Tots blog (family biking): www.twowheelingtots.com

Rascal Rides blog (family biking): www.rascalrides.com

Biking in the Park, DC Public Schools' First-Year Report, listed on the district's Cornerstones page: https://dcps.dc.gov/page/cornerstones

NOT YOUR MOTHER'S HOUSEHOLD:

ENERGY EFFICIENCY, WASTE REDUCTION, AND RENEWABLE ENERGY

"I'm bringing the compost outside. Anyone want to help?" I said. Silence. "I'm bringing the compost outside." Still no response. I grabbed the compost containers off the kitchen counter and started walking toward the back door.

"I want to help!" said a little voice behind me. Turning around, I saw Ethan.

"Okay," I said and looked for some newspapers to put in the compost along with the food scraps. Digging around in our pile of reusable bags—nothing. *Maybe in the recycling bin?* I shoved some cardboard cereal boxes aside and spotted a paper bag. *Bingo.* I pulled it out as I heard that same little voice behind me: "I want newspapers!"

"Sorry, hon. I can't find any newspapers. This is what we have. Come on," I said, opening the back door. He followed me out the door, down the deck stairs, and to our spinning composter. The large black cylinder sits on top of a square weighted base. Ridges run around the whole thing and there's a hole in the bottom to drain extra liquid. I opened the top and took the lids off of the reused quart yogurt containers we use to store our food waste. Dumping the rotting food into the bin, I wrinkled my nose.

Ripping off a piece of paper bag, I handed it to Ethan. "Rip this up, please."

He pulled at the paper handle, twisting it one way and the other. His small voice piped up: "I can't do it."

My husband, who was getting something out of the car, said, "Go the other way," then demonstrated how to rip it.

Ethan shredded the paper into thin strips before handing them to me one by one. "Put them in there," I said, gesturing at the open composter. He tossed them in on top of the vegetables and eggshells.

I shut the lid and slid the silver hook into place. Curling my fingers, I grabbed two ridges and pulled the composter toward me. The big cylinder barely moved. I pulled harder. It slowly spun. As it moved, the liquid that seeped out the bottom into the base started to coat the rest of the container. Around and around I turned it, touching it carefully to avoid the gunk.

Opening the lid, I peered in. There were rotted newspapers, food, and yard waste, all covered by a thick layer of black goo. "See, look at all of that great black compost forming!" I said to Ethan. He looked in, touching the lid. I winced, knowing what was on it. "Come on, let's go inside and wash our hands," I said.

Knowing that our food waste is on its way to help grow our garden always makes me feel a little better, even if the process can be gross. The alternative is worse though.

The average American produces about 4.5 pounds of waste per day, as of 2015, the most recent year with data available. Unless you compost or recycle it, waste goes into landfills. Garbage dumps take up valuable space, produce the greenhouse gas methane that contributes to climate change, and are frequently sited in low-income, minority communities. In communities that burn their waste, incinerators produce large amounts of pollution that contribute to poor air quality. The random waste that doesn't get to the landfill is destructive too; it often ends up in rivers, lakes, or oceans, polluting our water and hurting wildlife. While recycling reduces some garbage going into the waste stream, many facilities are receiving so much material for recycling that they can't process it all. Much of the time, they're just dumping it into landfills. In addition, each time plastic goods are recycled, they decrease in quality, limiting the number of times you can recycle them.

Besides waste, households are a major contributor to energy and water usage. Households use about 38 percent of the electricity produced in the U.S. The average household also uses more than 300 gallons of water a day, with 70 percent of it used inside.

Fortunately, reducing household waste, energy consumption, and water usage is one of the easiest things with the biggest impact you can do to reduce your individual environmental footprint. Household conservation is also one of the easiest concepts for children to understand and participate in. Being able to see the concrete results of household sustainability makes the impact real. Kids can learn to throw away less garbage, use less water, turn off lights, open windows instead of turning on the air-conditioning, and value renewable power. Using less water and throwing out less waste are simple for even the youngest children to comprehend. In fact, schools frequently start teaching the three Rs—reduce, reuse, and recycle—early and often. Many have ecological concepts baked right into the curriculum.

MEET THE GREEN TEAM

William Tyler Page Elementary in Silver Spring, Maryland, takes that emphasis to new heights. The school has a long-running "Green Team" that's involved kids in ecological activities for the past fifteen years. The Green Team's activities include making crafts out of recycled materials, planting flowers outside of the school, running school-wide recycling projects, making morning announcements about sustainability, and learning about solar energy.

These days, the club is incredibly popular. In a school of about 420 students, 81 students participated in the Green Team in the 2018–2019 school year—nearly a quarter of the school's population. There are so many students who want to participate that Rima Barrett, who runs the team, needs to split them into two groups.

"All of the kids that would like to join are pretty much welcome," said Barrett, who is a kindergarten teacher at the school. Currently, she has one group of students who are kindergarteners through second graders and a separate group that are third through fifth graders. Each group meets once a month.

While the team itself is an after-school club, an entire culture of conservation, waste reduction, and ecological awareness permeates the school. Each classroom has a Green Team leader who goes through the classroom at the end of the day to ensure they are saving as much energy as possible. The leader turns off lights, closes the window blinds, and turns off the computers.

In 2017 the U.S. Department of Education awarded the school the U.S. Department of Education Green Ribbon School designation. As each state can only nominate up to five schools a year, it's an impressive honor.

As I wanted to see the Green Team in action, I peeked in on a meeting of the third- through fifth-grade group. A diverse group of about thirty kids gathered in Barrett's kindergarten classroom, with even the biggest kids sitting in the miniature seats. Following the end of the school day, the children chatted among themselves, sometimes raising their voices in enthusiasm.

LEARNING BY CONTRIBUTING
TO A SHARED GOAL

Like any good teacher, Barrett started the session by getting the kids' attention. After clapping her hands and having them clap in return, she introduced the activity for the day. Their task was to tape customized covers onto classroom light switches to remind teachers and students to turn off the lights when they leave the room. The printed paper covers said: "The lights in this room use ___ watts of electricity." Each blank was filled in with a number, representing the energy use of the individual room. The students had calculated each room's energy consumption as part of an activity earlier in the year. These labels applied work students had done earlier to ensure it made an impact.

Once the kids received their instructions, they were raring to go. As Barrett called up each group, the kids rushed to the table, gathered their supplies—labels and pieces of tape—and formed a line at the door to get their room assignments. Because each label had an individualized number, it was essential to put them in the right rooms. Each group of three or four students scattered throughout the school.

The small groups walked through the school after the other kids had already gone home, something that always makes you feel responsible as a kid. A few peered into rooms they weren't allowed in, hoping to get special access. One of the teachers acting as an assistant shooed them away, commenting, "No, you can't go in the teacher's lounge." For the most part, the students were focused, appreciating their special role. They collaborated to figure out where to go and who had supplies like tape. To reward their hard work, one of the teachers allowed a group to take the freight elevator back down to Barrett's classroom—a special privilege indeed.

This sense of contributing to a shared goal is a common trait among children who are involved in hands-on community- or family-oriented tasks. The Green Team activities involve minimal formal teaching and heavy interaction. In many ways, they're similar to a method of learning that psychologists and educational researchers call "Learning by Observing and Pitching In." This method of learning is the most common in Indigenous groups in Central and South America as well as families of people descended from those groups. In contrast to conventional teaching in schools, it involves seven main characteristics:

➤ Learning is done in community with adults and children working together toward common goals.

▶ Learners want to belong and contribute to the larger community; adults act as facilitators.

▶ Teachers and learners work in collaborative, flexible groups with activities adapted to children's needs.

▶ Teachers pass on practical skills as a way of building overall responsibility and fulfilling future roles in the community.

▶ Children learn skills through observation and story in addition to or instead of formal teaching.

▶ Communication is largely informal and built on shared understanding.

▶ Assessment is based on what both the learner and teacher can do to help make the learner's final product closer to the teacher's version.

According to psychology researchers at the University of California and ITESO University in Mexico who have studied cultures that embody the principles of Learning by Observing and Pitching In, one of its major advantages is how it involves kids in family and community life. Carving out space for even the smallest of children offers them opportunities to make real contributions to a larger effort. This responsibility in the adult world puts activities in a bigger context, elevating them above rote chores.

One study led by a researcher from ITESO University observed children in two communities in Mexico, one urban and another rural and Indigenous. While household work was seen as a social activity done with parents in the rural, Indigenous community, city families were much more likely to assign individual chores to children. The children in the rural community actively chose to help; the city kids almost never did household work without their parents nagging them. That feeling of collaboration and responding to the needs of others fostered both short-term interest in helping and a lifelong mindset of cooperation in the Indigenous children.

Studies of children in the United States who do chores also provide proof that working toward a common goal creates meaning and purpose for kids. A study by University of California Los Angeles (UCLA) researchers of more than 750 ninth graders in three public schools in Los Angeles found that children who helped more in the household found their role in the family was more fulfilling than those who helped less. Helping more was also associated with being happier.

In the Learning by Observing and Pitching In approach children also have more self-direction than in other teaching styles. In observations by a University of California Santa Cruz researcher, European and American parents tended to guide toddlers and work to control interactions more than traditional Mayan mothers from Mexico. The Mayan mothers were more likely to allow children to lead without changing their direction. Having a level of control and independence can be quite motivating to kids. Self-direction allows children to problem-solve and gain confidence in their skills.

Likewise, collaborating with teachers and students across grade levels makes the Green Team learning more egalitarian than traditional classrooms. "I think they learn to help each other. They learn to guide each other. Be kind to each other," Barrett said. "I think the little ones really enjoy the big ones. The big ones really enjoy the little ones."

While most household sustainability activities don't need to involve kids, both the work of the Green Team and the social science research provide good reasons to do so. Although most research is on normal household chores, I think the ecological aspect of conservation activities makes them even more interesting to kids. The Green Team kids were enthused about contributing to the greater goal despite an activity that could have been boring.

Personally I've seen this in my children too. While my kids have zero interest in picking up their toys, their level of enthusiasm for composting or assisting in the garden is much higher. The feeling that "we're all in it together" as we work toward making our household more sustainable helps.

Welcoming and appreciating kids' contributions to the household early and often are key to cultivating this mindset, according to Barbara Rogoff, one of the main researchers who has studied Learning by Observing and Pitching In. Anyone who has kept plates safe from a toddler wanting to "help" can tell you that young children want to be involved with adults' activities, no matter what. An experimental study by University of Pittsburgh and University of Tennessee researchers observed forty-six parent-toddler pairs. In an activity of line-drying cloth napkins, only two children never helped. The young children responded to parents asking for help 73 percent of the time.

While it can seem annoying, working together with very young children to accomplish tasks sets the foundation for helping more later on. "Involving the kids in what you're doing makes it more possible to get things done," said Rebecca Stallings. A mom of a fourteen-year-old and five-year-old, she's been doing eco-friendly activities for years (and writing about them on her blog), long before her kids were born. When her older son was born, she was in charge of bringing home recyclables from her church. In Pittsburgh, where she lives, curbside recycling is only for family residences, not businesses or churches. With her son watching, she would bring the cans and bottles home, rinse them out, and smash them flat. "I have a picture of me with him, about two months old in a sling carrier, and I'm stomping aluminum cans on the kitchen floor. He just grew up with that," she said. As her son grew older, Stallings recruited his help. By the time he was two, he knew which items went in recycling and which went in the garbage. "He's always wanted to do what the grown-ups were doing and know how to do it right," she said. "I think having him help with a lot of volunteer activities has given him a good sense of what he can do and how he can help."

Kids chipping in can not only give them the impression of making a significant contribution but actually reduce parents' burden. Stallings said that she was able to use cloth diapers rather than disposables for her daughter—who is nine years younger than her son—because her son did his own laundry. Many other conservation activities, like using cloth towels instead of paper, making food from scratch rather than buying packaged, washing reusable containers rather than using disposable ones, and line-drying laundry rather than using a dryer, take more time and effort than their convenient but more wasteful alternatives. Often these efforts fall on the person who is already running much of the household—too often the mom. Minimizing that burden gives either more rest time to the parents or more time spent together as a family. Either makes everyone happier in the long run.

ENVISIONING THE BIGGER PICTURE OF INDIVIDUAL ACTIONS

Once the Green Team finished taping the labels to light switches, they met back in Barrett's classroom. To celebrate their final Green Team meeting of the year, Barrett handed out ice pops. She then invited the kids to share their experiences on the Green Team with me. They offered a variety of insights into their work:

- ▶ "We get to learn about the Earth and the planet." —Lilliana

- ▶ "I like that we get to help the environment." —Jaylynn

- ▶ "We got to learn about the Earth." —Chelyn

- ▶ "Multiple people are polluting and we need to save the Earth." —George

- ▶ "If you trash something that's reusable, you're trashing your money." —Abdullah

- ▶ "If we help the environment, it will help more people." —Alison

Many of these comments demonstrated how well the children understood that what they were doing was good for society and Earth. As a parent of kids who picked up random garbage when they were younger (and one who still does), I especially appreciated Jeda's comment explaining why the team cleans up trash: "When babies go to the park, they pick up random things." Exactly—ugh.

This association between activities the students do and the greater good isn't coincidental. Barrett works hard to help students make these connections through a heavy dose of discussion time. She starts by building off of the students' natural enthusiasm.

"They're very caring students," she said. "They have an interest in taking care of the Earth." She thinks that some of that interest comes from hearing about environmental issues at school, at home, and on the news. Children often pick up on what's going on in the adult world, even when adults don't realize it.

Keeping that inherent concern in mind, Barrett creates age-appropriate activities. With the younger students in kindergarten through second grade, she focuses on reducing, reusing, and recycling. The group talks about how the garbage they throw away fills the landfill or gets burned by incinerators. For the third through fifth graders, she moves on to composting, gardening, energy conservation, and water conservation. They also talk about how their Green Team actions affect wildlife around the world, including endangered species.

For some of the abstract concepts like energy, Barrett leads the group in an interactive play. In an activity called "Sun to Switch," students each take on part of the energy system, from the source providing energy to the electricity running through wires to the lights and appliances using it. They talked about how much of Maryland's energy is from coal and the pollution it creates. They also discuss how the school gets some of its electricity from solar panels on its roof. The play allowed students to understand their energy sources and what's needed to bring energy to their house when they turn on a light. "They may not have realized where energy came from," said Barrett. "They have a better sense of belonging to the Earth, belonging to the community."

These discussions also spark critical thinking about each step in that system. "Rima opens the world up," said Jim Stufft, who works for the district's School Energy and Recycling Team, which supports the school's Green Team. "She really is like, 'Why aren't we using more solar?' Those questions will come out. . . . It gets them thinking about the big picture and using natural resources wisely."

These types of lessons aren't limited to the classroom. Parents who work to run their households more sustainably said that they've used these types of activities to discuss the bigger picture with their kids.

When her son was around seven years old, Stallings started introducing the purpose behind their eco-friendly behavior. Children both gain a better understanding of consequences and become particularly invested in animals around that age or slightly older. Their activities include line-drying clothes, buying in bulk to avoid packaging, and running recycling programs for their community. In particular, her son wanted to know what he could do to help endangered animals. She said, "You know how I talk about how I don't buy this thing because of all of this plastic? To say, when plastic is made, that's pumping oil that disrupts animal habitat. And making plastic pollutes animal habitat. And then when plastic is discarded, that pollutes animal habitat." Explaining the "why" behind her actions helped her older son take more responsibility. "It didn't totally stop every begging for a plastic product, but it helped to remind him of why we're doing this," she said. "It's not just that Mom has some unreasonable grudge against plastic." Even when her son still wanted something unsustainable, that information helped him stop and think before acting.

Pam Mercer writes the blog *Greenily* and lives in Bethesda, Maryland. Although she started her eco-journey when her kids were older, she thinks that it's had an impact on their ways of thinking about the world. She largely focuses on waste reduction, from composting to avoiding disposable products. While her twelve-, fourteen-, and sixteen-year-olds are still normal adolescents, she believes they have a bigger sense of the world beyond themselves than most teenagers. "They have a better sense of being able to step back from things and say . . . I am not the center of the universe," she said. Backtracking to the "why" helps them reconsider how they affect others. "It helps their perspective, which is what I think the whole thing is about," she added. "If you have a different perspective, then that's going to affect your choices."

Many parents use movies as an introduction to these concepts. Bea Johnson popularized the "zero waste" lifestyle, which involves

producing as little waste as possible. Living in the Bay Area in California, her family produces only a small jar of garbage a year. When she
started her work, her sons were only five and six; they're currently
sixteen and seventeen. To explain to them why the family was changing their lifestyle, they together watched both fictional movies like
Wall-E and documentaries like *Home*. "Those really kind of show you
how beautiful the Earth is and [that] we should be taking care of it,"
Johnson said. For younger children, nonfiction picture books and mag-
azines such as the National Wildlife Federation's *Ranger Rick* magazine can also be useful.

The combination of explaining and modeling behavior really makes
the lessons sink in. "Kids are really sponges," said Johnson. When her
family started going zero waste, they first eliminated using plastic
bags at the grocery store. About two or three weeks into the process,
a person working the checkout line put Johnson's groceries in a plastic bag. Johnson's son looked at her and exclaimed, "Plastic bag!" in
horror. The cashier was quite surprised! "It was great [that] it came
out of the mouth of a kid and not me," Johnson said. "It has way more
power when it comes out of the mouth of a kid."

Even when the "why" seems obvious to adults, small children
often don't make those connections on their own. One Earth Day, my
older son came home from kindergarten and I asked him if his class
had talked about it. He said the teacher asked the class, "How can
we be kind to the Earth?" I responded, "What did you say?" and he
answered, "I don't know." I sighed and wondered if any of what I was
teaching was sinking in! As it turned out, he didn't make the connection between the concepts of "making less pollution" or "making less
garbage"—how we usually talk about these things—and being good
for Earth.

Johnson told me a similar story. Her family had been using the bulk
section of the natural foods store for about six months when her son's
school took a field trip there. When the teacher asked, "Why is it good
to buy in bulk?" Johnson's son just stood there, looking like he didn't
have a clue. While she was initially frustrated, she realized the change
hadn't affected him in a bad way. After all, he liked the food they got,

no matter what form it came in. Often what seems like a sacrifice for adults is actually quite minor to kids.

While we don't want to harp on the extra effort, it's useful to point out both how and why we're undertaking sustainable activities. We want our kids to notice! Helping children notice what our family does can set an example and provide context as to why we're doing it. If this work is invisible to them, they won't get the full benefits of it now or have the skills to do it for themselves later on in life.

BUILDING A CULTURE OF SERVICE

While only the official members of the Green Team come to the meetings, the Team's influence reaches much further throughout the school. As the group wrapped up, Barrett reminded the kids to point out the light switch labels to their fellow students and teachers. It was their responsibility to explain to others what the labels meant. She commented, "I bet the kids will notice this, don't you think? They'll ask what it's about."

That spirit of sharing information with and serving others is baked into many of the Green Team's activities. Each Wednesday, the Green Team has a spot reserved in the morning announcements. A student shares a "Green Team fact" with the entire school, often talking about energy- or water-saving activities. In addition to raising environmental awareness, it gives the Green Team students an opportunity to directly educate their classmates. "They kind of got hooked on that," said Barrett.

Similarly, the entire school anticipates the annual Green Team assembly. With the help of art and music teachers, the Green Team students sing environmentally themed songs and put on short sketches. Talking about the assembly, one of the students, Rejuna, said, "Everyone talked about saving energy . . . I'm pretty sure that helped people understand!"

As the students gathered up their items and walked out, Barrett and Stufft waved goodbye. "You had a phenomenal year. You were a fantastic Green Team," Barrett said. "It was a privilege to work with you." Stufft added, "You have done so much to help the school help the environment and help the planet."

This stance of service toward others is essential for being a good community member and citizen. Just as the Green Team members participate in activities around their school, participating in chores around the home is associated with building this attitude. In studies both in the United States and abroad, UCLA anthropologists found that engaging in household tasks early in life builds a sense of moral responsibility toward others.

One study by UCLA researchers compared children in Samoa, the Peruvian Amazon, and Los Angeles, California. They found that children in the Peruvian Amazon and Samoa performed far more household tasks and were much more receptive to meeting the needs of the family than the children in Los Angeles. The children in the Amazon reflect their egalitarian culture's values of working hard, sharing, and being self-sufficient even at a young age. By the time they reach puberty, they know and carry out all the same household tasks as adults. In contrast, even the older children in Los Angeles regularly demanded parents do simple tasks for them like getting a fork. Looking at the different cultural factors, the researchers concluded that much of the difference came down to two things: the emphasis the culture made on turning your attention toward others' needs, and being consistent (or not) about enforcing expectations about household contributions. The amount that the parents in Los Angeles managed their children's lives and didn't expect them to step up fostered the children's self-centeredness. Another study by a researcher at Simon Fraser University showed that when parents involved young children in cleaning up, the children were more likely to help an experimenter later with a separate task. Helping their parents set the stage psychologically for the children helping others outside the family as well.

Overall, helping around the household facilitates children in developing the ability to notice and respond to other people's needs, a key to healthy relationships. As a quote frequently attributed to Mother

Teresa says, "Wash the plate not because it is dirty nor because you are told to wash it, but because you love the person who will use it next."

Participating in household conservation activities can help build not just attitudes oriented toward one's family and community, but actual connections. In Washington, DC, U.S. Climate Action Network director and writer of *The Zero Footprint Baby* Keya Chatterjee lives in a super eco-friendly home with her husband and eight-year-old son. The house has no air-conditioning and a very small hot water heater. This minimalistic approach allows them to run the house off of just a few solar panels. Chatterjee said that because her house tends to be hotter in the summer and cooler in the winter than more conventional homes, her family gets out into the neighborhood more. "We are much more anchored in our community because we're out and about," she said. In the summer, instead of playing with Legos in his room, her son plays with them outside. That provides them in-person time with neighbors that they might not have had otherwise. When they're inside, the family often gathers in the warmest or coolest room in the house, depending on the season. Chatterjee said, "We're much more in touch with each other in the house because we're often in a shared space."

CULTIVATING COMPETENCE, CONFIDENCE, AND SKILLS FOR LIFE

With the year coming to a close, Barrett reflected on what participating in the Green Team meant to students. "They're very happy to be in the Green Team. They're always asking me, 'Is it Green Team time today? Is it this week? Is it next week?'" she recalled.

Barrett and Stufft work to reinforce that sense of pride and excitement. This year, they introduced name tags for all of the kids that they hung on special Green Team lanyards. The children loved having a special symbol of their participation. One child even asked Barrett if they could have certificates at the end of the year. She thought it was a great idea and planned on handing them out at an end-of-year ceremony.

Even after students graduate from William Tyler Page Elementary, their Green Team experience stays with them. Over the fifteen years that the Green Team has been around, Stufft reported that he's seen a number of students continue their environmental activities long past fifth grade. "They are matriculating up through the grades and they are still very excited about it," he said. One seventh grader who is a Green Team alumna comes over from the nearby middle school to drop off plastic bags for recycling. Many students have gone on from Green Team activities to participating in activism.

Knowing that they can make a difference in their school helps Green Team students be more confident in their abilities over the long run. Children who contribute to their households are more likely to be responsible and feel competent. This isn't just in the U.S.—it's true around the world. In one study, researchers from Pitzer College observed nearly 200 children, ages three through nine, across multiple cultures: Kenya, Belize, Nepal, and Samoa. They found that the children who were more involved in household work were more likely to make responsible suggestions and be nurturing. Similarly, a study of nearly 10,000 children in the U.S. by researchers from the University of Virginia Children's Hospital found that children who did chores in kindergarten felt more competent and capable when they were surveyed three years later than those who didn't do chores. On the older end, a survey of nearly 300 undergraduate students in California led by a researcher at California State University found that the students who had done housework regularly as children felt more confident in their ability to follow through on goals and accomplish work as needed.

Parents of older children who have worked to teach their kids about waste and energy conservation say that they've seen those efforts pay off. Bea Johnson said she was particularly proud the first time her son, then seven, turned down a goodie bag at a birthday party. That action really took a level of self-control and foresight. Before then, they had talked about how the toys in those bags break easily and quickly end up in the garbage. He just said, "No, thank you" to a very surprised party host. Johnson said, "In the end, it's up to the kid to learn to do that." Similarly Pam Mercer said that even her teenagers—who consider her incredibly uncool—follow her example. They turn down straws on their own, use reusable towels, and choose to compost with minimal complaining. "That's the proof that it's working," she said. "I truly think they get that it's the right thing to do because it's important, not because Mom said it's important."

Some kids even bring their household activities into the community. Rebecca Stallings said that starting in third grade, her son organized a marker and pen recycling program at his school. Even though two of his friends who were helping changed schools two years ago, he's continued it through eighth grade.

Besides learning everyday household skills, like folding laundry, washing dishes, composting, and recycling, energy and water conservation also offers opportunities for children to learn more abstract life lessons. Purchasing a new washing machine or dishwasher is a great opportunity to talk about comparison shopping, point out how to evaluate energy usage, and explain what the Energy Star label means. Installing insulation in your attic or weather stripping is a chance to teach some handy home maintenance skills. Switching to buying renewable energy or installing solar panels on your roof is a good time to explain how to read a utility bill. (Our utility is legally required to list their energy sources on the bill.)

While I don't usually whip out the utility bill for my six-year-old to read, he actually brought up the subject one day on his own. Dylan asked, "Does playing Mario cause pollution?" He wanted to know the environmental impact of playing his beloved video game. I replied, "Not really. You know the solar panels on our roof? Those provide about half of our electricity. We buy the other half from places that make wind power. And soon, we're going to get a lot of our energy from solar panels that they built on an old landfill. So that's really neat." He breathed a sigh of relief. As someone who thinks about my environmental footprint a lot, I was glad that he didn't have to feel bad about one of his favorite activities. Now if I could just figure out how to get him to turn it off without putting up a fuss . . .

What to Know

Conserving Energy

One of the biggest parts of conserving energy is buying energy-efficient household appliances, such as light bulbs, dishwashers, refrigerators, washing machines, air conditioners, and programmable thermostats. Compared to conventional models, Energy Star dryers use 20 percent less energy and Energy Star washing machines use 25 percent less. Reducing energy usage can save you a lot of money in the long run. Even though energy-efficient appliances can be slightly more expensive in the beginning, they pay themselves off through savings on your utility bill. Because most of these appliances list the energy usage right on the label, comparing them only adds a little bit of extra effort to the buying process.

Even if you rent your apartment or home, replacing incandescent light bulbs with compact fluorescents, or even better LED bulbs, can make a significant difference. According to the U.S. Department of Energy, swapping out non–Energy Star light bulbs with Energy Star ones in the five lights you use most frequently can save $45 a year. Because of advances in technology, LED light bulbs now produce light that's just as warm as any other kind of bulb.

In terms of behavior, turning off lights, line-drying clothing, washing clothes in cold water, and unplugging unnecessary electronics can all help over time. Because heating or air-conditioning makes up such a large part of the energy bill, turning it up or down even a few degrees makes an impact. Getting snuggly or letting in a natural breeze will save you money. Open the windows in summer and pile up the blankets in winter!

Buying Renewable Energy

Purchasing renewable energy instead of electricity made by burning fossil fuels is one of the easiest and most effective things you can do to lower your individual environmental impact.

About half of all households now have the option to purchase renewable power (mainly wind, although some places also have solar).

In some cases, this purchase will be an add-on to your usual utility bill. In others, you can sign up through a separate service that purchases power on your behalf while still getting your actual electricity through the traditional power lines. In some cases, these services may even provide renewable electricity that is cheaper or more reliably priced than what you would normally get through your utility. Large-scale solar or wind co-op projects that you can buy a piece of are increasingly popular as well. Just search Google for "renewable energy," "wind energy," or "solar energy" and your location. Even if you don't have control over your utility bill, you can buy "renewable energy certificates" that support these projects. These are an additional cost on top of your utility bill.

If you own your own home, installing rooftop solar is becoming increasingly simple and affordable. What was once more than $10,000 up front can now be spread out over many years via a lease or loan. In some cases you can even hand the cost and maintenance off completely to the solar company. For our solar panels, we signed what's called a power purchase agreement. The solar company owns and maintains the panels. In exchange for hosting the panels, we signed a contract to pay the company for the electricity the panels produce. It's locked into a fixed fee for a certain period of time, which protects us against spikes in prices from the utility.

Conserving Water

Water conservation generally involves buying and installing water-efficient appliances, including toilets, showerheads, dishwashers, and washing machines. An increasing number of these appliances include information comparing their water usage.

Even if you live in an apartment or otherwise can't switch out your appliances, making behavioral changes can help reduce your water consumption. Washing only full loads of clothes or dishes, turning off the water when you aren't using it (when you brush your teeth), and rinsing dishes off as little as possible will help minimize water usage.

Because 30 percent of water is used outside, this is one of the places you can make the biggest difference if you have a lawn. Choosing not to water the lawn is easy and saves a lot of money! This is especially true if you live in a dry area where water companies charge more for each extra gallon used past a certain point. If you're in an area where a lawn needs to be watered, replacing your lawn with native plants or a rain garden can cut down on outside water usage. If you want to water a garden, consider getting a rain barrel that collects rain instead of needing to draw it from municipal sources. Many cities and counties offer reimbursements or discounts for such purchases so they can fulfill their water conservation strategies.

Reducing Waste

Reducing waste is probably the area that kids can be the most helpful. In *Zero Waste Home*, Bea Johnson expands the three Rs (reduce, reuse, recycle) to five Rs: refuse, reduce, reuse, recycle, and rot. Refusing involves turning down items that cause unnecessary waste, including plastic bags, junk mail, and free stuff at events. Reducing requires minimizing the amount of stuff that you buy, which reduces packaging and leaves you with fewer items to deal with. Reusing means that you replace disposable items with reusable ones. Using cloth bags, glass jars, mesh bags, and reusable bottles to buy food and other goods in bulk will cut down on garbage from packaging. Reusing also involves buying durable items that can last and be repaired. Because recycling itself takes energy and many places are throwing away certain materials instead of recycling them (especially plastics), it's a last resort.

Then there's "rot," another name for composting. For food and yard waste, composting is far more sustainable than throwing it in the garbage. There are a number of different composting systems, from simple and often free bins for yard waste to expensive under-the-counter systems. (*Zero Waste Home* has a great table comparing different systems.) In general the simpler the composter, the cheaper it is. The simplest systems are either a pile of yard waste in the corner of the yard or a black plastic mesh cylinder, rather like a laundry basket for waste. However, simpler systems can't always handle food waste without attracting rodents or bugs. Just putting a pile of rotting food in the corner of the yard with some leaves in a wooden box is guaranteed to attract unintended visitors. If you're only composting yard waste, there's a lot less to worry about. Just make sure your pile is out of the way and has plenty of time to break down.

We have a large tumbling composter that handles all of our fruit and vegetable waste as well as eggshells and coffee grounds. It keeps out animals that might like poking around in garbage. If you're composting food, the key consideration is to balance the food with dry, carbon-rich materials, like shredded black-and-white newspaper, dry grass, or dry leaves. If the compost is too wet, it will smell horrible, break down incorrectly, and breed flies.

If you don't have the ability to compost at your house, an increasing number of cities have companies that will pick up your compostable materials and turn them into compost for you for a fee. In many cases, they allow you to drop the materials off at a central location.

Next Steps

Frame Eco-Household Activities as Family Activities, Not Individual Chores

One of the biggest aspects of getting kids involved in chores—whether eco-friendly or not—is to make it a collective family activity. In the case of the Green Team, they build a sense of "family" by going on a field trip at the end of the year to a state park. In your family, just doing these activities alongside your kids is most likely enough!

Framing household responsibilities as something the entire family cooperates on to get done gives them more impact and makes them more fun. Inspired by my research for this chapter, I've started having "household cleaning times" once a week. On either a Saturday or Sunday, everyone in the family pitches in for twenty to thirty minutes to clean the house. Dylan vacuums or folds laundry and Ethan wipes down counters (and even the bathtub!), while my husband and I guide them. I personally hate cleaning, but the time working together is enjoyable. Plus, the family working together for a half hour gets so much more done than just my husband and I would have been able to do on our own. Although these chores aren't specific to being ecologically friendly, cleaning together frees up time to garden, bike or walk places, and spend time outside.

In contrast, having children be individually responsible for chores frames them as a dull obligation. And paying an allowance for chores generally reduces children's inherent motivation. A number of studies on external rewards—like paying for chores—have shown that while they're effective at motivating behavior in the short term, they reduce long-term interest in continuing it.

Make It Part of the Family Culture

Children are used to what they grow up with. For example, even though we don't grow much food compared to what we eat, my older son asked me, "Wait, some people get all of their food from the grocery store?" I had to keep myself from chuckling. If you embrace an eco-friendly lifestyle, children will accept it for the most part, especially if you start it when they're young. "When you grow up a certain way, you take it for granted," said Bea Johnson. "For our kids, zero waste is totally normal and automatic." Treating how you live as normal will make it feel like normal, even if some aspects seem hard at times.

Even at the school, Barrett said that environmental sustainability went beyond the Green Team because the school fostered eco-friendliness. "It just was very embedded in the culture here," she said.

Set Up Your House in a Way That Encourages Success

It's hard to be sustainable if everything in your household encourages waste. Keya Chatterjee chooses not to have a dryer, while Bea Johnson doesn't even have a garbage can. While you may not be that radical, having a smaller garbage can or getting rid of an extra energy-inefficient fridge can help.

In contrast, having the right tools can make all the difference. William Tyler Page Elementary has recycling bins all over the school, including the cafeteria and hallways. Keeping reusable bags in your personal bag and keeping cloth towels in your kitchen can serve the same purpose. Making sure those towels are accessible to kids can help them reach for a cloth towel instead of a paper one next time they spill something. Shopping at places that minimize packaging, like farmers markets and stores that have bulk sections, keeps you from needing to buy items with packaging. Installing a programmable thermostat or a tool to turn your appliances on or off automatically can help you save energy without needing to keep track of it. Some utility companies even encourage you to sign up to have your air-conditioning turn off on days the energy grid is under the greatest pressure.

Take Small Steps That Build Long-Term Habits

Many of these activities rely on habit-based behaviors. Barrett said that students not only got used to doing eco-friendly activities at school, they also started to tell their parents about them. "This is just part of the normal, everyday happenings at school. Repeated every day," she said. "It carries on to their home too." Modeling these everyday activities for your kids over and over again will help them pick them up. Always turning off the water when you brush your teeth or putting apple cores in the compost container sets an example. Other habits include turning off lights when you leave the room and unplugging electronics that still draw electricity from the wall when they're off. (Many appliances stay on "standby" mode that uses energy even when you have turned them off.) Like anything, demonstrating it alone isn't a guarantee. For the amount I complain about turning off the lights, I regularly sound like a stereotypical 1950s dad—"This uses energy, you know!"

Help Your Family See Concrete Results

Being able to see exactly what you've done motivates you to do more. "I think the tangible things are the things that have the most impact and we focus on the most," said Pam Mercer. Being able to physically see the impacts of your actions is most obvious when it comes to reducing garbage. Scaling down from a garbage can of waste a week to one every two or three weeks is easy to see! At William Tyler Page Elementary, they ran a clothes recycling drive. The company weighed the clothes and gave the school cash in exchange. With the money, the school bought a bike rack for the front of the school. The rack serves as a physical reminder of the students' efforts.

Even with water and energy conservation, there are ways of "seeing" those differences. Taking a look at the utility bill and comparing from month to month is one option. The U.S. Department of Energy has a nifty infographic showing various visualizations of energy use (www.energy.gov/articles/how-much-do-you-consume). Sticking a large container in the sink while kids brush their teeth with the water running can give them a sense of the water savings.

Don't Overcomplicate It

It's easy to think that you need to do everything at once when it comes to household conservation and waste reduction. Start with the simplest actions with the biggest impact. If you can't see being able to do that action every day for several months, focus on something that's sustainable for your family as well as the environment.

Doing these things shouldn't require buying a lot of stuff. Johnson said the key to going zero waste for her family was simplifying: buying less, making less complex meals, and downscaling their possessions. Even if you're far from zero waste, trying to do the simplest things that work for you will be the most beneficial for your family and the environment.

FAMILY ACTIVITIES:
Household Energy Audit Scavenger Hunt

Mark off the different items in your house to see where you can improve! This doesn't replace a professional energy audit. However, it can help everyone in your family realize all the different ways we use and potentially waste energy. As you go, fill in the answers to the questions in this book or on a separate sheet of paper.

LIGHT BULBS

➤ How many incandescent light bulbs do you have?

➤ How many CFLs (fluorescent light bulbs) do you have?

➤ How many LEDs do you have?

APPLIANCES

➤ How can we use the refrigerator more efficiently? (Possible ideas: Keep the fridge door closed, think about what you are going to get out of the fridge before opening the door)

➤ How can we use the dishwasher more efficiently? (Possible ideas: Only run it when it's full, do as little rinsing as possible before putting dishes in the dishwasher)

➤ How can we use the washing machine and/or clothes dryer more efficiently? (Possible ideas: Use cold water when possible, only run full loads)

INSULATION

➤ Is your hot water heater wrapped in insulation?

➤ How many doors and windows have leaks? (To test for a leak, shut the door or window on a dollar bill. If you can pull it out very easily, there's probably a leak.)

SINKS AND SHOWERS/BATHS

➤ How many sinks are leaky?

➤ How many showers or baths are leaky?

▶ Does your toilet run even when no one is using it? (This is an indication of a leak in the toilet.)

▶ What are ways we can reduce our water use? (Possible ideas: Turn off the water when brushing teeth, take shorter showers, run water in the sink for shorter periods of time)

ELECTRONICS

▶ How many electronics are currently plugged in? How many can you unplug without resetting anything?

▶ Are there portable electronics or their chargers still plugged in after they have finished charging?

▶ Can you plug a number of electronics into a power strip? (This would allow you to turn them all off at once when you are finished charging them.)

WASTE AUDIT

Keep track of what you throw out for a day! Or if you're really ambitious, keep track of it for a few days or a week.

Establish three containers: one for garbage, one for recycling, and one for compostable materials. (If you don't compost, this can give you an idea of what a difference it would make.) If you need to sort your recycling out into different containers, such as paper and cans, have separate containers just for this project.

Before you start, discuss with your kids what types of materials can go in which container. Any food that doesn't have animal products in it can go in the compost container. While it will differ depending on your location, printer paper, newspaper, magazines/catalogs, cans, bottles, and certain plastics are often recyclable. Plastic bags, electronics, and batteries can be recycled but need to be brought to special facilities to do so. Everything else should go in the garbage. Throughout the day, work with your kids to ensure that everything you throw out goes in the right container.

At the end of the day, go through the waste container. Talk about the following questions with your children: What garbage could be eliminated by not taking it in the first place or replacing it with something reusable? Is this from packaging we could avoid if we bought a slightly different product? What could be swapped out for something recyclable or compostable? Are there things you put in the recyclable or composting container that usually go in the garbage?

Then, look through the recycling container and ask the same questions. While recycling is good, trying to eliminate the materials earlier in the process is even better.

At the end, put the compost materials in your composter or in the garbage. Put the garbage and recycled materials in their appropriate bins.

Books

PICTURE BOOKS

Energy Island: How One Community Harnessed the Wind and Changed Their World, by Allan Drummond: A lovely book about an island in Denmark that chose to switch to 100 percent clean energy. It's a great true story about finding an alternative path and adopting renewable energy.

One Plastic Bag, by Miranda Paul and Elizabeth Zunon, and *Rainbow Weaver*, by Linda Elovitz Marshall and Elisa Chavarri: Both of these books offer stories of girls and women who found new ways to reuse plastic bags in their areas (Gambia and Guatemala) by integrating them into their weaving. They each have evocative illustrations with colors that reflect their respective cultures. *Rainbow Weaver* is also available in a dual-language version with both Spanish and English.

What a Waste, by Jess French: This infographic-packed book is full of fascinating facts about waste. It can also be a little overwhelming, so take this one in pieces, especially with younger children.

CHAPTER AND ACTIVITY BOOKS

Renewable Energy: Discover the Fuel of the Future with 20 Projects, by Joshua Sneideman, Erin Twamley, and Heather Jane Brinesh: While most of these projects are on the science and technology side (not the household conservation side), this book provides a solid introduction to the many types of renewable energy.

The New 50 Simple Things Kids Can Do to Save the Earth, by The EarthWorks Group: Even though the updated version is now eleven years old, the classic of my childhood still holds up. It provides succinct, compelling descriptions of problems along with straightforward ways to take action.

The Everything Kids' Environment Book, by Sheri Amsel: This book provides a good introduction to ecological and conservation issues. A lot of it focuses more on the science side of ecology, but it can help answer a lot of the "why" questions when it comes to energy and water conservation.

The Boy Who Harnessed the Wind, by William Kamkwamba and Bryan Mealer: Despite needing to drop out of school and living through the horrors of a famine, William Kamkwamba taught himself how to build a windmill out of reused materials to light his family's home. Hearing the story in his own words highlights both his brilliance and humility. While this book is available in both a full and a picture book version, the young readers edition is perfect for older children and preteens.

Resources

TEDx talk on Radical Collaboration by Barbara Rogoff of UCLA on Learning by Pitching In and Observing: https://www.facebook.com /watch/?v=1116724285019770

Zero Waste Home, by Bea Johnson

The Earthling's Handbook blog, by Rebecca Stallings: http://articles .earthlingshandbook.org

Greenily blog, by Pam Mercer: www.greenily.co

Save Energy, Save Money, U.S. Department of Energy: www.energy .gov/energysaver/energy-saver

Water Sense, U.S. Environmental Protection Agency: www.epa.gov /watersense/start-saving

Reduce, Reuse, Recycle, U.S. Environmental Protection Agency: www .epa.gov/recycle

Energy Star, U.S. Environmental Protection Agency/U.S. Department of Energy: www.energystar.gov

Buying Clean Electricity, U.S. Department of Energy: www.energy .gov/energysaver/buying-and-making-electricity/buying-clean -electricity

Solar Estimate: www.solar-estimate.org

Shared Renewables (community renewable energy): www.shared renewables.org

National Geographic Kids Save the Earth: https://kids.national geographic.com/explore/nature/save-the-earth-hub/

BREAKING FREE OF "STUFF":
REJECTING MATERIALISM

"We really need to have less junk in the house," I declared. This is not an unusual statement for me. We have a small house and my children enjoy dropping things randomly on the floor, including toys, craft supplies, and utensils they steal from the kitchen cabinet. I often follow this statement up with fantasizing about getting rid of everything.

"I like junk!" piped up Ethan.

"Do you even know what junk is?" I asked him.

"No," he said.

"Junk—or at least what Mommy's talking about—is cheap plastic stuff," explained my husband. "Toys that break easily, stuff that you play with only once, that sort of thing. So do you still like junk?"

"I like junk!" he exclaimed with just as much enthusiasm as the first time.

We have some work to do.

Our family is certainly not the only one to suffer from an excess of stuff. In the U.S., children receive $28 billion worth of toys each year, averaging about $380 per child. American kids have 40 percent of the toys produced worldwide even though we only have 3.1 percent of the population of children. In a sociological study by UCLA researchers of thirty-two families in Los Angeles, they found the average family had 139 toys visible, not including those in closets or under beds. Three-quarters of the families couldn't store their cars in their garages because there was so much clutter in them.

Much of this glut comes from the pressure to buy more and more. While advertisers have long targeted kids, they've gotten particularly intense in the last decade. Although advertisers focused on moms in the past—think "Mom-approved" cereal—now children are the driver of American consumer culture. One company estimated that four- to twelve-year-olds drive $330 billion worth of sales to adults per year. And it's not just about toys. Advertisers push children to have opinions on everything from cereal to what kind of cars their parents should drive.

This onslaught of material goods comes with a big environmental and social footprint. All of those toys and other products use natural resources to produce, especially plastic toys that require oil production. Electronic toys use batteries or require electricity to run. Most of these toys are made in countries with poor labor standards, where people are overworked and underpaid. Sweatshops for clothing and toys have gotten increasingly nimble at evading inspectors and hiding mistreatment.

Disposing of these material goods is also difficult to do ethically. When electronic toys break, they're nearly impossible to fix. Even when things are still usable, dropping your unwanted goods off at the local secondhand donation center is often not a great option. With a lot of people decluttering, Goodwill and Salvation Army shops are getting far more stuff than they can handle. If they can't sell these goods, they just end up going in the garbage anyway.

But the impact of all of this stuff goes beyond physical objects. Materialistic attitudes of "more, more, more" also extend to other aspects of life, like buying larger houses, signing kids up for activities to boost their résumé, or focusing on what kindergarten children get into so they can get into a "good" college.

The push to get your children "the best" teaches them consumption and self-focus, perpetuating the cycle. Materialism develops either from growing up economically deprived or from following materialistic role models, including parents and celebrities. In a survey of moms and teens, of the seventy mothers who rated financial success as important compared to self-acceptance, 71 percent of their kids said the same thing.

In one sense, this competitive attitude is very privileged. Many people don't have the financial resources to worry about having too many material possessions or one-upping each other over educational opportunities. However, this stance has deep effects beyond the people directly involved. Even among people who can't afford to participate, it creates stress. It also reinforces systems of privilege. These systems further hurt groups that society has denied and continues to deny educational and economic opportunities. The families who have enough privilege to deal with this problem also have a responsibility to address it.

Passing along these attitudes extends the impacts from today far into the future. In an experiment, participants played a game where they decided how much of a forest to cut down as a group; people who were more materialistic were more likely to cut down larger sections of the forest to benefit themselves. As the book *The High Price of Materialism*—based on decades of psychological research by its author, Tim Kasser—states, "Materialistic values also conflict with concern for making the world a better place, and the desire to contribute to equality, justice, and other aspects of civil society." Simply put, materialism gets in the way of being a good person.

A RADICAL EXPERIMENT

Knowing materialism's influence made me particularly intrigued by the story of Scott Dannemiller and his family. In 2014 Scott and his wife, Gabby, decided they were sick of being on the consumption treadmill. One day Gabby simply asked, "What if we didn't buy anything for a year?" As they contemplated the idea, it became more and more of a concrete thing that they should do. In the book he wrote about the experience, *The Year Without a Purchase*, he said, "We have been living life by accident. Allowing our schedules and possessions to define us.... The time has come to live by a set of rules to help bring us back into balance, reconnect us with our mission. To live life on purpose, with purpose." They decided to buy nothing except consumable goods like food and toiletries for an entire year.

To set up the challenge, they made a few rules. If it was something that would be used in a year, that was okay. If something broke, they would fix it. If it was unfixable and absolutely needed to be replaced, they would try to buy it secondhand. All gifts would be charitable donations or experiences. Perhaps most importantly, they wanted to frame it as a year of stepping out of immediate gratification and the need to buy stuff. They wanted to embrace other ways of finding fulfillment than buying things.

Talking to Scott and hearing his family's story illuminated a number of benefits to getting off of that materialistic treadmill for all of us.

FOCUSING ON YOUR FAMILY'S CORE VALUES

Comparison is a liar. But we all do it, especially in the age of social media. The worst part is that our kids catch on to those comparisons. Purposely rejecting materialism can help quiet the voices that tell us to ignore our values. Interviewing Dannemiller five years after the book came out, I heard from him what the experiment had taught them in the long run.

"It was about getting back in touch with what's important," Dannemiller said. "We noticed ourselves getting back on the hamster wheel of consumption and trying to get in the rat race of working for the wrong reasons."

The Dannemillers found themselves caught up in this cycle. It's far too easy for "stuff" society says we need to crowd out what we believe is actually the right thing for our families. Buying and valuing physical objects less can be a step toward living out those values more. Christine Koh (who lives in Boston, Massachusetts) and Asha Dornfest (who lives in Portland, Oregon) write and talk about finding your inner voice apart from social pressures in their *Minimalist Parenting* book and *Edit Your Life* podcast. When I talked to her, Dornfest pointed out that much of the conventional wisdom around purchasing is arbitrary. For example, many people have the idea of a "starter house." Once you have kids and accumulate more stuff, you scale up in size and price. But so often, when people scale up, they end up filling the new house with more unneeded stuff. In addition, they spend more time taking care of it. "Needing more 'storage space' can be a trap. Always, always challenge that impulse," Dornfest said. "Do you really need that? It's easy to get rolling along with that without stopping to think about [it]."

Instead, tuning in to our own values can help guide our actions. "It's about trusting yourself as a parent to make the decisions that work for your family," Dornfest said. "That involves a certain amount of developing confidence in your own values and your own decisions and choices."

If our actions don't match up with our values, our kids will notice. Children have hypocrisy radar. "If you know your values are all about living a balanced life and having balanced stuff and then there's stuff everywhere, you're not modeling living your values to [your] kids," said Kim John Payne, author of the book *Simplicity Parenting*. He lives with his two children in western Massachusetts. "Little kids kind of get that you're speaking and see your lips move. But what they really see and take in, in terms of values, is the practical world." What small children see is what they know and understand, even if it conflicts with what you're telling them. If parents say they value time as a family but spend more time taking care of stuff than with each other, children simply won't get it. Older kids are even sharper. If the reality of life speaks louder than your words, they'll know which one is real.

As Dannemiller said to me, "You have to put your values into action. Otherwise, it's just a saying that you think is really neat."

SPARKING CREATIVITY AND IMAGINATION

While it seemed easy for the Dannemillers to not buy stuff for themselves, a few situations threw them for a loop. One of the first was figuring out what to do when their son was invited to a birthday party. Everyone who has ever had to get a present for a child's classmate knows how difficult it is. What kind of things does the child like? What if you get them something they already have? What will not annoy the crud out of the child's parents?

As Dannemiller considered the options, each seemed increasingly unacceptable. Six-year-olds don't really appreciate charitable donations in their name, even if their parents might. Bringing your own kids to the children's museum is wonderful, but no one wants to force that on someone else. And getting nothing? That's awkward.

But then he realized much of his anxiety was his alone—not his kid's. Once he shoved aside the cultural baggage associated with birthday gifts, he and his wife started to get creative. Instead of purchasing a traditional toy, they put together homemade "science experiments" with ingredients from the grocery store. Things like combining Mentos and Diet Coke or sticking a bar of Ivory soap in the microwave. They also included a gift card to a local frozen yogurt shop. Despite Dannemiller's worries, it turned out that their gift was one of the birthday girl's favorites. She loved doing it together with her family.

Later on, their experiment motivated them to get creative in other ways too. When Dannemiller forgot to bring more than one pair of socks on a business trip, he washed them in the sink each night. Instead of buying their niece a physical present for her graduation from an online high school, he and his wife organized a full prom, complete with music.

Having more physical, mental, and emotional space allows creativity, problem solving, and competency to blossom. This is just as true for kids as it was for the Dannemillers as adults.

In fact, owning too much stuff can actually limit the quality of children's play. If there are too many things to pay attention to, children get distracted, jumping from toy to toy. In both a 1979 study and a similar 2018 study, researchers found that the more toys available to toddlers during an experiment, the less time the children spent playing with each one. The researchers from the University of Toledo who ran the 2018 experiment reported that the kids who had four toys switched back and forth between toys half as much compared to the children who had sixteen toys available. They also played with each toy twice as long. As a result, children in the condition with fewer toys explored more thoroughly what each toy could do. Playing with toys longer and figuring out different ways to play with them helps young children develop imagination, creativity, and understanding of cause and effect.

Even in older kids, having less stuff that requires more effort fuels creativity. Payne told me a story that he heard from a mother in one of his Simplicity Parenting workshops. The mom didn't have much money and both of her boys wanted new mountain bikes. However, the bikes simply didn't fit in the budget. But one day, they were driving by a yard sale. The kids spotted a 1970s dragster bike for sale—banana seat, high handlebars, all of it. They desperately wanted it. But it was a piece of junk, totally rusted out. Despite her qualms the mom bought it for five dollars; the seller threw a second one in for free. Seeing the bikes' potential, the boys spent months rebuilding them. Staff members of local bike shops and spray painters helped them restore the bikes. The kids learned the ins and outs of how bicycles function, from swapping out pieces to decorating them. The end result was beautiful—so much so that the boys wanted to keep the bikes in their bedrooms every night. By the end, they had learned so many skills that they opened a shop in their garage to help other kids repair their own bikes.

"She's given them the gift of creativity, the gift of construction, and most of all, a feeling of competency," Payne said. "That competency can go in all sorts of different directions." If either the mom or kids rejected the bikes because they weren't new or fancy enough, the boys would have missed out on major life lessons.

Rather than harkening back to some hallowed past, this type of problem solving is increasingly important in our current and future economy. A growing number of people are self-employed, which requires a high amount of organization, independent problem solving, and self-reliance. As Payne said, "The power of less gives kids the power of more competency [and] self-reliance, which is the future. The power of less is not about the past." Unlike materialistic goals, reaching goals related to personal growth can help build feelings of self-esteem and competence.

DEVELOPING A CORE SENSE OF SELF

As Dannemiller and his family continued their experiment, he noticed how many purchases aren't based on actual needs. Instead, they're about presenting a certain image to others. This is most obvious in advertisements that use sex or fantasy to sell a product. However, it's even true for products that portray themselves as practical.

This contrast became particularly clear to him when he had to use an item society judges as inappropriate for a businessman rather than buy a new one. When his suitcase for business travel broke, he didn't have a backup. The only one in the house was a lavender, "ladies" suitcase that was far different from his no-frills black one. But no buying is no buying and he needed something to travel with. So the lavender suitcase it was. Despite getting some odd looks at the airport and hotels—as well as an unexpected conversation with a stranger—he put up with the awkwardness.

While this lesson is hard enough to deal with as an adult, it becomes exponentially more difficult when you're making that decision for your kid. As part of Dannemiller's son's end-of-year basketball tournament, a number of his son's teammates received special red socks. Of course, it felt like everyone on the team had them. Except the Dannemillers. Scott and Gabby decided that the socks weren't enough of a true need to break the challenge. In addition, they didn't want their son to feel like he had to buy things to fit in. "We cover our kids up with so much shiny junk that it's virtually impossible to see the person inside," Dannemiller said in the book.

Through these experiences, Dannemiller realized that even if we don't care about what our stuff looks like, people will judge us on it. Whether we like it or not, our possessions signal a number of things about us to others. Facing up to that truth and inwardly dealing with it will help us build a stronger sense of self. In addition, that uniqueness will make us more vulnerable, which increases our chance to make real connections with others.

In general, people who are materialistic are more worried about other people's judgment of them. As a result, they feel less able to be who they truly are. Materialism and self-expression directly conflict with each other.

Even though the Dannemillers did the challenge five years ago, it seems like this message has stuck with their son into adolescence. Dannemiller told me that when he and his son went shopping for athletic shorts recently, his son picked the cheaper store brand over shorts from Under Armour or Nike. "He realized, 'I just need to cover my butt. Any of these things are going to do.' It's not about the message that sends," Dannemiller said. For a thirteen-year-old, that's pretty damn insightful.

Unfortunately we as parents can actually undercut messages about sticking to your values through external rewards like buying material gifts for good grades or behavior. These rewards can actually decrease children's internal motivation. Instead of seeing these behaviors as inherently good, children start to think they can't and shouldn't bother doing them without a reward. As a result they're less likely to explore their own passions, strengths, and personal areas of interest.

In contrast, having experiences helps people define who they are apart from others' opinions. Researchers from the University of

Chicago and Cornell University wrote a paper describing a series of studies about how people's experiences are more important to their core identity than their possessions. People drew Venn diagrams of how important experiences and things were to their identity, incorporated experiential and physical purchases into their life story, and imagined deleting memories of a physical object or an experience. In all three, the importance of their memories consistently trumped the importance of objects. Experiences will set a much stronger foundation than physical possessions for helping children understand who they are.

MAKING TIME AND SPACE FOR RELATIONSHIP

Of course, experiences are the most meaningful when they're shared with others. As he started to give experiences for presents instead of material goods, Dannemiller realized the true power of this switch.

He first saw it with his kids. Normally when his mom came to visit the kids, she would bring a present. It often was something she picked up at the thrift shop. As the rules didn't forbid other people from buying presents, Dannemiller and his wife thought it was fine. That was, until the one trip when she didn't bring anything. The kids asked, "What did you bring?" and were quite disappointed when they realized she came empty-handed. At that point, both Dannemiller and his mom realized something had gone wrong. Fortunately, she was there to bring them to the zoo. Although it seemed like material goods were going to stand in the way of building connection, the good experience of the day washed away their disappointment. That's the power of time spent together.

The more you value material goods, the less you tend to value people. Survey research shows that people who are more materialistic have shorter, more negative relationships and feel more disconnected from others. An experimental study from McGill University with four- and five-year-old children compared kids who watched a television show with two commercials for a specific toy to those who watched a show without commercials. Of the kids who watched the commercial,

65 percent would play with a "not so nice" kid who had the toy in the commercial over a "nice boy" who didn't. In contrast, only 30 percent who didn't watch the commercial would play with the "not so nice" child. In addition, children who watched the commercial were far more likely to pick playing with the toy over playing with their friends in a sandbox compared to the kids who didn't watch it.

When I talked to Dannemiller, I asked what his children thought of getting experiences instead of physical gifts. Part of his and his wife's strategy was not sharing their plan with the kids during the year and seeing if they figured it out. When it was all over, they had a family meeting. They told the kids, "Did you notice that last year we didn't buy any stuff?" At first, their children were confused; they pointed out that they bought food and tickets to experiences. Then their son said, "You mean, we didn't buy anything that was worthless?" In hearing that, the Dannemillers realized that their kids really did appreciate the experiences far more than any physical thing. While the kids were back to asking about Legos in the next breath, the connection still stuck.

Even now, their children are more likely to ask for experiences than physical things. Dannemiller has done a number of road trips with his teenage son where they spend time together that they wouldn't otherwise. He said, "It's something that one day when I'm gone from this planet, my son is going to say, 'Yeah, me and my dad, we spent time together.'"

Personally I've experienced this in my own family as well. My husband and I take the kids for special one-on-one kid-parent time about once a month. They're often my favorite memories and I suspect they're my kids' favorite ones too.

Despite the pressure to buy physical objects, science backs up the idea that experiential gifts are far more meaningful. In general, the "shine" wears off of physical stuff much faster than experiences. In contrast, your memories of an experience keep the enjoyment around for longer, even though the experience itself is shorter. In addition, most experiences inherently involve other people.

Through a combination of surveys and experiments, researchers from the University of Toronto and UCLA found that experiential gifts—even experiences done without the giver—fostered stronger relationships than physical gifts. They asked parents who received gifts on both Mother's Day and Father's Day how they felt about their relationship with their children before and after the gift. Those who received experiential gifts reported their relationship with the giver strengthened more than those who received objects. In other experiments, the researchers gave participants money to buy a physical gift or experience for a friend. The researchers then asked the friend about the relationship before and after. These too had similar results, with the friends receiving experiential gifts having their relationship strengthen more than those who received material ones.

Having less stuff can also give you more time and money to spend with your family. As Asha Dornfest put it, "The less time you spend having to deal with your stuff in your house, the more time there is to do stuff with the people in your house." She said that while she "felt like I was a servant to my house" when her kids were younger, she's now pleased that simplifying has made dealing with her household less burdensome.

Getting rid of physical clutter can make more physical and emotional room for families to connect. Christine Koh said that her family's favorite part of the house is a room they call the "zen den." Unlike other rooms that have more stuff, this room simply has a bed with some board games, books, and family video games. The family gathers here just to hang out and be together.

Although she lives on the more extreme end of this spectrum, Brynn Burger sees many of the same benefits. Motivated to radically simplify because of her son's behavioral challenges, her family lives in a thirty-six-foot camper trailer. While they spend some of their time traveling around the country, the camper is most often parked in Ohio. She said spending less money buying things and less time cleaning has freed up resources, allowing them to connect with each other more. In addition to reducing the number of physical possessions, they've also minimized their obligations. "When you get in the rat race of every day 9 to 5, working late, pick up the kids, take them here, take them there, it's easy to neglect that sort of thing," she said. She said that because her kids spend so much time outside and with their family, they don't complain about their lack of toys.

These times of simple connection are consistently what people list as their favorite childhood memories once they've grown up. In his Simplicity Parenting workshops, Payne often asks participants about their "golden memories" of childhood. People never answer with fancy vacations or physical gifts. "The answer is always human connection," he said. When parents substitute the ease of buying things for the complexity of relationships, they stand in the way of creating memories. He said when overscheduling and overconsumption take over your life, "You're crowding out the very thing that makes us human."

BORROWING FROM AND GIVING BACK TO THE COMMUNITY

Caring about and accumulating less stuff both makes you rely on your community more and gives you the time to contribute to it.

The Dannemillers found that they enjoyed sharing and borrowing from others, including using the library more often. They also started walking to school with some of their neighbors and appreciated that time spent together. The idea of "the village," where people make an effort to take care of each other, began to feel more real to them.

Turning to neighbors for help reinforces social ties, which ripples through society. Outside of formal structures like community centers and libraries, informal networks also have a role to play. Buy Nothing groups and websites such as Freecycle provide community members ways to give away items that are no longer needed and pick up second-hand items from others. Barbara Greene Alfeo is an art instructor at an environmental education center in Seattle as well as an environmental blogger. Many of her projects with students involve making art out of garbage or recyclable materials. She relies on her local Buy Nothing group to collect supplies, such as bottle caps. Her kids, who are two and a half and four years old, come with her when she picks up items or attends picnics with the group. She also makes further connections through a Seattle Green Families group, where the participants switch off watching each other's children during events. Speaking about her children having these experiences, she said, "My hope is that they're seeing all of these things and it's sinking in in some way that this is what citizenship looks like, this is what participation looks like."

When you make an effort to spend less time and money on things, you can spend it on helping your community instead. The Dannemillers wanted to purposefully give back. As part of the year-long challenge, they started volunteering with local groups focused on reducing hunger. The first time they volunteered, the kids loved packing up green beans in bags and giving them to folks who would eat the food or distribute it to others. The second time they volunteered didn't go as well. They were packing potatoes into a truck, which didn't have the same emotional impact. But the third time, it truly hit home. The family was packing backpacks full of food for schoolchildren. Initially, the kids saw it as another fun activity. But on the way home, they started talking about how hard it would be to survive off the food in the backpacks for the entire weekend. Dannemiller's son asked, "Do any kids at my school get backpacks like that?" His wife answered, "Probably so. We'd never know. Those backpacks look just like yours. And they're attached to kids who look just like you." That shocked the children into silence. Later on, having seen the bigger picture, the kids declared that they wanted to help again in the future.

In contrast, people who are materialistic rarely take the opportunity to think about or serve people around them. When researchers from the University of Missouri and University of California, Davis asked more materialistic people what they would do with $20,000, they said they would donate less than half as much to charity as less materialistic people. Perhaps not surprisingly, materialistic people are also less likely to do volunteer work. In general, materialistic people are more likely to treat people as a means to an end rather than individuals. As the character Granny Weatherwax says in fantasy author Terry Pratchett's book *Carpe Jugulum*, "Sin, young man, is when you treat people like things." Being materialistic results in acting in ways that are opposed to working collaboratively to benefit society, particularly those who are less privileged.

Even folks who aren't inherently materialistic fall prey to this self-focus if their materialism is triggered. In one study by researchers from the University of Chicago and Cornell University, they asked one group to think of a material purchase, another to think of an experiential purchase, and a control group to think of something unrelated. Participants then played a game where they decided how much money to keep and how much to give away. The group that thought about material purchases was the least generous of the three, while the group that thought about experiential purchases was the most generous.

BUILDING GRATITUDE FOR WHAT YOU HAVE

Even if it's by choice, not buying stuff when you want to can make you feel like you're missing out. It's easy for middle- and upper-class people to feel entitled to the things they have rather than appreciative of them.

Finding ways to increase your gratitude can reverse that perception. Being grateful is the opposite of being materialistic. Seeing things through a lens of abundance rather than scarcity helps us embrace what we have instead of being frustrated by what we don't. It also helps build emotional and mental connections to the people and community associated with the good things in our lives.

To shift his view, Dannemiller did what psychologist Martin Seligman calls an "appreciation audit." It's simply writing down three things you're grateful for every day. In a number of studies with children and adults alike, this simple exercise or ones like it result in being happier, more satisfied, and more likely to be kind to others. Being grateful fulfills a number of psychological needs, including feeling like you have control over your life, the ability to "be yourself," and being connected to others.

Dannemiller wrote down five items a day he was grateful for. While he started by focusing on the items around him, he soon switched to include intangible things such as a flexible job, music he enjoys, and his children. At the end of a week of doing this exercise, he said that reading those thirty-five different items resulted in "a flood of gratitude."

Another way to build appreciation for what you have is to regularly state your gratitude in front of your children. Rebecca Stallings, who lives in Pittsburgh with her two kids, grew up in a very anti-materialistic household. Her family has a long history of passing along goods; most of her furniture and children's clothing is secondhand. She tells her kids, "Isn't it great that we found this shirt at Goodwill that we like so much and it only cost two dollars?" or "This is the great soup pot that Uncle Carl gave us." Attaching the object to a person or situation with an emotional aspect helps increase gratitude. She said, "I feel like there's a lot of abundance in our lives without having to buy a lot of new and wasteful stuff. I think there is a lot of appreciation for what they have."

Forcing children to wait to get an item they want increases their patience as well as their appreciation once they actually get it. Payne calls this waiting "the gift of anticipation." Immediate gratification creates a cycle where a child gets a brand-new thing, plays with it for a short period of time, then wants another new thing shortly after. But half the fun of receiving gifts is having the excitement build up beforehand. Waiting also helps children build self-management skills, including the ability to control impulses, tolerate frustration, and delay gratification. In the short term, these skills help kids feel capable. In the long term, they're essential to maintaining relationships and making healthy life choices.

When we appreciate our items more, we often respect and take care of them better. Dannemiller says that after the experiment, they continued to repair items they owned rather than just replace them. When their basketball hoop rusted out, he found a welding shop that could make the piece they needed rather than purchase a new one. He said, "If you have it, own it. Take care of it. It's not disposable." Doing these things with our kids brings the lesson home. When I showed Dylan how to repair a hole in pair of pajama pants, I both taught him a new skill and illustrated that we appreciate our possessions enough to fix them. While it hasn't stopped my kids from leaving things on the floor (yet), I'm playing the long game.

Being grateful helps us better appreciate not only our stuff but the people in our lives as well. In an experiment by researchers at North-eastern University, they found that when a participant received help from another participant (who was trained by the researchers), they experienced a surge of gratitude. The first participant was then sig-nificantly more likely to help both the person who helped them as well as a second, unrelated person who needed assistance. In other studies, participants have consistently rated the grateful people they know as more generous or helpful than others.

FOSTERING EMOTIONAL WELL-BEING

Perhaps not surprisingly, people who are materialistic are simply less happy than those who are grateful. Even though it sometimes feels like having more stuff will make us happier, it does the opposite in reality. Both an excess of physical stuff and the desire for it can create stress and frustration. In the UCLA study of families in Los Angeles, parents who felt stressed about clutter had higher levels of the chemical corti-sol in their blood. Cortisol is associated with depression. The research-ers found a direct link between having a high number of objects in the household and physical health.

Burger's family moved to their tiny trailer for the sake of her son's mental health and well-being. Her son has severe attention deficit hyperactivity disorder as well as a sensory processing disorder. Moving out of their large farmhouse into a simpler, less overwhelming space reduced his stimulation. With fewer choices and less to manage, he's far less overwhelmed. "He's able to think through things a lot better. He's able to have better impulse control," she said. "That has been a huge help for us." When they visit relatives who have a large number of toys, he finds it overly stimulating and needs to decompress for a few days afterward. The "busyness" of the surrounding atmosphere is more stressful than their simpler lifestyle.

Even for children without disabilities, having too much stuff can limit emotional development. According to Payne, having relatively few toys helps children learn the various stages of play: solitary play by themselves, parallel play next to other children, sociodramatic pretend play, and game play. Moving through these different stages helps children build essential social and emotional skills. "If they don't develop . . . a full range of social and emotional skills, they don't succeed in life," said Payne. "The jury is in on that one."

Being involved in consumer culture—the active desire to buy things—further reinforces this stress. Children who are more materialistic are more at risk for anxiety and depression, as well as less likely to feel connected to others. They're also more likely to engage in risky activities. A survey led by a researcher from Hofstra University of more than 1,000 high school students in Long Island found that the teenagers who were more materialistic were more likely to be envious of others. In contrast, students who were more grateful were more likely to be satisfied with life, more connected to others, and less likely to be depressed. Similar studies of teenagers have found a relationship between valuing financial success and lower levels of energy, trust in others, feeling like they could be themselves, and likelihood to contribute to society.

Between the combination of materialism, overscheduling, and social pressure, children from affluent, well-educated families are now considered at high risk for mental and emotional health issues. In a 1999 survey by researchers at Columbia and Yale universities, about one-fifth of adolescent girls from suburban upper-middle-class and middle-class families scored as clinically depressed. This was much higher than the national average of 7 percent and even higher than the percentage of depression for inner-city girls, which was 18 percent. Since then, parents and teachers have reported these issues continuing to get worse.

★ ★ ★

Even though my kids are still so in love with their stuff that they freak out when I suggest donating toys, I have hope for the future.

On Martin Luther King Jr. Day, Dylan had the day off from school. The local bounce-house had a special, so we went there for a few hours of mom–son bonding time. As the day is also a national day of service, we stopped by our community center later on to check out their activity. Even though the event was supposed to run for another hour, everyone had packed up except the volunteer organizing it. But he had plenty of materials left, so he invited us to participate.

The event involved writing notes of encouragement to women in homeless shelters—not exactly the most kid-friendly activity. But we sat down anyway and went to work. I discussed what to write with Dylan and then wrote it on the cards. He added a sticker to seal the envelope and a bow for decoration. We did about ten before we ran out of materials and packed everything up.

That night at bedtime, I asked him, "What was your favorite thing today?" Obviously, it was going to be the bounce-house. But instead he answered, "Writing the notes." I smiled and replied, "That's wonderful, honey. Me too." Sometimes it takes time for lessons to sink in, while others are there for you to see right away.

What to Know

Our society is so materialistic that it's often hard to hear your inner voice over the noise. Developing specific skills can help you and your kids see the bigger picture.

Consider Your Real Reasons for Buying or Scheduling Things

While we think we "need" specific items, buying is more often about fulfilling a psychological need than a practical one. Fear or sadness can drive our purchases. When children hear us saying we "need" a nonessential item or see us engaging in "retail therapy," they start to see buying things as a way to solve mental or emotional problems.

Thinking about the deeper motivations behind a purchase—whether for ourselves or our children—can help us buy what we truly need instead of what we feel compelled to by social pressure. Are we buying a toy for our children because we've been working long hours and feel like we have to make up for it? Are we buying new clothes to make ourselves feel better after a hard week? Are we considering buying a larger house because that's what you do at this stage in life?

In contrast, facing our fears about being "weird" or not having "the right thing" can model to our kids how to reject materialistic messages. While Dannemiller worried about what other kids would think of his son's lack of special basketball socks, the kids didn't have a problem with it at all. "At the age they were at, it didn't even register with them. We realized we were the ones projecting all of that on them," he said. This is especially true at the holidays. Some families celebrate the holidays a certain way because that's "the way it's always been," regardless of whether it's right for them or not.

In some cases, children may not even want the things parents think they "need." "Parents feel real pressure to get their kids on the best track possible in order to do x, y, or z, whatever that may be. They feel bad if they don't get their kid the things that the other kids have," said Koh, who co-wrote *Minimalist Parenting*. "This was something that I wrestled with a lot when I first became a parent because I grew up low-income and really struggling." At first, she wanted to sign her kids up for all the activities that she was never able to do as a child. In reality, her kids wanted to do very few of those things. Instead, they were much happier with extra free time.

Model Thoughtful, Conscious Buying

Impulse buying is one of the biggest contributors to an excess of stuff. Just pausing before buying something can halt a lot of unnecessary purchases. Burger recommends leaving the store and then waiting until the next day to make a purchase if you're still interested in it. She said that tactic often keeps her from purchasing stuff and then forgetting she even bought it in the first place. Things seem far less tempting outside of the store than when they're staring you in the face.

When we make a purchase, talking through the reasons behind that purchase models good buying habits for our kids. Dannemiller said that during and after the challenge, he changed how he talked to his kids about why they chose to buy or not buy certain things. Before the challenge, he would usually say that they weren't buying something because they couldn't afford it. Essentially, he was saying that if you have enough money, you can and should get anything you want. "I was like, 'Wait a minute, that's not the message we want to send,'" he said. "Instead of saying we can't afford that, we started saying we don't need that." Now before buying something, they ask questions like, "Do we have one like this at home already?" "How long will we use this?" and "How much time and energy will it take for me to maintain this item?" Switching from thinking about what you could buy to what you actually need helps put purchases in perspective.

Other families take similar tactics. Stallings said that her parents only purchased items once there was no other choice and walked their kids through the process when they did. When they bought a washing machine, her parents considered whether to get it new or used, if they could get it on sale or not, and which one would use the least energy. She's continued this tradition with her own kids. When her children ask for grocery items that she wouldn't normally buy, she discusses the cost with them, as well as if the ingredients are healthy or not. Personally, I ask myself if the item I'm going to purchase is available secondhand and if it's not, if it's made in as ethical a way as possible.

Even if it feels awkward talking through these things, the lessons really do sink in. Stallings said that she was very proud of her preteen son when he came home from the store and told her about how he was comparison shopping for chips with his friends. "All these years of thinking out loud in the grocery store have rubbed off on him," she said. Similarly, I was shocked and pleased when Dylan decided to comparison shop for the Rubik's Cube he wanted.

Having this attitude also keeps you from shopping for the sake of shopping. As Dannemiller said, "Buying is not bad, but if I turn that into a hobby, then I've got to ask myself a question, 'What do I get out of it? Should I take up crocheting?'"

Use Specific Tactics to Limit Impulse Purchases

When your kid asks for the same thing for the five millionth time, it's really hard to say no. It's handy to have some go-to answers in your mental back pocket.

Our biggest tactic is to only buy toys on three occasions: Christmas, birthdays, and a souvenir on vacation. If my kids want something outside one of those occasions, I take a photo and say that they can add it to their birthday or Christmas list. This works surprisingly well even if the event is months away. When we visited Disneyland on vacation, Dylan wanted a *Cars* toy even though he had already purchased his souvenir for the trip. I took a photo, which sat on my phone until December. Having to wait often takes the shine off of things that seem new and exciting when kids first see them.

Other families have similar philosophies. Some have a "one in/one out" rule that if an item comes into the house, a similar item must be donated. Having to sacrifice a toy in exchange makes the purchase mean a lot more. For the holidays, the "Four Gifts" tactic is popular: something the child wants, something the child needs, something the child can wear, and something the child can read. Of course, purchasing experiential gifts rather than physical ones is a great option. My parents have bought my children gift certificates to a play area and rock-climbing gym as birthday presents.

Next Steps

Minimize Exposure to Advertisements and Teach Kids to Look at Them Critically

One of the biggest predictors of consumerism and materialism is the amount of media and advertisements kids are exposed to. The average kid above the age of two sees 25,000 advertisements a year, according to *Adweek*. In addition, television shows and YouTube influencers often trigger insecurity because they show people who are much more attractive and wealthier than the average person. Having less screen time overall and watching shows on services without ads helps reduce exposure to commercials.

Critiquing advertisements can also reduce their influence. While children under six are typically not critical thinkers, you can help them develop this skill earlier if you work on it. Our older son has been watching football games with my husband from a young age, and they are full of advertisements. From the start, we simply said, "Commercials are trying to sell you things." As he grew older, we described different tactics advertisers use. We explained how advertisers show photos of cute babies in diaper commercials to make parents feel like this diaper would make their baby happy. Likewise we talked about how ads of SUVs driving over mountains try to send the message that if you get this car, you'll be adventurous. Building kids' skepticism toward advertisements' claims makes them less susceptible to the over-the-top promises in many ads. Knowing that a toy car can't actually drive through flames makes it a lot less appealing.

Reducing our own exposure to advertising and systems that encourage impulse buying helps too. The Dannemillers canceled all catalogs and unsubscribed from email coupons. Koh said that cancelling her Amazon Prime subscription made a big difference. Not having that "order now" button reduced the temptation to do so. "It has not been hard and it has totally changed our habits," Koh said. "We're just not doing that kind of loose, mindless spending that was sort of slipping into our habits because of the accessibility of that platform."

Find New Ways to Appreciate What You Have

Rather than buying more stuff, find new ways to make old stuff feel new again. Any parent who has ever declared, "You haven't played with this in ages! Maybe we should pass this on to someone else," and then had a child immediately start playing with a toy knows this approach works.

One way to minimize clutter while creating this feeling of "newness" is to have a toy library. With this tactic, certain toys are available while others are put away in a closet, at a relative's house, or other hidden-away place. You then periodically switch out the toys.

In addition, you can help your children find new ways to play with toys they already have. Perhaps an abandoned doll can find new life if your child crafts her some clothes or a toy car can be more exciting with a custom-built ramp.

There's also the classic standby of letting your children play with kitchen utensils or other non-toy items. No matter how many toys are available to my kids, they still love swiping our spatulas and chopsticks to bang on things or fly around as spaceships.

Let Your Children Experiment with Money

While giving your children money seems contradictory to de-emphasizing materialism, it helps them understand how much things actually cost and how much it takes to earn them. When children just get purchases when they ask for them, they don't have a sense of scarcity; money is always there when they need it. In contrast, if they are responsible for making decisions, it can get them out of the "if I ask enough times, Mom/Dad will buy it" mode. If they buy something that's junk and it breaks, they'll be more likely to realize what a poor investment it was.

Koh said that a few years ago, her daughter (who was eight at the time) wanted an American Girl doll. As Koh's "crusty New England self" didn't want to buy the pricey doll, she told her daughter that she would help her earn the money to buy it. Cobbling together money from selling a number of her own toys and gift money saved from the holidays, her daughter finally had enough money to buy the doll herself. At the end, her daughter was so grateful for the help Koh provided that she offered to take Koh out for ice cream. "There was so much learning in that one experience," Koh said. "I feel like that has carried through for her for so many other things."

Have Strategic Conversations with Relatives

Even if you don't buy much yourself, extremely generous relatives can flood your home with toys. Talk to them honestly about your values and practical limits as parents. For holidays or birthdays, sending them links to simple and useful gifts can help avoid a large number of toys. Some people may also prefer to give experiences or contribute to a larger item that the child is saving up money for. Of course, some people are more than happy to give practical gifts, like money toward college.

As Much as Possible, Buy Multi-Purpose, High-Quality Items

Buying high-quality, simple items that hold up over time instead of trendy toys helps them be more valuable in the long run. My children have used their toy kitchen for more than five years and I expect to get a few more years of use out of it. In addition, it's less likely that high-quality items will break; if they do, it's more likely that you'll be able to fix them. Admittedly, buying high-quality items isn't easy; they tend to be more expensive. But because they hold up well, you can sometimes buy them secondhand.

Make a Habit of Building Gratitude and Serving Others

One source of materialism is feeling like your emotional needs aren't being met. Materialistic teenagers generally have less nurturing families, which can make them more susceptible to commercial messages. In contrast, less materialistic teenagers have families who encourage self-acceptance and serving the community.

Practicing gratitude can help fulfill these emotional needs. Cultivating gratitude works best when it becomes a habit. At our dinner table, we say thanks every night. In addition to a general thanks, we show appreciation for everyone who helped get food to our table. At bedtime, we discuss something that made us happy that day, so we end by remembering something good.

Finding ways to serve the community regularly can be a little more challenging, especially with young kids. Emphasizing community service is particularly useful during the holidays, when kids are the most obsessed with presents. At Thanksgiving, my husband and older son bake an extra apple pie for the free lunch program at our church. During the holidays, we pick out a toy together to donate to Toys for Tots as well as "donate" an animal like a goat or pig through a charity.

FAMILY ACTIVITY:
Make Your Own Toys out of Discarded Goods

Toys from the store often do only one or two things, motivating kids to want something new after a short period of time. But what if we could empower kids to make their own toys? If they're built from things we would throw out or recycle anyway, we can show kids that fun doesn't require buying anything at all.

COLLECT AND LOCATE THE ITEMS YOU WILL USE TO MAKE YOUR TOY

Over a few days, set aside and keep objects that you would otherwise get rid of. You may want to consider keeping bottle caps, toilet paper tubes, pieces of string, rubber bands, cereal boxes, milk jugs, broken crayons, used paper, egg cartons, and more. If you throw away very little, you can expand to include natural materials from the outdoors, such as acorns, pine cones, and sticks.

BRAINSTORM WITH YOUR CHILD WHAT KIND OF TOY THEY WANT TO MAKE

Ask them open-ended questions that can help spark their imaginations. Some ideas include: Is your toy a character, like a robot or animal? Is it a game that you can play together? Is it a construction toy, like a marble run or Lincoln Logs? My husband and son once made a home-made Rube Goldberg machine. Encourage your child without rejecting ideas out of hand. Even if what they suggest is impractical, they may find a way to build it with a heavy dose of imagination.

COLLECT ADDITIONAL BUILDING/CONSTRUCTION MATERIALS

Figure out with your child what tools they need to make the toy and gather those in one place. These may include scissors, masking or duct tape, glue sticks, paint, colored pencils, or crayons.

SIT BACK AND PROVIDE ENCOURAGEMENT

Let your child lead the way as they design their toy! You can ask occasional questions or point out areas that you think they're being particularly thoughtful about. But for the most part, let their creativity run wild.

Books

PICTURE BOOKS

A Chair for My Mother, by Vera B. Williams: While it's named after a possession, this book is really about the power of working together as a family. After a little girl's family loses almost all their possessions in a fire, she helps her mother save money to purchase a chair that everyone can use together.

Last Stop on Market Street, by Matt de la Peña and Christian Robinson: This book follows a young boy and his grandmother's bus ride through the city as he discovers how interacting with people can be more fulfilling than owning stuff.

Sally Jean, the Bicycle Queen, by Cari Best and Christine Davenier: This lovely book is very similar to the real-life story that Payne told about the two boys restoring the bikes, even down to establishing a community bike shop. Sally Jean loves her bike, but when she gets too big for it and her parents can't afford to buy her a new one, she uses community and ingenuity to build one herself.

Bear Says Thanks, by Karma Wilson and Jane Chapman: Bear doesn't have anything in his cabinet to share, but his friends are more than willing to help out with what they can bring to the table. This book does a great job illustrating gratitude and the power of community.

My Heart Fills with Happiness, by Monique Gray Smith and Julie Flett: This beautiful book celebrates the small things that bring us true joy, from making music to spending time with family.

Resources

A Year Without Purchase, by Scott Dannemiller

Simplicity Parenting, by Kim John Payne

Minimalist Parenting, by Christine Koh and Asha Dornfest

Edit Your Life podcast with Christine Koh and Asha Dornfest: www .edityourlifeshow.com

Sunshine Guerilla blog by Barbara Greene Alfeo: www.sunshine guerrilla.com

Live Simply Right Now, by Brynn Burger

GETTING DIRTY
WHILE DOING GOOD :
ENVIRONMENTAL
VOLUNTEERISM

"What is that?" I squinted and asked my three-year-old, Ethan. He was holding something, but I couldn't see exactly what it was. I was sitting at a picnic table, finishing off my dinner while he was playing in a random corner of the picnic space. We were at a baseball stadium, so it was likely something he wasn't supposed to have.

"Here, have it," he said. I took a closer look.

"Augh, no! It's toilet paper! Put that down," I said, batting at his hands to drop it. I sighed and rolled my eyes a little. "Ethan, please don't pick up garbage."

That was far from the first time we've had that conversation. Tissues, soda cans, bottle caps—he's picked them all up at our park and other places. He means well; he wants to help out. But that doesn't mean you should pick up trash—especially toilet paper—with your bare hands.

However, that desire to make our outdoor spaces better can be awesome if applied correctly.

As our little litter-picker-upper demonstrates, there's still a lot of garbage in the outdoors. Despite anti-litter laws and enforcement, there's 51 billion pieces of litter that appear on roadways—not including parks, sidewalks, and other areas—per year, according to Keep America Beautiful. Garbage also contaminates wetland, beach, and stream habitats, which are fragile and essential ecosystems. Of course, it can hurt animals that swallow it, including whales and sea turtles.

In addition to the environment, it's crummy for the community too. Litter reduces a neighborhood's property values by as much as 7 percent. Picking up litter costs more than $11.5 billion a year. Garbage in public spaces like beaches and parks makes them less attractive and even unsafe to visit.

Litter can even be a public health issue. Garbage that ends up in streams, storm drains, and drainage areas can pollute water, reducing water quality. Freshwater rivers and streams provide two-thirds of America's water supply. Certain types of litter can also attract pests such as rats, especially in areas that already have poor public services. Cleaning up parks, streams, and beaches can be a powerful way to serve your larger community.

While picking up litter is one of the most popular ways to volunteer outdoors, it's far from the only one. In fact, there is a huge variety of possible ways to give back to your community in outdoors settings. With city and state environmental agencies often underfunded and understaffed, volunteers can help fill major gaps.

Outdoor volunteerism projects include tree planting, trail building, measuring water quality in streams, pulling invasive plants, and caring for plants in your city. TreePeople, a volunteer group in Los Angeles, planted nearly 2,000 trees and took care of 9,500 others in

2017 alone. Volunteer stream monitors are essential to keeping an eye on changes in water quality.

Youth are often leading the way in these efforts. Many Girl and Boy Scout troops work to improve or maintain outdoor spaces. Roots & Shoots, a group established by conservationist Jane Goodall, specializes in engaging children in volunteerism to help people, animals, and the environment.

SCOUTING GARLIC MUSTARD

Conservation has been part of the Boy Scouts of America's mission since it was founded in 1910. So tagging along with a local group seemed to be a great way to see youth volunteerism in action. One sunny spring morning, I joined up with a Cub Scout pack in Northern Virginia that was working to earn the Hornaday Award. The award is named for William Hornaday, the conservationist who helped prevent the extinction of the American bison and founded the National Zoo. Either individual Scouts or units can earn it. Of the unit awards, only twenty-two units out of thousands in the country receive the award each year.

"It's a very prestigious award," said Sara Holtz, a local Leave No Trace coordinator and advisor for the Hornaday Award. She was helping the pack organize their events; she's also helped other Boy Scout groups earn it in the past.

To earn the unit award, 60 percent of a Boy Scout troop or Cub Scout pack has to participate in a substantial conservation project. It must be sustainable and have a long-term impact. Eligible projects include planting trees, pulling invasive plants, and establishing pollinator gardens.

This pack's focus? To clear as much garlic mustard as possible from nearby parks and county land. Garlic mustard is a highly invasive plant species that doesn't provide the same types of ecosystem services, like food and shelter for native animals and building good soil, that native plants do. It's also incredibly aggressive, crowding out native plants and reducing the light and nutrients available to them. Garlic mustard even puts out chemicals that reduce the growth of other plants. Places it grows actually have a lower diversity of native plants. Its hardiness is legendary as well. The average plant sends out 600 seeds at a time that can stay in the ground dormant for more than five years.

Meeting up with the group, I arrived at a small county park, a ribbon of wild-feeling land surrounded by large suburban houses and lawns. A dirt path led down it, winding over a stream and through a forest floor thick with plants. A blue Adopt a Stream sign stood at one side of the path and a green sign declaring that "Invasive plant removal and habitat restoration in progress" stood at the other.

Not long after, the Cub Scouts (first through fifth graders) and their parents arrived. Many were wearing "Take Back the Forest" T-shirts from past garlic mustard pulling excursions, with images of English ivy tendrils (another invasive species) winding up the back. Wearing hiking pants, sweatpants, leggings, boots, and sneakers, they were prepared to work. While the parents chatted in small groups, the dozen or so kids bounced around in excitement. One boy messing around in the drop-off from the road to the park declared, "I'm walking up the trench of doom!"

BUILDING AWARENESS OF THE ENVIRONMENT

Gathering the kids and parents together, Holtz gave a short presentation. Looking out from under her blue Cubs baseball cap, she mixed enthusiasm with gravity, trying to help the kids realize the importance of what they were doing. Holding up a sign with photos labeled "Invasive Plants," she described how they can take over an ecological niche. Pulling up a stalk of garlic mustard conveniently next to the path, she held it up as an example. As a long, tall, green stalk growing numerous thin branches and heart-shaped leaves, it was easy to spot. "This is the danger," she said, pointing to the seedpods. "These seeds grow fast, aggressively. They can take over where natural plants would be."

As the seeds can stay dormant for so long, the group wasn't going to mulch or compost the plants. Because people use the mulch or compost in their yards, disposing of them that way would just spread the seeds further. Instead, the group would bag the plants before bringing them to the dump. Unfortunately, there was no lack of garlic mustard to pull. The last time the group met, they filled twenty-two bags' worth of garlic mustard.

Searching for these plants required the kids have a keen eye and awareness of their surroundings. Because the project required going off-trail, Holtz cautioned, "If you see ferns and obvious plants, try not to step on them."

Almost immediately, the Scouts got it, even those who hadn't been at the previous event. Finding his first plant, one Scout declared, "I got a handful!" I overheard one mom whose kids had attended previous sessions saying, "My kids didn't stop talking about plants for like five days afterwards."

The scavenger hunt aspect helped. Once you knew what you were looking for, it was easy to spot almost everywhere. Holtz really wasn't exaggerating its aggressiveness.

This opportunity to get out and experience nature in their neighborhoods is increasingly unusual in children's lives. With so much time devoted to school, organized sports, and other structured activities, a lot of kids just don't spend time exploring their backyards and local parks. As a result, fewer and fewer children are familiar with their surrounding environment, especially plants. People are much less likely to notice and recognize plants than they are animals, leading to less interest in plant biology and conservation.

In contrast, learning about the local environment was an inherent feature of these events, both formally through Holtz's talk and informally by getting hands-on in nature. "It gets them out and it gets them curious," said Greg Pinto, one of the Cub Scout leaders in the group. On previous excursions, the children had seen box turtles, snakes, frogs, dragonflies, spiders, and giant luna moths. By engaging their senses, the outdoors environment sparked their inherent interest and awareness.

Holtz said that once the children start looking, they begin to pepper her with questions. As they spot a variety of organisms, they want to know more. They notice invasive species other than the ones they're looking for, matching what they see to the plants on her shirt or sign. "They're face to face with the ground. They're face to face with bugs and insects and worms," she said. "Because you're in direct contact, it's hard to avoid the curiosity that overcomes kids in a situation like this." In the process, they pick up an understanding of their local environment, as well as the vocabulary to describe it.

Similarly, Anna Sharratt, who founded the Free Forest School movement out of Minneapolis, said that becoming familiar with a specific place builds a level of comfort in children. "Rather than a one-time adventure to a new place, returning to the same place helps a child really feel a sense of ownership for and love for nature," she said. "Without you talking about it, they internalize the cycles of nature, change of the seasons, and their connection to something larger than themselves. In a natural setting, there's so much that stimulates them and challenges them that we simply can't provide indoors."

That awareness and interest help build a sense of place in children. Having a level of familiarity makes them want to return to the same place over and over again. Atiya Wells is a pediatric nurse and the director of the Baltimore chapter of the Free Forest School. She's also the founder of Backyard Basecamp, an organization devoted to introducing, educating, and connecting families in Baltimore, especially those of color, to local outdoor spaces. Although Wells's daughter disliked formal hikes and excursions, she very much enjoys coming back and playing in the same places again and again. Wells said that it's great "how observant they get about everything. How fascinated they get with everything. Once you feed that and you don't push them away from picking up worms or digging through the weeds or anything like that, they get really driven and they can't wait for you to come back." Her new project, BLISS (Baltimore Living in Sustainable Simplicity) Meadows, a ten-acre green space and urban farm, is designed to provide that sort of space for children and adults alike in northeast Baltimore City.

DEVELOPING A SENSE OF RESPONSIBILITY TO THE LOCAL ENVIRONMENT

With support, that sense of place can translate into a sense of caretaking toward the local environment.

The kids tackled the project with gusto, running back and forth between where the plants were and the nearest adult with a garbage bag. They hauled handfuls and armfuls of garlic mustard to and fro.

After running through the initial site in only a few minutes, we moved on to two more sites in the same neighborhood. As we walked to the next one, I overheard one mom say, "My kids didn't want to do it last week, but were like, 'Can we come back this week?'"

That enthusiasm extended beyond this set of scheduled experiences. Pinto said that when his son was on a field trip, he spotted garlic mustard and wanted to pick it there as well. He was showing his friends how to identify it and told them about how easy it was to pull it out. The child also told Holtz about seeing it, asking her if he could return and pick it. "When we become engaged, particularly in the environment, particularly in our neighborhood or the place where we live, we have ownership," she said. "Moving forward, it becomes a norm. It becomes like what you do, who you are."

Action is an essential part of the equation. Talking about the Scouts, Pinto said, "They have an investment in whatever it is they're doing." He pointed out that these activities move children from being spectators to being engaged. For example, his group previously participated in a stream cleanup. When the Scouts pass by that stream now, they still point it out and recall how they helped.

That sense of responsibility to your local community is common when people engage in volunteerism. Social responsibility generally develops between the ages of nine and eighteen, motivating how people approach their community commitments. However, it's not an automatic process. It's influenced by how much people in the preteen or teenager's life encourage and support it.

Fortunately, once it's developed, those values generally persist into adulthood. A study by researchers at the University of Rochester, the Search Institute, and the University of Wisconsin-Madison shows that volunteering is a great way to build that value. They conducted a survey of more than 800 fifth through twelfth graders over the course of three years. Children who had participated in volunteer work were more likely to say it was important to help people who were less fortunate, others in the community, students in school, and society at large.

Outdoor volunteerism projects in particular build this commitment to community. Researchers at the University of Maryland examined attitudes and activities of people who volunteered for the Watershed Stewards Academy project in Maryland. This project trains nonscientists to monitor water quality, educate their neighbors, and minimize pollution in the Chesapeake Bay watershed. The volunteers said they particularly appreciated having a hands-on way to make a difference in their local communities and engage with their neighbors. Researchers found that volunteers were much more likely than the average citizen to have participated in other civic activities, including attending town hall meetings, signing petitions, and contacting elected officials. The authors said, "We argue that participation in environmental stewardship activities is helping to diversify democracy by rooting citizens to their localities in individually and socially meaningful ways." A related study by University of Maryland researchers looking at volunteer tree-planting initiatives in New York City, Philadelphia, and Washington, DC, found similar results. Volunteers were more likely than the average person to engage in a number of civic activities, including participating in protests. The more experienced volunteers were more likely than those who were less experienced to be involved in other local environmental organizations.

That attitude of service develops naturally when children become attached to a place, according to Sharratt. From her experience with the Free Forest School, she's seen children start picking up garbage on their own and expressing disgust when they see litter. "They just develop this ethic of care organically without you ever having to explain it to them," she said. Raising committed citizens may start with connecting them to the places they live and play.

Engaging in these activities also reduces entitlement and helps children appreciate the hard work that goes into maintaining public spaces.

"They learn that things don't happen by magic or somebody else doing it," said Pinto, who pointed out that helping is a core value of the Scout ethos. "They learn not to take it for granted. They learn that they have to do their bit and if everyone does their bit, it's a huge impact." Along with managed parks or natural areas like streams, these spaces can include public playgrounds, community gardens, schoolyards (as long as you have permission from the school), trees planted in sidewalks, and informal green spaces. Anywhere that someone could experience nature in some capacity, residents can chip in to help out.

This work comes in many forms, something that Erika Nowlin has seen firsthand. She runs Austin Allies, a group in Austin, Texas, that organizes and connects families with volunteer opportunities. They've run a number of volunteer days focused on the environment, including taking care of trees in local parks, cleaning up leftover Christmas decorations on trees, and planting flowers with residents at a local nursing home. "It's nice for kids to get out and kind of take ownership of parks that they maybe play in. And they're like, 'I didn't think I could come out here and make my park better,'" she said. The children participating realize that even though they're not usually the ones who do this work, someone must do it. Collaborating with local groups to monitor the water quality of local streams, remove invasive species, and plant native species are other ways of building that investment.

As much as they provide a direct connection to nearby spaces, these activities also widen children's understanding of what constitutes their backyard. As Nowlin said, "It gives you more of an ownership too of your city." Volunteerism can extend a child's relationship from that one special spot to the entire community.

"Once kids are aware of what's happening in their community, they just become much more engaged in what they can do to make a difference," said Misty Castañeda. She runs For Purpose Kids, a company out of Los Angeles that teaches children service and kindness through subscription boxes with relevant activities that families receive each month. "Not being disconnected from the community lends that sense of responsibility." When they see the impact they have, children understand that their actions matter. No matter how young or small, they can make a difference.

REINFORCING COMMUNITY CONNECTIONS

Of course, that connection often goes far beyond nature. It's about building relationships with your human neighbors too.

At the second location of the Cub Scouts' cleanup, a neighborhood homeowner met us in the street. To get to the county land, we had to cut through some private property, so the neighbor wanted to give us an introduction to the area.

As we stood in a cul-de-sac, the white-haired and white-bearded neighbor verbally guided us through the landscape. Pointing out the steepness of the nearby slope, he commented, "We need some billy goats here." He told us about some of the local wildlife too, including a resident skunk and snakes. "They are not dangerous," he clarified, referring to the snakes. Before sending off the Scouts, he thanked them for their help and service.

As the group moved on, other neighbors also showed interest. They came out into their yards and chatted over wooden fences. One shirtless gentleman pointed out, "I live right over there." He offered us water and food, a gracious offer considering the swampy weather. One Scout dad countered, "How 'bout a beer?" The neighbor wasn't quite that generous.

The very nature of serving outdoors makes these projects more obvious to neighbors than projects that are indoors. People naturally want to see what you're doing and why. For the Boy Scout events, Holtz ensures that even if people don't see them in person, they're likely to see them virtually. She posts photos to her neighborhood Facebook groups and always gets very positive responses. "Everyone is like, 'Thank you,' 'This is great,' 'This is awesome,'" she said. Often, seeing others serving the community spurs further action. "When people see kids working like this, your inclination is to at least do it on your own property," she said. "It's building momentum."

Some of the Boy Scout projects even require commitments from the local community. If a Scout wants to earn the individual Hornaday Award, they're required to put 500 to 1,000 collective hours into the project. Of course, they can't do that themselves; they have to enlist help from neighbors. Holtz said that often half of the hours come from non-Scout participants.

Building these community ties is essential to developing social capital. Social capital is the network of people around us that we can rely on to solve problems. It's particularly important for solving local environmental problems. The amount, strength, and intensity of people's relationships in a community determine its social capital. With the rise of digital communities and increasing physical isolation, many social science researchers have bemoaned a decrease in local social capital compared to the past.

But having shared experiences, such as volunteer activities, is a major way to build it. A study of volunteer stream monitors in Wisconsin looked at the social capital the program helped build. Surveying 155 experienced volunteers and 105 new volunteers, scientists found that the more experienced volunteers were more likely to provide information to their neighbors about stream health and monitoring. The longer people participated in the program, the more connected they felt to other community members interested in water and stream quality.

This type of social capital is incredibly valuable for children. It harkens back to the idea of "the village," where everyone in a neighborhood felt collectively responsible for taking care of local kids. After moving from Sweden to the U.S., Linda McGurk missed much of that feeling. She wrote the book *There's No Such Thing as Bad Weather* to share lessons about parenting that Americans could learn from the Swedish. "If we know that our neighbors are out there, sort of keeping an eye on the kids as well, we're doing it as a community," she said. "That I think will help give kids more freedom outside as well."

Likewise, Wells founded BLISS Meadows in part to meet the needs of her neighbors. She said that outdoors volunteering builds a special bond. While she was building bonds with fellow participants on hikes and workshops, she wanted to engage in it with the people in her immediate area. She also wanted to bring it to marginalized communities that often don't have access to these opportunities. "No matter how much time you spend in community with people, it's just like being outdoors doing that kind of adds another level to it," she said. "You'll never forget that moment or you'll never forget this place and time because you were out there in community, village-building."

CREATING QUALITY TIME WITH FAMILY AND FRIENDS

These types of experiences can offer family members a chance to connect as well. Unlike very structured activities that separate children and adults, outdoor volunteerism usually involves a leader giving directions and the volunteers collectively carrying them out. In a world where adults are often spectators on the sidelines to children's activities, it can be empowering to work together to carry out a shared goal.

During the Scout event, parents and children collaborated to get work done. Parents held the increasingly full bags while children darted back and forth pulling plants.

Nowlin said that she sees this bonding take place at her Austin Allies events as well. "When they come out and do it together, it's often something they haven't done before," she said. "They laugh, they have fun, they're working hard together." Volunteering becomes one of their regular family activities.

Interviews with families who volunteer by researchers from Indiana University show that volunteering together builds bonds, increases life satisfaction, and helps children focus on others' needs. Children reported that after volunteering, they respected and appreciated their family members more. Parents thought these activities helped the family act more like a team, especially siblings.

The outdoors element only adds another layer to the relationship. Without the distractions of housework or electronics, parents and children can focus on each other and jointly share in emotional experiences. Children's inherent curiosity can help parents see natural areas through new eyes. "When kids and parents spend time in nature together, away from cell phones and other distractions, there's a deepening of the parent-child relationship," said Sharratt.

Of course, there are times that are frustrating too. I heard one mom yell to her kids—who were mucking around in the forest with shorts on—"I'm 100 percent sure you're going to end up with poison ivy." It sounded like something that might come out of my own mouth. (Along with, "If you step in that puddle, your shoes will be wet all day.") It's just a chance you take with these activities.

DEVELOPING PSYCHOLOGICAL AND EMOTIONAL CAPABILITIES

While Holtz and the parents gave the Scouts directions, ultimately the activity was up to them. The kids determined how much they collected, how focused they were, and where they looked on the property.

As we worked, I saw them collaborating to get the work done. Some carried armfuls of plants while others picked. One Scout was even directing others to split up to thoroughly cover the area.

In addition, many of them were testing and expanding their physical and mental capabilities. Scrambling up and down the steep slope near the neighbor's house helped them work on balance and judgment. Leaping across a small stream that meandered through the property helped them judge distance and risk. Other children explored a fallen log, some teetering on top of it while others played limbo under it, singing "Limbo limbo limbo!" Another group of children were stopping and observing nature, like the kid who exclaimed, "It's a waterfall, a tiny waterfall!"

The outdoors is an ideal setting for children to build a number of psychological competencies, from executive function to risk evaluation. Executive function is an umbrella term for the skills to mentally plan and control behavior, including focus, working memory, emotional regulation, and the ability to think about the same thing in multiple ways. The flexibility and inherent lack of structure of being outside create a need and opportunity for children to develop these skills.

Much of that development may occur because exposure to nature helps restore attention. Being able to direct your attention toward a particular thing and away from everything else—whether that's an intense emotion, irrelevant information, or random stimuli—is essential for executive functioning. Any long-term effort that requires directed attention will lead to fatigue, as anyone who's ever done careful, close work for long periods of time knows. In 1995 psychologist Stephen Kaplan from the University of Michigan proposed that time in nature may reduce fatigue and restore the ability to pay attention. He described nature as having four parts that help fill this role: being inherently fascinating while also calming, creating a feeling of being "away" from work, taking up space in your mind, and fitting your personal emotional needs.

Since then, several psychological studies at a variety of locations have backed up these ideas about nature and attention. One study by a researcher currently at Cornell University followed a group of seventeen children (seven to twelve years old) in a public housing development. All the children changed houses during the study period, with the new houses having significantly more views of and access to green space than the old ones. The researchers measured the children's ability to pay attention before the move and a year after. They found the children who previously lived in places that had the least exposure to green space (and therefore the biggest change when they moved) also had the biggest increases in their ability to pay attention. The change in greenness accounted for about one-fifth of the increase in attention year-over-year.

In a similar study, University of Illinois researchers interviewed residents of Chicago public housing to look at the differences in attention between children in housing with more views of green space versus fewer views. While some buildings had grass and trees between them, others had pavement. By testing seven- to twelve-year-olds in 169 families, they found a strong positive relationship between the amount of green views near their home and girls' levels of concentration, ability to inhibit impulses, and ability to delay gratification. (Oddly, none of the results were significant for boys. The researchers thought this may be because boys play further away from home than girls. As such, they may be less affected by the level of greenness near their homes.)

This connection is far from limited to Chicago. A study in Barcelona, Spain, by researchers from Centre for Research in Environmental Epidemiology examined data from more than 2,500 second through fourth graders who took cognitive development tests. These tests measured things like working memory and ability to pay attention. Using mapping software to assess greenness around the school, the children's homes, and the routes between the two, researchers found that the students who had more greenness around their school had significantly more progress in working memory over the course of the year than those whose surrounding areas were less green. A different but related study in Barcelona by many of the same authors also found that children who played more often in green spaces had better relationships with their peers and fewer emotional issues.

Part of attention restoration is the fact that being in nature is relaxing. While biologist E. O. Wilson popularized the idea of biophilia—that humans have an inherent affection for nature—psychological research has supported it. People who see natural scenes or have more natural views heal faster in hospitals and recover from stress more easily. Levels of cortisol, a hormone associated with stress, are lower in people who are looking at scenes of nature.

As Wells said about her experience with her own children, "Just getting unstructured time . . . they can decompress a little bit. With their observation skills and focus skills building, they can sit quietly either by themselves or around their friend and they're fine." While her children tend to bicker inside, they're much more self-sufficient and calmer when playing together outside.

McGurk reported the same thing with her children. She described getting outside as a "calm down technique." She said, "It's not always easy to get there, but once we're outside, I feel like nine times out of ten at least, nature does have that sort of soothing effect on them. We usually can turn a day around just by going outside and exploring and playing. It's been a really effective tool in my toolbox as a parent." I've definitely had the same experience. My older son can be quite intense. When he goes outside, he visibly relaxes. The pent-up energy just seems to dissipate.

Nature's influence on attention and stress reduction can be especially powerful for children who have trouble with highly structured, adult-led settings.

"One thing I love about unstructured play in nature is that there's no wrong way to do it," said Sharratt, who sees this in her Free Forest School activities. "Outdoor play is powerful in that it creates a place where all children belong, learn, and develop at their own rate." She said that she worked with one student who would often have multiple staff people chasing him down the hall inside the school. But when the class moved outdoors, he was able to focus in a way that he never did inside.

Psychologists are considering playtime outside as a possible treatment for children with attention deficit hyperactivity disorder (ADHD). As people with ADHD are especially prone to attention fatigue, anything that can help them restore that attention may be a powerful tool. Researchers from the University of Illinois asked more than 400 parents of children who were five to eighteen years old and diagnosed with ADHD to rank a variety of leisure activities and whether the children's ADHD symptoms were better, worse, or the same after engaging in those activities. The parents also ranked the "greenness" of the settings of the activities. Parents consistently ranked symptoms as less severe than usual after children were in "greener" outdoor settings. Symptoms were also less severe after activities in natural settings compared to activities in indoor or built outdoor settings. In the experimental side of the same paper, seven- to twelve-year-old children diagnosed with ADHD and those without put together a puzzle for fifteen minutes. They then went for a twenty-minute walk. After walks in the greenest settings, both children with ADHD and those without it were better able to pay attention than when they walked in the other two settings. The second study of children in Barcelona also found that the more green space around the home of a child with ADHD, the more attentive they were and the less likely they were to have issues with impulsivity and hyperactivity.

While it seems like the complete opposite of being calm, being outdoors also allows children to take risks. Nature offers safe opportunities for taking risks (like walking on logs), creating a perfect place for children to safely practice doing so. Wells said that each time she brought her daughter to Free Forest School, she saw both her physical balance and confidence increase. Each stream crossed and tree climbed led to her daughter being a little surer of herself.

Allowing children to take those risks fosters independence—for both the child and the parent learning to let go. "I know it's transformative for many parents to just watch their child and realize how much their child is capable of," said Sharratt, describing what parents see when they step back and watch their kids. "Most people see something pretty remarkable happening."

CULTIVATING COMPASSION FOR ANIMALS AND THE ENVIRONMENT

If you talk to adult environmentalists, a key theme that emerges is how time spent outdoors led to their love of nature. I have many fond memories of fussing around with dandelions in my yard and hiding under the branches of our giant pine tree. Developing that sense of wonder was essential to my environmentalism. Of course, developing this respect for nature is a core part of the Scouts as well.

At the event, Holtz definitely emphasized this point. She told kids directly, "It's for the environment," and reminded them of how their work was helping restore the area's ecology. Pointing out that the garlic mustard seeds could end up in the nearby stream, she explained that if that happened, the seeds could flow downstream all the way to the Potomac River. In that way, she tied the activity to the ecology of not just the neighborhood but the larger region as well. She encouraged the Scouts to take pride in helping local plants and animals. "All along, you're making an impact," she said.

But nothing makes respect for nature more concrete than being in close contact with it. As we made our way along a dirt trail back at the original park, a group of the Scouts were randomly gathered together. As I glanced over, I saw some earthworms had come out of the dirt. One kid started poking a worm with a stick. One of the moms remarked, "Let them live. Don't mess with it." Despite the warning, the kid poked the worm again and killed it. Not surprisingly, that led to a lecture. "What outdoor code did we break?" asked the mom. "Respecting wildlife," answered the kid, sounding a bit ashamed. "They help nourish the soil," she reminded him. "We always respect wildlife. They have a right to live."

While that particular child didn't respect worms—at least not yet— that opportunity to learn wouldn't have happened if they weren't in a natural area. These instances help children develop empathy and understand the consequences of their actions. Talking about times when children hurt animals accidently, Sharratt said, "I think the children have a deep connection to whatever they've found because they're out in the environment and really seeing themselves as part of the place. It can be very impactful for young children to have that experience."

Just being exposed to nature helps students develop that empathy as well. In one study researchers from Western Washington University and the University of British Columbia interviewed students participating in an overnight outdoors program. After the program, students had a much stronger emotional connection to nature. They also showed more concern for wildlife. Even the children who started with negative notions about nature before the program, including being scared of wild animals, were much more positive at the end.

The service aspect of volunteerism adds even more significance. "It's a very good way to show kids how to give back to Earth and it's not just a place for us to entertain ourselves," said McGurk. "Nature is a place that needs caring for."

EXPLORING LIFE SKILLS

Volunteerism can be a great way for children to explore their passions and develop real-life skills. Holtz hopes that even if the Scouts don't continue with invasive species removal that they'll get involved in other environmental projects.

Traditional classrooms often don't offer opportunities to explore the same types of subjects or career paths that being outdoors can. Holtz said that as a result of these types of events, she's seen Scouts go into fields like environmental education and ecology. "You never know which of the Scouts will come forward as the person who wants to do this for a career," she said. In a survey of families who volunteer by Indiana University, two-thirds of the youth interviewed said volunteering helped them decide on a future career path.

Getting involved in organizing volunteer activities can teach even more. Nowlin pulls her children into the behind-the-scenes aspects of Austin Allies. They regularly greet volunteers and coordinate with the nonprofits the group partners with. "I've definitely seen a lot of growth in my kiddos that way," she said.

No matter what their career path, kids develop social and emotional skills from both volunteering and being outdoors that will help them in life. In the same Indiana University survey of families, 86 percent of volunteers said that it changed their perspective on the world. "Developing strong values like empathy and compassion, I think it's going to be the centerpiece of change," said Castañeda. "People who grow up to be more empathic and compassionate grow up to be better leaders, to be more successful, and more self-aware." While conversations about empathy can go a long way, getting out in person together is the most powerful way for children to develop it. Meeting your commitments for volunteering and feeling the need to carry out the task correctly also help build responsibility.

★ ★ ★

Much to my little volunteers' delight, our family participated in a stream cleanup last spring. To celebrate the National River Cleanup, our city was organizing several events across the town. Fortunately, one of them was at "the far-away park," a park about three-quarters of a mile from our house. My older son, Dylan, is particularly fond of this park, as we'd often stop there as he was learning to ride his bike on the road. Along with my parents, we hauled the whole crew over to the park bright and early on a clear April morning.

Picking up gloves, bags, and a trash picker from the sign-in desk, we headed off into the stream. Immediately, both kids wanted to use the trash picker, which looked like a much bigger version of the fake robot hand we have at home. With some help from the adults, both kids used it to pluck trash off the ground. As Ethan was too small and unsteady on his feet to wade in the stream, he stood on the banks and pointed out garbage for the adults to pick up. Often, he spotted things that we couldn't see from our viewpoint. With gloves on, Dylan reached into the water to wrestle out stubborn plastic netting and bottles. Of course, they all laughed at me when I stepped in deep water and swore as it poured in over the edge of my wader boots.

Looking over the stream afterward, we could truly see the difference. Although there had been plastic litter all over it to start, it was scrubbed clean at the end. My kids admired their handiwork for a few moments before running off to the nearby playground. But even now, whenever we go to the far-away park, we remember how we helped clean up the stream.

What to Know

Match Your Activity and Attitude to the Age Group and Abilities

The Scout activity worked so well because it was an excellent match for the skill level of elementary school students. Garlic mustard is easy to identify, pull, and bag. In contrast, other invasive species have thorns, are difficult to pull, or look too much like native species to consistently tell the difference.

Sometimes an activity is perfect, but children need a little more information than you would initially assume. Castañeda brought her three-year-old son on an informal beach cleanup while they were on a trip to Florida. At first he balked at leaving his toys. So she reframed the activity as a "scavenger hunt." Instead of garbage, the items were keys to a treasure. Putting an imaginative spin on it engaged him; soon, he was picking up trash left and right. But there was one more slight issue. Castañeda and her son were putting the trash—nothing dangerous—in his sand bucket to throw away. Much to her surprise, he ran into the ocean and dumped the bucket over! Although an adult would know the trash needed to go in the garbage, that thought simply didn't occur to a preschooler. Thankfully it was easy to pick out of the water. After that, the adults made sure to take the garbage out of the bucket and put it in a bag before her son headed back to the ocean. "It's not until you get out there that it really becomes real," she said. Children may need coaching about what to pick up and what to do with it before you start.

Having the right attitude can make all the difference in the world. Wells said that a few years ago, they signed up for the Baltimore County Nature Quest, where families do prescribed hikes around the area. But her daughter, who was four at the time, hated it. Wells said that she felt like, "Oh my gosh, we made our daughter hate nature." Obviously, she wanted to figure out what to do differently. When she started the Free Forest School chapter in Baltimore, those activities transformed her daughter's opinion. She started wanting to play in the forest. Just letting her daughter play freely without rushing her made a huge difference.

Follow Your Kids' Interests

Not every kid is going to be into planting trees or mucking around in streams. Heck, not all of them are going to be into environmental or outdoors service at all. You don't want volunteerism to be painful and forced. However, exploring a variety of options can help you and your kids figure out what they're interested in. Both Castañeda and Nowlin said they design activities that span a variety of subjects so they can spark a passion for service in children with diverse interests. In her subscription boxes, Castañeda includes a variety of recommended actions, from raising funds for conservation organizations to fostering animals. Nowlin's group has put together wildflower seed balls, placed mulch around trees, and planted flowers at a senior center.

Use Everyday Experiences to Spark Service

Volunteering or community service doesn't need to be a big event. Just taking action as a family can be very powerful.

Castañeda started For Purpose Kids in part because she was inspired by a friend's son named Dane. When Dane was walking with his mom, he saw a homeless person and started asking questions. While he and his mom had a good conversation, she didn't think much of it until a few weeks later. At that point, he approached her and said, "Mom, can you pull out your phone and take a video of me? I've been drawing these pictures." By selling his hand-drawn pictures, he raised nearly $800 for his local food bank. If his mom had brushed off those questions or not supported his efforts, he would have never been able to make that difference. Building off of real-life experiences helps nurture genuine passion that will last long beyond an individual project.

Parents can actually work service into everyday habits. Bringing plastic bags when you go to the park or on a walk makes it easy to incorporate cleaning up garbage into your routines. It also integrates the idea of service into children's very identities. "It becomes an ingrained habit for the kids from an early age," said McGurk. Seeing nature as around us and something we care for instead of separate from us also helps build that attitude of caretaking.

Base It on the Needs of Your Community

If you want to be part of a larger group or a formal event, check out what existing organizations are doing. Often they have events that welcome families. They also know what the biggest needs are in your area and the best ways to care for the local environment. Austin Allies has partnered with Keep Austin Beautiful and the Austin Parks Foundation to remove weeds from parks, mulch trees, and make wildflower seed balls.

Make It Concrete

Many outdoor volunteer activities are satisfying because it's very clear what you've accomplished. At the end of the Scouting event, the group had several bags of garlic mustard to display. They took a photo to both show off to the community and remind the participants of what they did that day. "At the end, you can actually see your impact," Holtz said. She also made sure to point out to the group that there was so much less garlic mustard at that event than there had been at the first event. Although some of it had grown back, it was powerful to see the long-term effect. Having a sense of the impact motivates kids to come back again and again.

Bring the Right Gear and Clothing

Outdoor volunteer events are like anything in the outdoors—having the right clothing and gear makes all the difference. For anything involving water, wear sturdy waterproof shoes. Waders are great, but hard to walk in. Sandals are ideal for warmer days. For tree planting, park cleanups, or planting flowers, wear comfortable closed-toe shoes. Dress in layers, so you can take clothing on or off as necessary, especially if there's a chance of it getting wet. While some events may be canceled in the case of a downpour, bring rain jackets in case it starts sprinkling. Of course, as with all outings with children, sunscreen, water, snacks, and hand sanitizer are always useful.

Next Steps

While not all outdoor volunteer activities are appropriate for children, most can be adapted to a variety of age groups. Some of the most common ones are cleaning streams, cleaning beaches, planting trees, pulling invasive plants, monitoring water quality, and performing other community science activities, where nonscientists collect data that can be used by researchers.

Many water conservation organizations hold cleanup days on an annual basis with events all around the country. For streams and rivers, check out American Rivers. For beach and ocean cleanups, take a look at the Surfrider Foundation and the Ocean Conservancy. For general park cleanups, check out local chapters of Keep America Beautiful. Many local governments also organize their own events focused on waterways, either independently or in partnership with nonprofit organizations.

For tree and flower plantings, some cities, counties, and local groups organize these types of events. In addition to the ones in major cities like TreePeople in Los Angeles and Casey Trees in Washington, DC, many Sierra Club chapters also do this work. In fact, the Scouts' plant removal efforts were part of a larger project that they were doing in partnership with the local Sierra Club chapter.

For water quality monitoring, many of these projects are run through the local or state government. Training is often organized by the state's Cooperative Extension Service. Try searching online to see if you have a group in your area or state.

To participate in community science projects, the apps iNaturalist, Project Noah, and SciSpy plus the Habitat Network website allow naturalists of all levels of expertise to take photos of animals and their habitats. The website SciStarter has a list of more than 1,500 community science events, including many in ecology.

FAMILY ACTIVITY:
Picking Up Trash at a Local Park or Green Space

Starting local and simple is a great way to introduce your kids to outdoor volunteerism. You don't even need an official event to get started!

GATHER YOUR MATERIALS

Grab several garbage bags, along with gloves for both the adults and children. Gardening gloves are the best, as they can protect against somewhat sharp objects. If you have any kind of tool (such as tongs) that you can use to pick up questionable objects, that's always useful.

GIVE INSTRUCTIONS TO YOUR KIDS

Designate one bag for garbage and one bag for recyclable items. If you compost, you can designate a third bag, although it may be difficult to empty things from a garbage bag into a composter. Talk your children through what items they can pick up themselves and what items they need adult assistance with. Water bottles, chip bags, aluminum cans, and plastic bottle tops are usually fine for them to pick up by themselves, especially with gloves on. Cigarette butts, broken glass, and any type of used paper product should be left to an adult. Of course, if you come across dangerous items like syringes, gathering those requires professional assistance.

MAKE IT FUN

Do whatever you can to be encouraging and make it exciting. Framing it as a scavenger hunt or running a contest to see who can pick up the most garbage in a set amount of time can help. Often the thrill of the search is enough to motivate kids.

DOCUMENT YOUR IMPACT

Take a photo at the end with what you've collected. If you want to be really fancy, you can take before and after photos of the space. You don't need to humble-brag, but sharing those photos on social media can inspire your neighbors and friends to do the same in their area.

Books

PICTURE BOOKS

The Tree Lady, by H. Joseph Hopkins and Jill McElmurry: A lovely non-fiction book about Kate Sessions, who overcame people's perceptions of who a scientist should be and what a desert ecosystem should look like to plant thousands of trees in San Diego, California.

Me . . . Jane, by Patrick McDonnell: By introducing primatologist Jane Goodall as a little girl who loves her stuffed monkey, then jumping to her as an adult at the end, this book does a great job showing kids how their passions now can change the world in the long run.

I Am Farmer: Growing an Environmental Movement in Cameroon, by Baptiste and Miranda Paul with Elizabeth Zunon: A beautiful, engaging true story about Farmer Tantoh, a leader in Cameroon who helped build more than sixty structures to bring clean water to villages. He also inspired other people in Cameroon to plant hundreds of gardens across the country.

City Green, by DyAnne DiSalvo-Ryan: By turning an empty city lot into a blooming community garden, a little girl named Marcy helps brighten up her neighborhood and heal an elderly neighbor's heart in this heartwarming book.

The Brilliant Deep: Rebuilding the World's Coral Reefs, by Kate Messner and Matthew Forsythe: This book's gorgeous watercolor illustrations bring the true story of Ken Nedimyer to life. It follows how his love of the ocean as a child led him to establish one of the biggest coral restoration efforts in the world.

Resources

Take Your Kids to Clean Up a Local Stream (Even If They Won't Clean Their Rooms): www.outdoorfamiliesonline.com/earth-day-tips/

Keep America Beautiful: www.kab.org

Surfrider Foundation: www.surfrider.org

American Rivers: www.americanrivers.org

Boy Scouts Conservation and Environment page: www.scouting.org/outdoor-programs/conservation-and-environment

Girl Scouts Environment page: www.girlscouts.org/en/about-girl-scouts/girl-scouts-and-the-environment.html

Roots & Shoots: www.rootsandshoots.org

Free Forest School: www.freeforestschool.org

There's No Such Thing as Bad Weather, by Linda McGurk

Last Child in the Woods and *Vitamin N*, by Richard Louv

SciStarter (community science database): www.scistarter.com

Children and Nature Network: www.childrenandnature.org

LISTEN TO THE CHILDREN:
ENGAGING IN ENVIRONMENTAL ACTIVISM

As I walked down a hall in the New York State Capitol building, I felt important. The hallway was decorated with historical photos; I felt like I was making history too.

Ahead of me, the group leader was holding a cake for our state senator. But it wasn't his birthday. Considering the cake was decorated with toxic waste canisters made of frosting, that would be a bit gruesome. Instead, it celebrated the twentieth anniversary of New York State's Superfund program. A precursor to the more well-known U.S. Environmental Protection Agency program, the New York State Superfund program cleans up some of the most polluted sites in the state.

This wasn't a simple celebration. It was a demand. The program was running low on funding—it would run out two years later—and we wanted it to have a larger budget. Because communities of Black and Hispanic residents are the most likely to have Superfund sites near them, this was a matter of social justice. I was proud to be part of the group.

While most people don't think of lobbying your state government as a kids' activity, I was only sixteen years old. I was participating in the Earth Day Lobby Day, a yearly gathering of environmental non-profits at the New York State Capitol. Even though I didn't talk to the senator myself—if I remember correctly, no one did—I walked away feeling like I used my voice for good.

Although I had done plenty of pro-environmental activities before then, I felt like an activist for the first time that day. I had opinions on policy and ways to make them heard. Since then, I've continued to lobby, contact my Congressional members, speak at city council meetings, and march in protests. That event started it all.

While recruiting teenagers for a lobbying event felt relatively unique at the time, young adults are now leading much of the climate and environmental movements. Fridays for Future and Climate Strike were both started and led by middle and high schoolers, including Alexandria Villaseñor in New York City, Autumn Peltier from Canada, Greta Thunberg in Sweden, and Isra Hirsi in Minnesota. These movements, which encourage young people to periodically walk out of school to protest climate change, organized more than four million people at 2,500 events in September 2019. In a study of a set of marches held on and around March 15, 2019, researchers found that 45 percent of the participants were between fourteen and nineteen years old. Before these movements started, the young plaintiffs in *Juliana v. the United States* have been suing the federal government for a lack of action on climate change since 2015.

As great as it is for individuals to lower their carbon footprints, the big changes need to come through policy. Only 100 companies are responsible for 71 percent of global greenhouse gas emissions. In fact, 25 corporations and state-owned organizations are responsible for more than half of all the carbon emissions produced since 1988. If we're going to significantly reduce our contributions to climate change and minimize its impacts, we need systemic change.

This responsibility to make change falls the most on people who have the most privilege, whether that's racial, economic, or social privilege. Privilege is the set of advantages a person has because of a specific characteristic they share with a larger group as well as the problems they avoid as a result of being part of this group. People with the most privilege also have an obligation to encourage their children to be activists. As Jameila "Meme" Styles (a civil rights activist in Austin, Texas) said, "If we don't do the work right now, if we don't grow socially conscious kids right now, then we're going to continue to repeat the same disastrous things." Although her activism focuses largely on anti-racism, this goes for environmental issues as well.

Activism and advocacy can help make systemic changes on the local, regional, national, and global levels. Activists focus on taking nonviolent action as often as possible on a variety of related issues. In contrast, advocates focus on a particular issue and apply a variety of tools to make change on that issue. There's a huge range of activities that fall under both, including calling or writing to elected officials, commenting on rules that the government is considering, in-person lobbying, testifying at local meetings, protesting, attending marches/rallies, and participating in nonviolent civil disobedience. Of course, groups always need people willing to organize and provide support for these actions beyond mere participation. There are also a variety of targets, including corporate headquarters, members of Congress, state representatives, county policymakers, city council members, and boards of education. Each tactic and audience has its advantages and disadvantages, depending on the specific campaign and goals. Each approach also has different levels of accessibility, especially to people who are physically disabled, face mental health challenges like anxiety, need childcare, or don't have reliable transportation.

If this seems overwhelming, there are groups that can help families get started. Moms Clean Air Force is a nationwide organization devoted to improving air quality and minimizing climate change. They work with more than one million parents to fight air pollution and protect children's health. The organization focuses on parents because of both our inherent concern about our children's futures and our potential political willpower.

Since 2013 the group has organized an annual Play-In for Climate Action. The event is a mix of family-friendly speakers, games, music, and more, all with the theme of fighting climate change. Families from all over the country gather to make their own and their children's voices heard. After the event on the National Mall in Washington, DC, families head to Capitol Hill to lobby their members of Congress.

"The idea that we're doing this with our children, for our children, is paramount to our work. I think that's what sets us apart," said Heather McTeer Toney, the Moms Clean Air Force national field director. Before this position, she was the first African American, first female, and youngest mayor of Greenville, Mississippi. In between, she was the regional administrator for the U.S. Environmental Protection Agency's Southeast Region. This is a woman who knows how to make change. She said that it's essential for our kids to see us in action and even participate themselves, as appropriate for their age.

To see how play can be protest, I joined the 2019 Play-In for the Climate early on a hot August day. As I exited the subway station and walked to the National Mall, I was soon surrounded by a sea of diverse families in red shirts led by a marching band. Laughing, I realized that I had walked right into the Play-In before I even got to my destination.

RAISING AWARENESS OF THE STRUCTURES OF POWER AND HOW TO INFLUENCE THEM

Reaching the National Mall, the drum corps spread out and finished up their song. With children of all ages running around, the group started what they called a "Welcome to the Land" ceremony. It looked like it was going to be kid-based street theater at its finest.

But first, they needed participants. In addition to the assigned volunteers, leaders recruited children watching in the audience to take on roles in the play. Some grabbed large cardboard trees while others donned colorful wings to become birds. Still others grabbed cardboard houses that looked like children's drawings, hilariously large compared to the kids holding them. After some logistical scrambling—organizing small children is always a bear—the play began.

With drummers in the background, the children holding houses gathered in a circle to represent a neighborhood. Children and adults pretending to be butterflies, bees, and birds flapped around them. Disrupting this idyllic scene, performers dressed as devil-looking monsters intruded—the specter of pollution. They brought with them clouds, algae blooms, and "sunny day flooding" (flooding when there's no rain). These threats surrounded the houses and started pushing them to the side.

But the elders came to the rescue! Older adults, many past retirement age, were dressed as butterflies. They marched up to a cardboard cutout of the U.S. Capitol and began singing, "Got to wake up / got to rise up / got to make a change—now now now!" With that bit of protest, they chased away the pollution. The negative consequences to the community departed as well. In the wake of them leaving, people carrying the sun and windmills emerged, restoring the community.

It was a simple play with little narration, but the message was clear. While the people who make laws hold the power, we can use that power to help our communities if we work together. It was a perfect illustration of three major skill sets identified by researchers from Vanderbilt University, Rutgers University, and the University of New Mexico. These skills help children and adults maintain mental health and take action even when change seems difficult or impossible. The first skill is critical consciousness, or understanding the foundational causes of social problems. The second is empowerment, which helps people feel like they're in control of their own lives. From a political point of view, empowerment involves understanding social and political systems well enough to feel that you can influence them. Empowerment generally develops as people get involved in their community. On the flip side, disempowerment is associated with chronic stress and depression. The third idea is "critical hopefulness." Instead of optimism based on a rose-colored perspective of the world, critical hopefulness is a clear-eyed view of power structures coupled with a realistic understanding of what you can do to change them. While this attitude is rare among adults, a study of almost 400 high schoolers in a diverse Northeast U.S. city found that about a quarter of them had critical hopefulness.

Activism and advocacy can help children and adults develop both the knowledge and the hope. Toney is living proof of this—she grew up in a household of activists. Her parents moved from Baltimore to Mississippi to participate in the 1960s voting rights movement. "I grew up in a household of social justice activism at all times," she said. In fact, she participated in marches with her parents when she was just ten years old. Overall she credits this involvement with inspiring her own career and path of public service. Toney sees herself reflected in the children participating in the current climate change movement. "I'm living witness of it," she said. "It will stay with them throughout their life and they will teach others how to do that."

Styles went through a similar learning process. She too grew up in an activist household, with her father and other relatives being involved in the Black Panthers and NAACP (formerly National Association for the Advancement of Colored People). Even further back, she's related to Booker T. Washington. While she said it was sometimes frustrating as a child to feel like she was competing for her parents' attention (a good reason to have a work-life balance), she sees its benefits now. "Very early on, you form a definition of what social good is and then later, what social justice is," she said. "It does empower me every day now to care about people." This emerges in her activism, much of which is devoted to running the group Measure Austin, which uses data to eliminate social disparities. She's also on the board of Earth Day Austin. These days, she sees this same passion in her daughter Jalisa.

Becoming aware of these power structures and gaining an understanding of how to tackle them were themes I heard over and over again when I talked to young activists and their parents.

At sixteen Hannah Testa has already had more influence over corporations than most of us will ever have in our lives. When she was only ten, a petition about black rhinos being poached caught her attention. "It broke my heart that these creatures I loved so much were dying because of us," she said, speaking not just of the rhinos but endangered species in general. "I couldn't sit back and watch it happen." She ambitiously promised the group that she would bring them 500 signatures for their petition. But she didn't just meet her goal; she far exceeded it, bringing them 1,800 signatures in the end. "That really inspired me that I can make a difference even at a young age," she said.

Since then, Testa realized that much of her passion is making businesses' practices more environmentally sustainable. Through her website, social media, and consultation, she's worked with Kashi, Starbucks, and other companies to reduce their use of plastic. She's also met with members of Congress, city leaders, and other policymakers. While she didn't even know the difference between the American political parties when she started her work at thirteen years old, she's gained a sophisticated understanding of it since then. Even though she's not old enough to vote yet, she insists elected leaders need to represent her and other young people in her district in suburban Atlanta, Georgia. "I've definitely grown and matured and been able to learn more about the world as a whole," she said. "I've definitely learned that young people have a voice and that we do have power in our voices."

Robbie Bond's work was similarly inspired by hearing that a natural thing he loved was in danger. When he was in fourth grade, he visited his first national park, the Grand Canyon. Shortly after, his family visited another national park and national monument. Then President Donald Trump passed an executive order to reduce the size of twenty-seven national monuments. "The executive order sparked my interest in environmentalism," Bond said. Talking about the parks and monuments he visited, he said, "They were super beautiful and amazing and I couldn't let them be reduced in size or just destroyed." To follow up on that passion, he started Kids Speak for Parks from his home in Honolulu, Hawaii. Although the group started as a Facebook page, his work has grown to include a number of speaking engagements and media collaborations. In fact he's partnered with Google Expeditions and Disney to do a virtual tour of certain national parks. He's even in a new television show and comic book called *Marvel's Hero Project* that features kids who are heroes in their communities.

Levi Draheim took a different path to activism. He's the youngest participant in *Juliana v. United States*, the lawsuit twenty-one young people brought against the federal government starting in 2015 to demand action on climate change. The group supporting the suit, Our Children's Trust, also supports legal actions on the state and international levels. When Draheim was only seven years old, he heard about the suit through his church pastor, who is involved in environmental issues. The pastor told Draheim's mother, Leigh-Ann, about the lawsuit and wondered if Levi would be interested in participating. After Leigh-Ann vetted the group and put a lot of hard thought into it, she asked Levi himself. He immediately said yes. "I want to have a voice. And people don't really look at kids having a voice and for kids to take action," he said. "So I decided I wanted and needed to take action if I wanted to have a future here on this planet."

Maintaining this empowerment is essential for helping kids deal with and make sense of problems covered in the media. Climate change is in the news on a daily basis, from wildfires to hurricanes. Hearing about these issues with no way to respond can lead to frustration and a feeling of helplessness.

Depending on where they live, young people may even be directly affected by climate change and other environmental issues. As the Draheims live on a barrier island in Florida, sea level rise is very salient to them. Leigh-Ann said that the constant presence of climate change's effects was one reason she felt it was okay to get Levi involved. "It's not something you can hide from or pretend it doesn't exist," she said. "So I decided not to shield my child from it and just give him the power to make a difference as opposed to not." Relatedly Lisa Hoyos—the head of Climate Parents, a climate change group hosted by the Sierra Club—said that for the past two years, her son's end-of-year soccer tournament has been canceled because of smoke from wildfires in California, even though the fires were miles away from her home in the San Francisco area.

Hearing about or suffering through problems and feeling like you can't do anything about them are stressful. However, taking action through activism can provide relief. Organizing allows people to identify problems, understand the systems that are causing the issues, and collaborate to solve them. Participating in social movements helps people feel more efficacy, the ability to do things and make change in their lives. It also helps them be more engaged in their communities. For teenagers, being involved in civic issues is associated with higher overall well-being and being less likely to engage in risky behaviors. Jalisa Styles said that her social justice activism has been essential for her mental health. "It just helped me cope with a lot of the things that happen in society and around the world," she said.

This critical hopefulness can even help young people develop their sense of identity. "This gives young people an opportunity to define themselves. Define themselves based upon the issue of their time and how they see it and what their ideas are," said Toney.

This positive identity can be particularly important for youth who society stereotypes as "troubled." Researchers from the University of Colorado Boulder and San Francisco State University found that activism can help build resiliency and empowerment among marginalized youth in particular. When other people dismiss your voice, finding ways to make it heard is very powerful.

Part of maintaining that hopefulness is realizing that action isn't one-and-done. Getting long-term results takes a long time. While Hoyos leads Climate Parents, she's not the only activist in the family. Her son testified at one of the U.S. Environmental Protection Agency hearings to repeal the Clean Power Plan, the policy to reduce emissions from fossil fuel-based power plants and increase renewable energy. According to Hoyos, he knew going in that his testimony alone wasn't going to change policy. But taking that step was still important. "He learned that 'I'm going to do my best in the situation. I don't necessarily have control of the outcome, but I'm going to stand on the right side of it,'" she said. "They learn a lot about political maturity. I think they learn about themselves and their own passion and their own power."

Another big part of empowerment is realizing that you aren't on your own—by working together, everyone can push in the same direction to make a difference. "It gave me the sense that collectivism really does make change," said Meme Styles, referring to her childhood. She said that although it feels like pushing back the ocean at times, a community can form a dam. "I feel like the more people that I'm able to bring together or mobilize around a certain issue or problem then the more likely it is I feel like we can solve it together."

Levi Draheim has seen that as well through his participation in the lawsuit. "If we get enough youth together, people are going to notice," he said. "So we need to take action and make the government and people in charge notice that we are actually here." A study on youth organizing in a Midwestern city by a researcher at the University of Colorado found that as students participated in the program, they shifted away from believing problems were caused by individual decisions toward seeing them as systemic issues that could be fixed if people worked together.

For youth, some of this empowerment via collective effort can come from feeling like they have adult support. All the kids said that support from their parents and other adults was essential. Testa said that receiving support from both her parents and children younger than her has helped her keep going. "It always comes down to hope. I know that sounds very common and something that people say a lot," she said. But despite the cliché, "That's what's really kept me going."

The key seems to be providing support without talking over young people or taking over their events. Discussing the students organizing events like the Climate Strike, Toney said, "We want to help them be the best that they can be in this process. And to be heard. We want to be the ones as adults to give them the microphone."

Similarly, Leigh-Ann Draheim said that Levi gets frustrated when people tell him that he's doing great but won't take action themselves. "Kids don't want people to stand in front of them, block their way, and prevent them from moving forward from this. But they also don't want them to stand behind them and just say 'Yay, good for you.' They want them to stand with them and take action," she said. In several different studies looking at groups encouraging students to organize, the most successful ones had young people leading the groups, with adults providing logistical and emotional support.

If properly supported, activism can transform a young person's relationship with their community. One study by Brown University researchers of 124 teenagers in seven different groups across the country found that students involved in youth organizing were more likely than a random sample of teens to participate in other civic activities, such as contacting their representatives, participating in marches, and solving other community problems. More than half said that they wanted to learn more about politics and stay involved in activism in the future. They also said that they understood issues in their community better after participating. In addition, 90 percent said they would be more motivated to complete high school and 80 percent said their grades improved afterward. In several case studies of different youth organizing groups, students reported that their organizing helped them feel like they had something they could contribute to their community and had the ability to make change.

Perhaps most importantly, these efforts pay off. It's not a false sense of empowerment. Fridays for Future and Climate Strike reignited the climate change movement. The local youth groups studied by researchers established anti-violence initiatives in schools, influenced school budgets, set up paid internships for high school students, and even led to school administrations reversing certain policies.

PARTNERING ACROSS DIVERSE GROUPS

After the skit, the focus of the Play-In for Climate Action switched to the main stage. After Toney revved up everyone with a "What do we want? / Climate action / When do we want it? / Now!" chant, she brought on Dominique Browning, cofounder of Moms Clean Air Force. Browning started off by saying, "I'm so glad we're working across several generations of people, from babies to mothers to grandmothers to great-grandmothers. Welcome, have fun, use your voices! Use your voices to demand politicians do the right thing!"

Next up was Vanessa Hauc, a host on Telemundo, the Spanish-language television network. "How are we doing today? *¡Bienvenidos!*" she said. "This is a vibrant crowd, coming from all over this country to make change." She discussed how she has seen devastation from climate change all over the world, including Puerto Rico.

But my favorite speaker was Great-Grandmother Mary Lyons, an Ojibwe wisdom keeper, water keeper, and United Nations observer on women's/Indigenous issues. Decked in a beautiful traditional beaded headpiece and black thick-rimmed glasses, she was physically small but had a mighty presence. She requested, "If you can each take a moment within your own language to speak up loudly, tell me good morning in your language." The crowd reverberated with several different languages. She spoke of working together across our cultural, age, racial, and other differences while also embracing them. "I sing the songs of my mother and my grandmother to my daughter, my granddaughter, and my great-granddaughter," she explained. Then she got a good chuckle out of the audience when she said, "I could go on forever. I have that right because I'm a great-grandmother." Referring to future generations, she rallied us with the words, "We can open the door to them and let the truth be told." (All the speakers had sign language interpretation, making the presentation more accessible to deaf members of the audience.)

The diversity of speakers—in addition to Moms Clean Air Force's partnership with organizations Ecomadres and Elders Climate Action—reflected much of the diversity needed in the environmental and climate movements. Early environmentalists who focused on wildlife and land conservation promoted racist and classist policies. Founders like John Muir held views of both Indigenous and Black Americans that were deeply rooted in prejudice. Much of the movement—including the founding of the first National Parks—pushed Native Americans off of land that they had already been forced onto because of colonialization and attempted genocide. While the environmental movement expanded in the 1970s and 1980s due to the work of Black people and Native Americans, it still has a long way to go. That effort continues today.

To perpetuate oppression as little as possible and build momentum to make change, environmental movements need diverse leadership and participation. Of the youth organizations researchers studied, several groups saw their racial, religious, and cultural diversity as key to their success.

Fortunately activism often exposes participants to diverse communities that they might not be a part of otherwise. Jalisa Styles said that even though she goes to a HBCU (historically Black college or university), she was amazed by the diversity of backgrounds and places her fellow students come from, including the Virgin Islands, Cayman Islands, and Nigeria. "That helped me connect a lot with what I'm trying to do and what it is that I'm trying to have a voice for," she said.

Her mom said that she sees her daughter demonstrating that empathy regularly. "We're so here-and-there, everywhere quickly, that we don't stop and pause and feel and understand what other people are going through," said Meme Styles. "But she is definitely one that does."

Other activists reported that they've been able to meet people from all over the world doing this work with them. "One of my favorite things is just meeting so many different people of all ages and all different walks of life wherever I go," said Testa. "That really gives me hope and really fuels my fire to keep going." Robbie Bond's mother, Michelle, said that people have reached out via social media from New York City, Canada, China, and Italy, saying that he has inspired them to start their own projects. Levi Draheim said that finding out how many other people care about these issues has been very encouraging, especially because there's not a lot of interest in climate action in his home state of Florida.

Working together on challenging issues helps bring people together into close relationships. Draheim has traveled all over the country with the other plaintiffs on the lawsuit, including to marches. "The other plaintiffs are the closest thing I will ever have to an older sibling," he said. "They always will have my back." In a study led by a researcher from the University of Wisconsin–Madison of an intergenerational youth organizing group, members said that they felt like the participants were a "second family."

Building this sense of community can be key for maintaining emotional and mental health for young and adult activists. Tying one's
identity to activism may cause stress during tough times, but creating social connections reduces some of it. Several studies show that a
"sense of community" is associated with better physical and mental
health. "Being able to find a community of other people has been so
helpful in so many ways," said Testa. "We're all out to help each other."

GROWING SKILLS FOR THE FUTURE

While Mary Lyons was the oldest speaker, Alexandria Villaseñor was
the youngest at just fourteen years old. At the time of the Play-In, she
had been striking in front of the United Nations headquarters in New
York City for thirty-one weeks. She's also the founder of the organization Earth Uprising, which played a major role in organizing the
worldwide Climate Strike and has youth ambassadors from sixteen
countries. She was just as engaging—if not more so—of a speaker as the
adults. "Speak your minds and not give up!" she implored us. "We need
to be out there, on the streets, lobbying, making sure our voices are in
the conversation."

In the crowd there were several students with signs and shirts
saying Fridays for Future. As it was a Friday morning, they must have
opted out of school to come.

Seeing these teenage activists illustrated how activism teaches
young people real-world practical skills that they otherwise might not
have the chance to develop.

Public Speaking and Persuasion

While public speaking scares about a quarter of adults, it's a skill that
activists learn early and often. Whether speaking at a rally or in front
of a school board, many activists quickly learn how to talk in front of a
group. Hoyos said that her son (who was in sixth grade at the time) was
the only person testifying at the EPA hearing without notes—and did

so beautifully. She said, "All of these people came up to him afterwards and were like, 'Wow, that was very powerful.'"

Bond similarly attended and testified at a number of Bureau of Land Management meetings on national parks. "When I first started Kids Speak for Parks, I was kind of self-conscious," he said. "Now I'm pretty confident, so I can totally rock a speaking event." I wish I had his sense of self-assuredness!

Beyond the public aspect of speaking, explaining complex topics in a persuasive way to a variety of audiences prepares young activists for the future. Speaking of what Levi Draheim had learned, his mother said, "One of [his strengths] is just being able to articulate to a wide variety of ages and opinions." He's presented to everyone from pre-school classes to adult climate deniers. He's given interviews to *60 Minutes*, *National Geographic*, and CNN. To prepare for these efforts, he's become an expert on types of hurricanes, the inner workings of the U.S. government, and climate change policy.

Being able to stand up and ask powerful people for what you want is extremely valuable as well. "It made me really bold," said Meme Styles, talking about growing up in an activist household. "I was extremely fearless as a kid to have conversations with people that typically others would not want to approach." Her mom told her, "All they can say is no," and she found that very empowering.

Fostering that confidence is particularly important for youth activists, whom policymakers often underestimate. Testa said that when she met with one of her state senators, he initially didn't take her seriously. "A lot of people just think, this is just maybe like a Girl Scout getting volunteer hours," she said. "You want to be able to walk out of that meeting and have them rethink the stereotypes they have in their mind and be like, 'I really underestimated them.'" She added, "Just speak your truth and speak your passion, and they'll realize that you're here for business and you know what you're talking about." Bond said that getting people to listen as a result of his age has been his biggest challenge as well. He hopes that through Kids Speak for Parks that he can help other kids realize that they can break through and make a difference.

Developing a thick skin to deal with rejection and criticism of your work is another part of personal growth. "No matter what you do, there will be backlash," said Testa. "Even if you think you're doing the right thing, there's definitely going to be people out there who might not agree with that. And that's okay." She encourages youth activists to focus on the supporters and their encouragement rather than dwelling on negative feedback.

All of these aspects of personal growth are reflected in the social science literature on activism. A deep-dive case study written by researchers from Stanford and Villanova Universities described how organizing groups encourage and teach students to use social science techniques such as interviews and surveys to understand local problems and develop solutions. The students then present their ideas to school leadership, city officials, and at community meetings. Similar studies in San Bernardino and Riverside, California, reported that participants said they learned public speaking skills, gained confidence, and had the authority to speak on social issues they had studied. Other studies described students gaining skills in framing messages, building trust with your audiences, and time management.

Organizing and Networking

While not every young activist will run their own group, most youth organizing efforts provide participants with the opportunity to get experience with running meetings, recruiting fellow volunteers, delegating tasks, and collecting signatures for petitions. In a study of student groups in Oakland and Redwood City, California, many of the participants said they gained organizing skills, learning from both their mentors' guidance and real-world experience in the group. In the nationwide survey, about 40 percent of students actually said that they would pursue a career in organizing.

Meme Styles said her first taste of activism was in third grade, when she decided that it was unfair that her cafeteria didn't offer chocolate milk. She started a petition and collected signatures, asking fellow students, "Why does all milk have to be white?" Because of her efforts at mobilizing students, the school started supplying chocolate milk. "That showed me that gosh, all you have to do is influence people around you to have them recognize that there is something good," she said. Later, in eighth grade, she successfully organized her fellow students toward a more serious goal—to rename her school after Martin Luther King Jr.

Testa also started her journey by collecting signatures for a petition. She said that she quickly became involved with the organization, learning the ins and outs of campaigns and events. As she established relationships, she expanded her social capital. "Even networking is a huge thing that I learned at a young age," she said. "It's really about who you know. They will definitely help you out in the long run." Those contacts have helped her get funding for projects and learn from others' experiences.

As an adult organizer, Hoyos said these skills are essential. Being able to use both digital and face-to-face events to build alliances and create campaigns is useful for both the nonprofit and business worlds. Even running conference calls or virtual meeting platforms is critical in many jobs. "That kind of cultivation of the skills, ability, and confidence to do that happens when you're real-life physically working with other people," said Hoyos.

In studies of youth organizing, researchers have reported that participants gained many real-world skills. One particularly important skill is strategic thinking. Planning out practical steps toward a long-term goal is important when tackling complex, systemic problems like educational reform or environmental issues. Understanding and balancing the needs of diverse groups with conflicting needs are essential to creating solutions. Being able to develop contingency plans as well as adapt those plans to unexpected situations helps tremendously in both activism and life.

★ ★ ★

Carrying my older son on my shoulders, I wasn't feeling quite as empowered as I was eighteen years earlier. It was 2017 and we were marching in the People's Climate March up Constitution Avenue in Washington, DC.

The morning of the march, Dylan and I made signs together with markers and crayons. My sign read "Clean Energy and a Healthy Climate for ALL Our Neighbors" with a black-and-white picture of the Earth from space on it. His read "I Love Trains" with a scribbled page from a Thomas the Tank Engine coloring book.

At the march, my husband carried Ethan in a baby backpack and Dylan held my hand. When he was tired, I hoisted him up onto my shoulders to see better. Starting with a view of the Capitol, we marched down Pennsylvania Avenue yelling in support of climate justice and renewable energy. Along the way, I tried to point out and explain the kid-appropriate signs to Dylan, especially the ones referencing Dr. Seuss's *The Lorax*. Everything went well, save a pang of mom guilt when some well-meaning older ladies pointed out that Ethan should have been wearing a hat in the blazing sun. We had one, but he kept throwing it on the ground.

Before we reached the White House, the heat forced us to quit. We retreated to sandwiches and ice cream at a local restaurant, surrounded by other families who had also participated.

Despite it all, I was glad to be there. Dylan didn't fully know what was going on—I didn't explain climate change to a three-year-old—but he understood that we were telling the president that we wanted clean air and less pollution. He knew that he had a voice, a place in our democracy, and could make a difference. While he doesn't have a clear memory of the march itself, we still talk about participating and why my husband and I brought both of them. In the future, I hope that they'll march with me again. I want them to know that no matter what, it is always worth standing up for what is right.

What to Know

Build on Your Kids' Interests

As with everything, you don't want to push your kid into something that they're not invested in. That's particularly important for activism, where enthusiasm is key. "Tap into the activist in your child," said Meme Styles. "Every child is going to have some form of passion."

For some kids, the passion is obvious from a young age. Even as a very little girl, Testa had a love for animals and plants. She loved growing her home organic garden so much that she grew tomato plants from seed for each of her kindergarten classmates. She even gave a presentation on Earth Day to her class!

Sometimes, parents can make those connections clearer for children. Levi Draheim said that he was always interested in the environment and nature, especially if it involved mud. For him, tackling climate change seemed natural. "When my mom told me that climate change was a problem, I realized how scary it was and that my future was at stake," he said. Similarly, Hoyos said in fourth grade her son started to really love lemurs. She used that interest to raise his awareness about palm oil, which is often grown in areas that had previously been rainforest and burned to make space for palm oil trees. With that information, he decided to avoid eating anything with palm oil in it for a while, including candy.

Help Them See It as a Natural Outgrowth of Current Skills

Teenagers tend to see their activities as a key part of their identity. They may think, "I'd like to try that, but I'm not like the people in that group" or "I'm not the type of person who goes to a protest." But anyone can be an activist.

A number of the same leadership skills that young people use in sports or student council apply to activism too. Hoyos said that when Climate Parents worked with students to testify in front of a school board about adopting clean energy, two of the four kids were in their baseball uniforms. They came to the meeting straight from practice. "You can build this into your life," said Hoyos. "You don't have to be 24/7 focused on this. You can be a normal kid and still do this."

Introducing children to the many different types of activism can help them match their skills to the right activity. While activism can be marches and rallies, it can also include lobbying policymakers one-on-one, writing letters, calling members of Congress, organizing behind-the-scenes for events, recruiting volunteers, and even creating art.

Don't Put It All on Them

Although adults sometimes say things like "The kids are our hope!" or "They can save us all," that's far too much pressure. It often makes children feel like they are responsible for problems that adults have caused. Just as Leigh-Ann Draheim said that Levi gets frustrated when adults do that, many other youth activists have pushed back against that sentiment as well. Addressing the United Nations in New York City, climate change activist Greta Thunberg said it well: "This is all wrong. I shouldn't be up here. I should be back in school on the other side of the ocean. Yet you all come to us young people for hope. How dare you!"

Next Steps

Get Involved Locally

Organizations that focus on local policymakers are more likely to affect decisions, making it more likely to see direct results of your activism. It's also much easier to understand and influence the power dynamics of the local school board or city council than it is the U.S. Congress. While very important, national and international activism can also be some of the most frustrating types.

But just because a group focuses on local people doesn't mean that they don't address national or global issues. Some of the most exciting progress on climate change, waste reduction, and air pollution is on the city and county levels. Hoyos said that right now Climate Parents is working on a campaign to move school districts to 100 percent clean energy. That type of change can have a huge cumulative impact.

Join Organizations Led by (or Welcoming of) Youth

Activism isn't an individual pursuit. To prevent burnout and be able to get stuff done, it needs to be done in community.

While traditional environmental organizations are led by adults, an increasing number of local and national groups are led by youth: Fridays for Future, Earth Guardians, Earth Uprising, Sunrise Movement,

U.S. Climate Strike, and more. Connecting with other kids who care about the same issues can be encouraging and build community in a way that is sometimes difficult with adults alone. Even if you don't have any local groups in your area, many of these activists meet over video conferencing services.

Testa said that finding kids who were interested in the same things she was would have been very helpful when she was younger. "When I first got started, I felt super lonely. Because nobody in my area was doing the same things I was doing. I was looked at a little differently," she said. "But when I grew my platform, I met so many kids doing the same thing and I didn't feel alone anymore. They really inspired me to continue the work that I do today."

Encourage Them to Partner with Experienced Activists

Working with experienced groups or individuals can help youth with less knowledge maneuver logistical challenges. For example, experienced activists can help make connections in City Hall, provide information on how to apply for a permit, or know the best ways to put together talking points. One of the youth organizing groups that researchers from the University of Illinois studied provided training to students that drew on lessons learned from past social justice movements. The group also helped students role-play skills like lobbying. While all groups provide some level of training, the iMatter youth group particularly focuses on equipping young people with the tools to be effective activists.

Help Your Kid Engage in Self-Care

Unlike almost every other activity in this book, activism can have its downsides. Because of the level of knowledge you gain as an activist, you're exposed to far more negative news and have a deeper knowledge of problems than most people. "You see a lot more of the terrible things that happen around the world," said Testa. "You're just more open to these terrible things than I guess a normal person can be. It can get really depressing," Dealing with public backlash can also be discouraging. In addition, preteens and teenagers tend to be all-or-nothing with their passions, which means they may take failures or struggles very personally.

A key part of maintaining critical hopefulness is taking time away from activism to engage in other activities. These other activities can be anything that's relaxing, such as hanging out with friends, spending time in nature, and doing other extracurricular activities. As there's always more to do in activism, help children learn to say no when necessary. Talking through feelings with parents, other activists, or other adults who care about them can also help. "Self-care is extremely important in activism," said Meme Styles. "As you're growing these little radicals, make sure these little radicals know how to prioritize their health and their own sustainability in their work."

Helping young people set realistic goals can relieve some of this stress as well. It's easy to get overly ambitious in the beginning and burn out when you can't reach those aspirations.

Be Prepared for Rallies and Marches

If you're going to bring your younger kids to a rally or march, talk about the event ahead of time. Explain that there may be adults who are angry and have signs that reflect those feelings. (I've seen many signs with very "colorful" language at marches.) As marches can be more chaotic than the average public event, it's especially important to discuss with your children what to do if you get physically separated. Write your address and phone number down and pin it to the inside of your child's jacket or shirt just in case.

If you're crafty, you can make and bring your own signs. Remember that someone is going to have to carry the sign the entire time. That can get awkward if you're also juggling the normal amount of parent paraphernalia.

At the march itself, watch your kids' behavior. Some topics like climate change can be very emotionally charged. Other times, there's simply too many speakers for children to be able to pay attention respectfully. (I start to get antsy at long events myself.) If it's getting too hot/cold, long, emotionally intense, or boring, make a strategic exit. Of course bringing snacks and drinks is always helpful. Even adults get cranky when they're hungry or thirsty.

If your teenager is going by themselves, ask them what they plan to do if there is some kind of civil unrest, including people getting arrested. This occurs extremely rarely (unless it's planned, which organizers will tell you ahead of time), but it's good to have a plan just in case.

FAMILY ACTIVITY: Research and Make Your Voice Heard on an Issue

HELP YOUR KID PICK AN ISSUE THEY CARE ABOUT

Possible issues may include reducing greenhouse gases that contribute to climate change, protecting endangered species, preserving the rainforest, reducing pollution going into local waterways, or improving local biking/walking infrastructure. It's often best to tackle problems that can have an impact on you personally, as you have the experience to speak to the problem and the passion to keep going even when it's difficult.

BRAINSTORM THE TYPE OF LOCAL POLICIES THAT COULD MAKE A DIFFERENCE ON THESE ISSUES

While many of these issues are global, local policies can make a big difference. Some local policies that affect climate change include the city government or school district buying renewable energy, giving homeowners incentives to install solar panels, or switching lighting in government buildings to more efficient bulbs. Policies that affect endangered species or rainforests include committing to using 100 percent recycled paper, only purchasing rainforest-friendly coffee or tea, or not purchasing products that use palm oil. For water quality or conservation, cities can offer refunds for rain barrels, rain gardens, and other water-saving approaches.

RESEARCH YOUR LOCAL GOVERNMENT'S CURRENT EFFORTS ON THESE TOPICS

Many cities and counties have sections on environmental sustainability on their websites, often with lengthy plans describing their strategies. Others have sustainability/environmental managers or volunteer committees who can provide more information. If you're having trouble finding information on your topic, feel free to reach out to this person or group. Even if they don't know the answer, they most likely know someone who does. If there isn't anyone like that, then contact the city or county clerk and see if they can find an answer. (It may also show how much work there is to do.)

IF POSSIBLE, RESEARCH WHAT OTHER GOVERNMENTS ARE DOING ON THIS ISSUE

Using case studies or examples from comparable cities can be really powerful. You may need to revise your policy after looking into what your own or other governments are doing. If so, that's great—you're learning how real policymaking works!

FIND THE RIGHT PERSON IN YOUR LOCAL GOVERNMENT TO CONTACT ON THE ISSUE

Even if you have an environmental manager, it may not be that person, depending on the topic. Many cities have transportation managers who deal with traffic, pedestrian, and bicycle issues. If it's a purchasing issue (like using energy-efficient lighting), it may be the procurement or building manager. If it requires a significant budget or change in policy, the best bet may be to reach out to the mayor, city council, or county council.

WORK WITH YOUR CHILD TO WRITE AN EMAIL OR OTHERWISE COMMUNICATE TO THE MOST RELEVANT PERSON

In the email, make it clear that the child is sending it (it often packs more of a punch), why they are passionate about the topic, what the city is currently doing, and what they think the city can do. If you have examples from other places, be sure to mention them and provide links if possible.

If your child is really enthusiastic or interested in public speaking, you may want to look into if there are any opportunities to speak in front of the city/county council or school board. Meetings are generally public and often have a citizen or community forum where citizens can state their opinion on any topic for a few minutes. Check to see if you need to sign up in advance of the meeting.

Books

PICTURE BOOKS

Seeds of Change, by Jen Cullerton Johnson and Sonia Lynn Sadler, and *Wangari Maathai: The Woman Who Planted Millions of Trees*, by Franck Prévot and Aurélia Fronty: Both of these beautifully illustrated books are about Wangari Maathai, a Kenyan activist who not only started a reforestation movement in her country but also fought the government in doing so. She received the Nobel Peace Prize for her efforts.

Sofia Valdez, Future Prez, by Andrea Beaty and David Roberts: In this clever and lively book, Sofia is a big-picture community leader. When her grandfather gets hurt walking Sofia to school, she decides that the local pile of trash should be turned into a park. But when she receives pushback from City Hall—because she's "just a kid"—she puts her problem-solving skills to work.

Pedal Power: How One Community Became the Bicycle Capital of the World, by Allan Drummond: Amsterdam was well on its way to being dominated by cars in the 1970s when one mom and her friends stood up to demand rights for bicyclists. Through a combination of savvy use of the media, protests, and civil disobedience, they were able to make the streets safe for cyclists of all ages.

We Are Water Protectors, by Carole Lindstrom and Michaela Goade: This gorgeously illustrated book follows a young girl who is a water protector, an Indigenous person who fights to keep water clean and healthy.

Spring After Spring: How Rachel Carson Inspired the Environmental Movement, by Stephanie Roth Sisson: Building off of a beautiful description of young Rachel Carson's love of nature, this book delves into her adult work to raise awareness of and fight against the widespread abuse of pesticides that were harming ecological and human health.

YOUNG ADULT BOOKS

We Rise: The Earth Guardians Guide to Building a Movement That Restores the Planet, by Xiuhtezcatl Martinez: This book provides both a comprehensive guide to the biggest issues in environmental justice today and a unique perspective. Martinez is a Mexica (Aztec) teenager who testified in front of the United Nations assembly when he was only fifteen years old.

You Are Mighty: A Guide to Changing the World, by Caroline Paul and Lauren Tamaki: This fun and informative book covers every possible form of activism one can think of, from guerilla theater to walk-outs. It has a lot of great examples of activism by young people and even covers important concepts like privilege and intersectionality.

Resources

Climate Parents: www.sierraclub.org/climate-parents

Kids Speak for Parks: www.facebook.com/kidsspeakforparks/

Moms Clean Air Force: www.momscleanairforce.org

iMatter Youth: www.imatteryouth.org

Youth Climate Strike: www.strikewithus.org

Sunrise Movement: www.sunrisemovement.org

Earth Uprising: www.earthuprising.org

Earth Guardians: www.earthguardians.org

Hannah 4 Change, Hannah Testa's website: www.hannah4change.org

How to Bring Your Children to the Families Belong Together Rally, According to Experts and Moms Who Advocate (good advice for any political rally): www.romper.com/p/how-to-prepare-your-children-for-the-families-belong-together-rally-according-to-experts-moms-who-advocate-9552806

ENVISIONING
A SUSTAINABLE
FUTURE

"**M**ost nine-year-olds in 1993 were worried about which Lisa Frank folder they were going to use in math class. But me? I was going to save the manatees," I recounted to Dylan. I was practicing for a live storytelling show, where I'd be telling a room full of strangers the tale of how I became an environmentalist in third grade.

But right then I was telling it to the small person in front of me. Unlike his bouncing around at bedtime or lack of eye contact when you ask him for his breakfast choice, he was looking straight at me. His attention was focused and true. He longed to know what I was like as a kid and how that led to who I am now.

At that moment he was the only audience who mattered.

I wanted to share my story with him because it was such a turning point in my thinking about the world. I fell in love with manatees and realized they were endangered on the same day. Love and grief comingled in my preteen brain. These mixed feelings led to a passion for the environment that's carried me through the current day. In addition I thought it might be a process my son would go through one day as well. While Dylan knows that some animals are endangered, I don't think the real meaning of that word has sunk in yet. As he too loves nature, he'll most likely face that same emotional struggle as he gains an understanding of the bigger picture.

KIDS ARE ALREADY AWARE

Although my environmental concern was a little unusual for a child at the time—the television show *Captain Planet* didn't launch until the next year—it's far more common among children today. In fact, environmental educators recognize this dissonance as a risk. While they're teaching students to love nature, they're also explaining how it's under threat.

Even if you haven't started talking to your children about climate change or other tough environmental issues, they'll most likely hear about them from other sources by the time they're a preteen or teenager. In a 2019 poll supported by the *Washington Post* of more than 600 students from thirteen to seventeen years old, 86 percent of teenagers said human activity causes climate change and 61 percent said it's very or extremely important.

Much of this information comes from the news, where climate change and endangered species are being covered more and more frequently. The same poll found that 53 percent of teenagers pay "some" attention to the news, while 14 percent pay "a lot" of attention.

Many preteens and teenagers also learn about these problems in school, with environmental issues included in many elementary and middle school curriculums. When I was in fourth grade, everyone in my class wrote a report on an endangered species, forcing us to face that reality. (Of course I chose manatees.) Currently 54 percent of students say that they've learned a lot or a moderate amount about the causes of climate change at school.

As adults talk about it more and more, children will pick up on the subject and ask questions at younger and younger ages. Rebecca Stallings, an environmental activist and blogger, said that her son started picking up on these issues when he was just five years old. One Saturday morning, they were watching television when an advertisement for an environmental group came on. The commercial showed polar bears falling in the water, blaming it on melting ice floes due to climate change. Her son asked her, "Is that true that the ice is melting and there might not be any more polar bears?" She used his question as an opportunity to talk about minimizing people's effects on ecological systems. A few years later, his worry intensified after watching a documentary about Nairobi, Kenya. It showed residents dealing with leopards that were driven into cities from habitat destruction. While Stallings herself found it rather fascinating, her son saw it as a tragedy. He said to her, "The poor leopards and they have nowhere to live and they live in the alley with the trash cans and this is terrible!"

Unfortunately the news and even schools aren't prepared to help children deal with the emotions that come with these subjects. News tends toward fear-based narratives that paint the world in apocalyptic terms. While they can draw attention to the urgency of climate change and other environmental issues, this tone can also cause a lot of anxiety and fear in both adults and children alike. Teachers don't always have the time or ability to talk through how students feel about these subjects. Much of the time, the curriculum only covers the science or, at best, some ways to minimize human contributions.

Even if schools talk about solutions, students can still feel overwhelmed. Thinking about big and complex environmental issues like climate change and endangered species can cause significant stress. In the same *Washington Post* poll, 52 percent of teenagers said they felt angry about climate change, 57 percent said they felt afraid, and 43 percent said they felt helpless. Environmental educators even have a word for the feelings of loss from witnessing negative environmental change: solastalgia. (It's a combination of the Latin words for comfort and pain.)

If children feel that these problems will put them or their families in danger (such as if they live near the coast), that stress is only multiplied. A majority—64 percent—of teenagers in the poll said that they thought climate change would hurt them a moderate amount or great deal in the future.

When people care about issues and then perceive others around them as apathetic, it only heightens the stress. While neither anger nor fear are bad in and of themselves, they can lead to chronic emotional health issues if children don't process them correctly.

If not managed, that feeling of being overwhelmed can translate into disempowerment and cynicism. As an educator at the American Museum of Natural History in New York City, Emily Edmonds-Langham deals with the challenges of teaching these concepts to children who attend after-school programs and summer camp at the museum. The museum staff members start talking about larger environmental issues like pollution and loss of habitat with the third-grade groups and continue it with the fourth-grade ones. At that time, a lot of kids struggle to know what they can do to help. "Many of them get bogged down by the fact that people are the bad guys," she said. "And we're screwing all of this up. And how can we possibly fix this?"

Unfortunately, this problem isn't limited to kids either—they see their parents feeling this futility too. Environmental blogger and art teacher Barbara Greene Alfeo said that she frequently sees that hopelessness in society at large. "How do you move people out of this sort of apathy?" she said. "So much of this apathy is self-defense against total despair. What does hope look like here? How do you keep it functioning?"

Fortunately there are approaches that educators and parents alike can take to address difficult environmental issues in ways that motivate and inspire children. The poll also found that 54 percent of teenagers said that climate change makes them feel motivated and 64 percent believe there are things they can personally do to make a difference.

To avoid despair and disempowerment, we need to teach our children emotional resilience. Helping our families care for the environment, our communities, and the world can help us link self-esteem, empathy, bravery, responsibility, and compassion. It's essential to be able to realistically talk about these issues while also maintaining a sense of hope and imagination. As we help our children become adults in the age of ecological change, finding this balance will become an increasingly important part of growing up.

EXPLORING HOW TO COPE

Developing resilience depends heavily on having healthy coping mechanisms. A study by researchers at Uppsala University in Sweden of about 300 high school seniors found that there were three main ways they emotionally coped with climate change: emotion-focused, problem-focused, and meaning-focused. Teenagers who used emotion-focused coping tried to avoid negative emotions by downplaying or refusing to think about climate change. This type of attitude leads to climate denialism, cynicism, or just plain apathy. It comes about in part from a lack of emotional resilience to deal with these problems. But helping young people reframe the problem can shift them away from this type of thinking. With problem-focused coping, teenagers reduced their stress by trying to fix the problem. However, with issues like climate change where you can't fix the problem or you have a limited influence, this can lead to even more stress. With meaning-focused coping, teenagers acknowledged the depth and scope of the problem but found personal meaning in dealing with it. They explored ways to find joy and hope in the situation without denying the negative aspects. Examples of this type of coping include appreciating the work that has been done to tackle the problem so far and having trust in others who are collaborating to solve the problem.

This approach is very similar to the definition of resilience that Leesa Fawcett from York University and Janis Dickinson from Cornell University provide in the book *Trading Zones in Environmental Education*: "learning from, tolerating, and transforming negative experiences into a fuller, positive self-image and to be able to engage with internal capacities of resourcefulness and renewal with social well-being in mind."

The Uppsala University researchers found that teenagers in this study and twelve-year-olds in a previous study used all three methods of coping. Both the preteens and teens who used problem-focused and meaning-focused coping were more likely to engage in environmental behaviors and feel effective in doing so than those who used emotion-focused coping. Unfortunately, using only problem-focused coping was related to having more negative moods, including more anxious and depressive feelings. While the researchers found that much of that difference in mood was due to personality—teens who were more likely to be worried about climate change were more likely to be worried about things in general—it still shows issues with using that strategy alone. In contrast, using meaning-focused coping—sometimes in combination with problem-focused coping—had a relationship with having more positive moods and higher life satisfaction.

Using meaning-focused coping can help as adults as well. Alfeo said that thinking about her kids helped turn frustration into inspiration. She said she imagined talking to her child in a way similar to what Mufasa does to Simba in the movie *The Lion King*. Indicating what Simba will inherit, Mufasa says, "All the light touches will be yours." But instead of the beautiful savannah the lion shows his son, Alfeo imagined it as a wasteland. "All of the things we're giving to our kids is a hot pile of garbage. I was like, 'Okay, I have to do something about this,'" she recalled. While she deals with her feelings by tackling problems, seeing the issue through her love for her children helps her make meaning from that problem solving.

BUILDING RESILIENCE, STRENGTH, AND HOPE

We can help our children develop resilience through a series of four strategies. In developing these strategies, I drew inspiration from four types of participation in environmental education described in *Trading Zones in Environmental Education*: direct interaction with nature, social learning, action, and deliberative dialogue. Each strategy maps to various stages of children's lives, from infancy to adolescence. They each provide a different way to psychologically and emotionally handle these issues both individually and as a family. Fortunately they're not exclusive to each other; each has its own strengths and is worth building on and returning to as children get older.

With all of them, be sure to follow your children's lead. Kids with different temperaments and levels of emotional maturity will be able to handle different steps at different times. In terms of discussing environmental issues with kids, Edmonds-Langham said that the most important thing is "knowing your child and knowing how much nuance they can handle and, honestly, how much bad news they can handle." She said, "Only you can know when it's right for your kid."

In fact environmental and science journalist Michelle Nijhuis said that she didn't discuss climate change in detail with her daughter for a long time because her daughter explicitly told her not to. In fact, when her daughter would overhear someone talking about it, she'd say, "That freaks me out." But after her daughter, then ten years old, watched a video at school about climate change, she started asking questions. Nijhuis said, "The important thing that I learned was to let her lead the way. Because our kids actually know themselves a lot better than we think they do."

Spend Time in Nature Together

The simplest thing you can do to build both resilience and hope from the beginning is to spend time in nature together with your family. Even babies and toddlers can play outside, touch natural objects, listen to birds chirping, and feel the breeze on their faces. Building these relationships with the natural world helps children establish a love and respect for it. Environmentalist Paul Shepard proposed that healthy people have three forms of attachment: to their caregivers, nature, and the larger cosmos. He argued that people in modern civilization are continually stuck on the first, never moving on to develop a fundamental relationship with nature, much less the cosmos as a whole.

While most psychologists and environmental educators are more positive than Shepard, many agree that developing that relationship can feed a deep human need.

An advocate of nature play, Linda McGurk believes strongly in the power of just being outside. "For little kids, the emotional connection is really the most important part to focus on," she said, "talking about the cycle of life and just all of the things that we see and observe in nature." Spending time in nature helps develop a sense of interconnectedness with humans and nonhumans alike. Even discussing something as simple as the Leave No Trace philosophy (which involves taking nothing but photos and leaving nothing but footprints) sparks thoughts on the sorts of rights and responsibilities we have toward other organisms.

Similarly Anna Sharratt, the founder of the Free Forest School, finds that spending time outdoors lays the foundation for future action. "For people who care about climate change and the environment and have young kids, there's nothing more powerful than helping to create community around nature play," she said. "Research shows that putting children in situations that stimulate and nurture their natural love of the environment is really the groundwork of creating environmental activists."

Spending time in nature also provides opportunities for parents to help their children build some of the most basic mental frameworks around ecology. Examining plants and animals is a pathway into talking about food webs, predator-prey relationships, ecological niches, and other concepts that are necessary to understand human impacts on the environment. Heather McTeer Toney of Moms Clean Air Force pointed out that drawing attention to even the most whimsical of similarities between humans and animals can start building those connections in young children's brains. For example, we can point out that both humans and fish blow bubbles. She added, "There are ways to do this with really, really small children that moms are very creative at coming up with."

Being outside also sparks children's natural scientific curiosity. Toney pointed out that by taking kids outside, "We're beginning at a very, very early age to teach our children to ask questions. . . . That is what will help them to develop that comprehensive knowledge and question building that we want them to have when it comes to talking about how the science impacts climate." Even though I have a graduate degree in environmental issues, my children ask way more questions when we're outside than I'm personally capable of answering. I'm constantly saying, "I'm not sure. I'll have to look that up." That desire to ask questions is essential to understanding the science itself and problem solving to reach solutions later on in life.

As children get older, this appreciation for nature can provide solace when dealing with stress from challenging issues. When I'm the most troubled about humans' effects on the planet's ecosystems, I find it deeply comforting to gaze into the stars and contemplate the universe's beauty. While meditative practices in general can support mental strength, moving that to outdoor settings can provide further stress relief. Finding spiritual and emotional restoration in nature can help provide meaning-focused coping and build resilience.

Social Learning in Family and Community Settings

Learning and problem solving in social settings provide the next level up to cope with these issues beyond free play in nature.

In environmental education, social learning engages students in decision making around natural resource conservation and management issues. It generally tackles problems that don't require major systemic changes to fix. These issues range from collaborating to build a community garden to deciding on the best ways to collectively manage a fishery. Learners work with each other to develop and carry out plans. They collaborate as they apply best practices to tackle local problems.

In the context of parenting, social learning happens all of the time. Any time families work together to discuss issues or solve problems, both parents and children can walk away with a deeper understanding of each other and the issue. Sports and community groups provide children opportunities for seeing other people's point of view and working together. Social learning is simply any learning outside of formal classroom activities.

As social learning is our bread and butter as parents, it's logical to connect it to environmental issues. Behaviors focused on sustainability can be just as fundamental as teaching the basics of polite dinnertime behavior or getting along with friends. "We have to teach them some of these things, the same [as] we teach manners and we teach other life skills and behaviors. This is a life skill of sustainability," said Toney, who has a three-year-old. "We're planting seeds that we know will develop a little later on in their life."

Explaining why we as a family engage in certain environmental activities, such as composting or taking the bus, opens the conversation up to discussing the bigger problems. This is a great way to tackle these issues with preschoolers and early elementary school children. "Looking at your choices as a family from the lens of conservation I think is the next best step," said Edmonds-Langham. "Because that brings it back around to 'What can we do? We can do this.'"

To expand that social learning, Edmonds-Langham encourages parents to involve children in the decision-making process. "[It] is something folks can decide as a family and give kids a voice in," she said. "Let them be part of that conversation." Thinking about how your actions affect other people and animals develops empathy and moral reasoning. Problem solving with your family provides practice in strategic thinking and listening skills.

While focusing on "solving" problems by itself can be an unhealthy coping mechanism for these large and complex issues, starting with individual actions can be a stepping-stone. The many side benefits of these activities, such as building community, strengthening family relationships, and providing purpose, help transform these activities from problem solving to more meaning-focused coping. They're also a good way to introduce younger children to these tough environmental problems before moving on to more complex ways to deal with them. Leading with how we already contribute to the solutions helps problems seem more manageable. When it comes to younger children, it also allows you to introduce the idea of problems without getting into the gory details of their impacts.

Taking Political Action and Influencing Power Structures

"Action-oriented participation" focuses on problem solving as a member of the local and global community. It's similar in both the environmental-education and parenting worlds: identifying problems, researching them, creating possible solutions, and acting on those solutions. Instead of a leader telling students what to do, it's all about helping people develop their own opinions based on evidence.

Keya Chatterjee thinks political action is one of the most important aspects of talking to children about climate change. As the director of the U.S. Climate Action Network and the mom of an eight-year-old, she's involved her son in action since he was a baby. "If you want to tell your kids about what's going on in the world, you also have to give them agency," she said. "So much of what causes anxiety and panic is a lack of agency."

For us as parents, political action can provide the perfect complement to individual action, especially for older children. While we may not give younger children information on the detailed impacts, older children will hear about them and need a way to deal. Through school and the news, they'll start learning about the systems underlying climate change, including economic structures and social factors such as racism. Individual action alone may start to feel inadequate. As they realize many systems—such as the focus on cars to the exclusion of other types of transportation—make individual action harder than it needs to be, they may even become cynical. Combining individual and political action can empower them and help shift from problem-focused coping to meaning-focused coping. The more that people feel they can do and actually accomplish, the more hope they have around an issue.

Chatterjee said that she finds deep meaning in the fact that she's able to buck the system both personally and as an activist. "We're the ones saying like, 'No, I refuse to be dependent on this sort of thing that all of society is built to make us dependent on,'" she said. "It's an active, joyful resistance for me to say . . . I refuse to capitulate to what a bunch of billionaires who pull the puppet strings of policymakers decide that our infrastructure is going to support."

Dialogue and Storytelling

While the other three approaches are focused on action, the last one is focused on communication. In environmental education, deliberative dialogue involves thoughtfully discussing issues with others. Participants are committed to listening as much as speaking. In contrast to social learning or activism, there is no goal of coming up with a final or agreed-upon decision. It's all about the process.

For parents, these thoughtful conversations can arise in many different ways. Having these discussions with children shows that we appreciate their point of view and won't force our perspectives on them. Questions from children can definitely spark these types of conversations, as can talking through ethical issues in our own lives or the news.

Storytelling is a powerful but underrated approach to these conversations. While reading books is essential, stories we tell each other as a family can be incredibly important, according to psychologist Elaine Reese in her book *Tell Me a Story*. The stories we tell about our past, present, and future shape our thinking about those subjects. In addition, cultural stories often pass down moral values and teach practical knowledge. Children who listen to stories rich in detail from a young age have better memory and language skills as well as more advanced emotional development compared to children who don't. For children of all ages, talking about experiences via stories helps them better understand their own feelings and develop empathy for others.

Telling stories is a good path into discussing hard subjects while avoiding didactic lectures that shut down two-way conversation. In addition, stories fundamentally help us process and make meaning from events, offering a way into developing meaning-focused coping.

But if news stories about climate change are so often apocalyptic, what's a better way to frame them? Considering the problems at hand, everything can't be flowers and sunshine. Plus, stories with negative aspects are more interesting and dramatic. Fortunately there are a number of different approaches we can take that are both realistic and empowering.

Making a local connection can help people feel like they can and should do something. Researchers from the University of East Anglia in the United Kingdom found that discussing local impacts was most likely to make climate change feel relevant to people. In contrast, images of severe but far-away impacts made people feel sad but disempowered. For children, telling stories about small but significant local impacts of climate change or habitat loss can help them grasp the concept without being overwhelmed by it. When talking about possible effects, respond only to the questions children are asking without adding in too much extra detail. Even beyond what they are directly saying, try to understand their perspective. Connect the effects with some way of finding hope or the potential to reduce the impact.

Another way of talking about climate change is to frame it as a "readiness" story rather than a disaster-based one. Toney compared talking to children about climate change to running a fire drill. "Kids are adaptive and they're resilient in their own right," she said. "If we're talking to them as if this is the end of the world, that's what they're going to think. If we talk to them as in these are things we need to do to protect ourselves, that is what they are going to think." She described how as a child growing up in Mississippi, she frequently had tornado drills at school. The drills taught her to be prepared without constantly being scared of the threat.

From an advocacy perspective, Toney added that it is important to take action while also preparing our children. She compared it to how she simultaneously works to take political action on gun violence and racial justice while also having serious conversations with her sons (who are Black) about interactions with guns and the police. "I'm going to teach them as children and what they need to know to do. Make sure they are prepared," she said. "But at the same time, I'm going to advocate to ensure they are in safe spaces. Climate is no different."

Similarly Nijhuis said that while parents want to be truthful with their children, they should also emphasize how we're working to keep them safe. "You want to remind them . . . that's part of who you are," she said.

One way to integrate a family story into the bigger story of the environment is for parents to talk about ways they made a difference in their communities when they were kids. Children from eight to twelve years old enjoy hearing stories about their parents' childhood, especially about how they handled different challenges. Unlike teenagers, preteens don't process negative emotions well by themselves; they need their parents to help guide them. As a result, listening to others' stories that validate their own experiences is important to them. Telling our own stories and the meaning we found in those experiences growing up can help them see the difference they can make and the potential meaning in it. Personally I found it really powerful to share the story about my third-grade activism around manatees with Dylan. While my husband is less of a go-getter, he too has relevant stories of how he made his community a better place as a child. In particular he led his Cub Scout troop to clean up a neighborhood stream where a construction company was dumping garbage.

Beyond our own stories, reading and listening to stories of people doing this work who are similar to them can inspire and encourage children. The 2019 Moms Clean Air Force Play-In for the Climate had a training session specifically for teenagers. Alexandria Villaseñor, the fourteen-year-old co-leader of the U.S. Climate Strike, spoke to participants about her experience. They asked her questions about protesting, including the consequences for skipping school to participate. They even discussed the social impacts of activism, such as having a potential boyfriend not understand why they cared so much about the climate. "When I listened, I learned how brave these kids were," said Toney.

Likewise Nijhuis said that her daughter finally started asking questions about climate change after hearing about teenage activist Greta Thunberg and watching a video featuring teenagers from the Alliance for Climate Education. Teenagers neither gloss over the problems nor present them as impossible to defeat. Describing the students speaking on the video, Nijhuis said, "Their attitude is, 'We didn't ask for this problem, but we . . . are doing amazing things and making amazing efforts to fix it and you can be part of that.' I thought the attitude was just right." Hearing other kids talk about the issues can help preteens and teenagers envision the role they too can play.

Hearing about these young people's accomplishments can be particularly empowering. Edmonds-Langham said that talking about success stories can help children see that there is a path forward even with problems that seem impossible to tackle. "They can see themselves in that story and feel like they have an active role and can participate in these massive movements," she said.

Perhaps the most empowering stories are the ones that we tell ourselves about ourselves. Parents influence the stories that children internalize. Telling children stories of both their positive and negative life experiences and how they dealt with them helps build resilience. These stories can provide children with an inner reserve of strength to draw on during tough times. Sharing these stories early and often helps children cope with future challenges, including environmental issues.

For teenagers in particular, having them write about their own experiences and fears can help them process difficult emotions better. Working through their stories helps them develop their own sense of self in relationship to others and the world. It also helps them draw more meaning from their experiences. Environmental educators working on resilience specifically encourage journaling to help process complex feelings about loss and anxiety.

Working together with our children, we can develop a collective vision of our future. Thinking of it together helps reinforce the message that we as adults are supporting them, not just leaving the mess we made to clean up. As Nijhuis said, "We should be really careful about making them feel like they're responsible for our neglect. We're still walking around. We're still on the job." We can only approach problems and make meaning together. It's way too lonely otherwise.

Fortunately we're all still telling the story of the environment and the role we have to play in it. Much of the story is written, but the ending isn't finished yet. We are the characters in our own stories and we have the opportunity to make our own meaning. We can tell the stories we want to hear and find ways toward the endings we want to see. While there is no guarantee of a happy ending, we can still find hope and joy in the very act of loving each other and taking care of our collective home.

FAMILY ACTIVITY: Envisioning the Future We Want

DESIGN YOUR IDEAL CITY OR TOWN

Ask your child what their ideal city or town would look like. They can draw it or just verbally describe features of it. Accept all suggestions, no matter how ridiculous. Gently ask questions about how people in the city would get around, where they would live, and how they would get food. If they don't mention it, ask your child where plants and animals would live and what kind of role they would play in this city.

THINK ABOUT YOUR CITY HOLISTICALLY

Explore how this city could be built in ways that reduce its contributions to greenhouse gases, air pollution, and water pollution. How would you change (if at all) the transportation, where buildings are built, where people get their food, and how energy is used?

EXPLORE DAY-TO-DAY LIFE

Ask your child to describe what their life would look like in this city or town. How would school be the different or the same? What about what you did on the weekends? How would your family life change, if at all? How would it be better than what you have now?

COMPARE AND CONTRAST WITH THE PRESENT

Ask your child which features of this city they would truly like to see in the place they live now. What are the similarities? What are the differences? Why would they want to keep what they keep? Why would they change what they change?

BRAINSTORM A PATH FORWARD

Discuss some ways that the place you live could become more like your imaginary city. Don't limit children to environmental issues—if they want free cotton candy every day at lunch, ask how they would do it! Talk about what you and they together could do as a family to help your hometown be more like their ideal city.

Books

PICTURE BOOKS

Care for Our World, by Karen S. Robbins, M. H. Clark, and Alexandra Ball: A sweet book about the many kinds of animals on Earth and our collective responsibility to take care of them. It's a great complement to bringing kids outside and has the cutest picture of a slug I've ever seen.

My Wounded Island, by Jacques Pasquet, Marion Arbona, and Sophie B. Watson: Written from the perspective of an Iñupiat girl who is affected by rising ocean levels, this moving book helps kids see how climate change is affecting children like them right now. The beautiful illustrations and intimate voice cultivate awareness of and empathy for climate refugees.

The Tantrum That Saved the World, by Megan Herbert and Michael Mann: Co-written by a children's book author and leading climate scientist, this book is about a little girl inundated by people and animals affected by climate change and what she does about it. It's particularly good about showing everyone working together to deal with setbacks and collaborating to make change.

YOUNG ADULT/ACTIVITY BOOKS

Heroes of the Environment: True Stories of People Who Are Helping to Protect Our Planet, by Harriet Rohmer: An inspiring collection of stories about people making a difference for the environment, with a heavy emphasis on environmental justice. While not all the example heroes are children, several of them are and they cover a broad array of environmental issues.

The Parents' Guide to Climate Revolution, by Mary DeMocker: This book provides 100 broad ways for families to re-envision what it means to have a "good life" while making real change. It's a great complement to this book!

Resources

Tell Me a Story, by Elaine Reese

Children and Nature Network: www.childrenandnature.org

Alliance for Climate Education: www.acespace.org

Kids at the Museum: Nature's Superheroes (videos about environmental problems by children participating in the American Museum of Natural History's programs): www.amnh.org/explore/ology/biodiversity/nature-s-superheroes

Climate Change Predictions Can Be Scary for Kids. What Can You Say?: www.usatoday.com/story/news/nation-now/2017/05/22/climate-change-predictions-can-scary-kids-what-can-you-say/335505001/

Five Tips for Talking to Kids About Climate Change (Without Freaking Them Out): www.rainforest-alliance.org/articles/how-to-talk-to-kids -about-climate-change

Beginning the Climate Conversation: A Family's Guide: www .climaterealityproject.org/sites/default/files/kidsandclimatechangee -book.pdf

On Talking to Our Kids About the Future: www.grist.org/article /2010-02-03-on-talking-to-our-kids-about-the-future/

How to Talk to Your Kids About Global Warming: www.parents .com/parenting/better-parenting/advice/how-to-talk-to-your-kids -about-global-warming/

APPEnDIX

ORGANIZING ENVIRONMENTAL ACTIVITIES AT YOUR CHILD'S SCHOOL

School-age children spend more than thirty hours a week at school. What they see their teachers, administrators, and fellow students doing influences their perspectives and behaviors. It's a perfect place to help students adopt behaviors that are more environmentally and socially sustainable. Having an entire school participate in a program multiplies its impact far past what your family can do alone.

At the same time, we're all busy. You want to ensure that you can create a long-term project while minimizing its burden on both you and the schools' staff members. Organizers of school gardens, Bike or Walk to School Days, and Green Teams shared their advice with me for developing school programs with the biggest impact.

RESEARCH THE PROBLEM AND POTENTIAL SOLUTIONS

The first step is to identify a problem you want to solve and research it. Cass Isidro is the executive director of the Safe Routes Partnership that organizes Walk and Bike to School Days nationally. She said that asking questions is key. "Once you start asking, 'How come nobody crosses that road?' then you start hearing about the barriers," she said. Be sure to ask a variety of parents and staff members questions. Parents of different income levels, ethnic groups, or geographic areas may have different concerns. Staff members may see different problems than parents do.

Next find out what the school has done to address these issues in the past. If they've tried a particular solution and it failed, it's good to find out why. Maybe there are new options available now that weren't before or you can learn from what they did.

Consulting best practices can help you avoid starting from scratch. In addition, having success stories where similar programs worked in other places makes it easier to pitch a program. For bicycling and walking programs, such as Bike/Walk to School Days and "Walking Wednesdays," the Safe Routes Partnership has a variety of resources. Similarly a number of organizations are devoted to supporting school gardens, including Slow Food USA and the Collective School Garden Network. Checking out the activities at schools that have earned the prestigious Green Ribbon Schools honor from the U.S. Department of Education can give you ideas for conservation and renewable energy projects.

DEVELOP SOLUTIONS THAT SOLVE MULTIPLE PROBLEMS

Environmental activities have advantages far beyond their sustainability benefits. Many environmentally oriented programs can solve multiple problems for schools and teachers.

"It needs to be solutions-oriented. If there's a program that solves something at the school that's a pain point, you've got a win-win right off the bat," said Isidro.

Biking and walking for transportation can help increase student attentiveness and rates of attendance. They can also reduce traffic congestion, especially at the much-loathed car drop-off line.

Energy-conservation activities can save schools money and reinforce themes in the classroom. The district that houses William Tyler Page Elementary (profiled in chapter 4), Montgomery County Public Schools, uses more electricity than any other single business in the entire county. Its electricity bill totals $27 million a year. Environmental activities can also fulfill or reinforce curriculum requirements in certain states. "Students learning about the environment and caring about the environment is so critical to the whole child and the whole person as they grow up," said Jim Stufft, who works for the county's School Energy and Recycling Team. He also supports the Green Team at William Tyler Page Elementary. "Schools that take it beyond that . . . it makes for a full, rounded education."

BUILD A TEAM

Trying to take on a project by yourself leads to burnout. Even if you're able to sustain it alone, other people won't be able to maintain it once your child graduates or you're otherwise unavailable. It's always better to have a team from the beginning.

Having a fellow parent on board to share the work is a great start. It's especially important to have another parent as a partner if the school isn't initially interested. Ask people in your PTA or other parents you know who are interested in similar issues. If you have an older child, it's good to pair with someone who has a younger child. In theory they should still be there to continue the work when your child graduates.

It's also useful to have a contact inside of the school, either a teacher or another staff member. In the case of encouraging biking and walking, the person in charge of transportation may be your best bet. For a garden, someone who manages the food service or school grounds may be essential. To start energy-conservation activities, you will probably need to connect with a facilities person. Because most schools will not have a paid staff member assigned to the activity, finding someone who has job responsibilities that line up with the project will make it easier.

Ideally, this school staff member will be your champion who provides internal support. Even if they aren't completely excited by the project, it's essential to get this person on your team early to avoid late-stage barriers.

"What we need is a team to share the joy and the burden of keeping a living garden alive," said John Fisher, director of programs and partnerships at Life Lab. "To make a garden thrive and work, you would need a team."

The more teachers and staff members you can recruit to your team, the better. William Tyler Page Elementary's Green Team partners with both the school art and music teachers to put on their yearly assembly. The music teacher works with the Green Team to prepare songs; the art teacher helps them make props and decorations. Involving a variety of people throughout the school integrates your program into the fabric of the school, making it more sustainable in the long run.

TEST THE WATERS

Don't start with a grand project that requires a ton of upkeep. Instead, try out a smaller idea that you can repeat if it works well, tweak if it needs improvements, or start over if it's a total flop.

If you want to start a walking school bus, where a few adults accompany a group of children to school, try it for the first time on National Walk to School Day, the first Wednesday in October. If you're interested in creating your own Green Team group, organize a one-off event to determine if students would even like that type of activity.

Use these events to gauge interest and start conversations. They're also a great way to judge the barriers that may stand in the way of launching a big program. If you want to start a school garden but the facilities person won't let you have potted plants in the classroom, you know that's an issue you need to tackle early.

MAKE IT APPEALING TO KIDS

The most important part of any school activity is ensuring that kids will want to participate! Getting kids initially interested may require some encouragement. As long as there aren't food restrictions at your school, snacks are always a winner.

For one-off events like Bike to School Day, giving stickers to participants instills pride. Another way to build excitement is to enter all of the participants in a raffle to receive a prize pack.

For longer-term programs, having a special recognition ceremony at the end of the year can help students feel special. Similarly a custom item to indicate their participation (like the Green Team's lanyards) helps reinforce their sense of identity as a volunteer.

PARTNER WITH LOCAL BUSINESSES, GOVERNMENT AGENCIES, AND OTHER SCHOOLS

Organizing events is never free, whether they require money or time. Both are always in short supply in schools. Working together with local businesses, governments, or other schools can help lessen the burden.

Local businesses can contribute goods relevant to your project, from bike helmets to gardening supplies. "Most community businesses are very interested in supporting things like garden-based learning," said Fisher. "I don't think you would have any businesses say, 'Nah, that's not a good idea.'" From participating in a national recycling program, the William Tyler Page Elementary Green Team even earned enough money to purchase a bicycle rack for the school.

Government officials can show up to events to demonstrate their commitment, which makes the school more likely to support the project in the long run. School leadership generally recognizes how important relationships with local political leaders are.

Working with other schools can help you pool your resources and share best practices. William Tyler Page Elementary is partnering with another nearby elementary school to teach them lessons learned from the success of their Green Team.

SET UP SYSTEMS TO MAKE IT SUSTAINABLE

Thinking ahead to what you will do in the next season or even next year is essential for long-term sustainability. For a school garden, considering what will happen during vacations can save you from last-minute scrambling to look for someone to water the garden. For a bike club, deciding on the coldest or hottest temperatures you may go out in can save you from having kids miserable because of the weather. With a walking school bus, creating a plan for more children wanting to join than the group is capable of handling can save you heartache from turning people away.

Resources

Slow Food USA School Garden Resources: www.slowfoodusa.org/school -gardens/

Walk and Bike to School Days: www.walkbiketoschool.org

Green Strides (environmental activities at schools): www.greenstrides .org

Montgomery County Schools (William Tyler Page Elementary's district) Energy and Recycling Team: www.montgomeryschoolsmd.org /departments/facilities/greenschoolsfocus/index.aspx

Green Ribbon Schools program, U.S. Department of Education: www2 .ed.gov/green-ribbon-schools

BIBLIOGRAPHY

CHAPTER I: CULTIVATING KINDNESS

"As an article titled 'Ethical Parenting'..."
Miller, Lisa. "Ethical Parenting." *New York*, October 4, 2013. http://nymag
.com/news/features/ethical-parenting-2013-10/

"A 2014 survey of 10,000 middle and high school students..."
Harvard Graduate School of Education Making Caring Common Project. "The
Children We Mean to Raise: The Real Messages Adults Are Sending About
Values." 2014. https://mcc.gse.harvard.edu/reports/children-mean-raise.

"People in places with the world's longest life expectancies..."
Buettner, Dan. "Power 9: Reverse Engineering Longevity." *Blue Zones*, June 5,
2019. https://www.bluezones.com/2016/11/power-9/.

"According to self-determination theory..."
Skinner, Ellen A., Una Chi, and The Learning-Gardens Educational Assessment
Group 1. "Intrinsic Motivation and Engagement as 'Active Ingredients' in
Garden-Based Education: Examining Models and Measures Derived from
Self-Determination Theory." *Journal of Environmental Education* 43, no. 1
(2012): 16–36. https://doi.org/10.1080/00958964.2011.596856.

"Competence is feeling like..."
Froh, Jeffrey, and Giacomo Bono. *Making Grateful Kids: The Science of Building
Character*. West Conshohocken, PA: Templeton Press, 2015.

"Prosocial means doing things..."
Malti, T., and S. P. Dys. "From Being Nice to Being Kind: Development of Prosocial Behaviors." *Current Opinion in Psychology* 20 (Apr. 2018): 45–49.
https://doi.org/10.1016/j.copsyc.2017.07.036.

"Morality involves knowing the right thing to do . . ."

Wray-Lake, L. and A. K. Syvertsen. "The Developmental Roots of Social Responsibility in Childhood and Adolescence." *New Directions for Child and Adolescent Development*, no. 134 (2011): 11–25. https://doi.org/10.1002/cd.308.

Wray-Lake, Laura, Amy K. Syvertsen, and Constance A. Flanagan. "Developmental Change in Social Responsibility During Adolescence: An Ecological Perspective." *Developmental Psychology* 52, no. 1 (Jan. 2016): 130–42. https://www.ncbi.nlm.nih.gov/pmc/articles/PMC5634966/.

"A number of different characteristics . . ."

Birchak, Stephen. *How to Build a Child's Character by Tapping into Your Own*. Unionville, NY: Royal Fireworks, 2004.

Lickona, Thomas. *How to Raise Kind Kids: And Get Respect, Gratitude, and a Happier Family in the Bargain*. New York: Penguin, 2018.

Brooks, Robert, and Sam Goldstein. *Raising Resilient Children: Fostering Strength, Hope, and Optimism in Your Child*. New York: McGraw-Hill Education, 2002.

McCready, Amy. *The Me, Me, Me Epidemic: A Step-by-Step Guide to Raising Capable, Grateful Kids in an Over-Entitled World*. New York: TarcherPerigee, 2016.

"This warmth and responsiveness is associated with . . ."

Berkowitz, Marvin W., and John H. Grych. "Fostering Goodness: Teaching Parents to Facilitate Children's Moral Development." *Journal of Moral Education* 27, no. 3 (1998): 371–91. https://parenthood.library.wisc.edu /Berkowitz/Berkowitz.html.

National Scientific Council on the Developing Child. *Supportive Relationships and Active Skill-Building Strengthen the Foundations of Resilience: Working Paper No. 13*. 2015. http://www.developingchild.harvard.edu.

"Coal plants tend to be located in low-income neighborhoods . . ."

Wilson, Adrian. "Coal Blooded: Putting Profits Before People." Report of the NAACP, Indigenous Environmental Network, and Little Village Environmental Justice Organization. November 2012. https://www.naacp.org /climate-justice-resources/coal-blooded/.

"Psychologist D. W. Winnicott proposed the idea . . ."

Winnicott, D. W. *Playing and Reality*. New York: Routledge, 1971.

CHAPTER 2: CONNECTING WITH OUR FOOD

"In 1971 the Youth Garden . . ."

"Who We Are and What We Do." Washington Youth Garden. n.d. Accessed June 2, 2019. http://www.washingtonyouthgarden.org/our-mission-and -history

"One study out of Texas A&M looked at the effects of a gardening curriculum . . ."

Klemmer, C. D., T. M. Waliczek, and J. M. Zajicek. "Growing Minds: The Effect of a School Gardening Program on the Science Achievement of Elementary Students." *HortTechnology* 15, no. 3 (July–September 2005): 448-52. https:// journals.ashs.org/horttech/view/journals/horttech/15/3/article-p448.xml.

"A project run by Louisiana State University in urban schools . . ."

Smith, Leanna L., and Carl E. Motsenbocker. "Impact of Hands-on Science Through School Gardening in Louisiana Public Elementary Schools." *Hort-Technology* 15, no. 3 (July–September 2005): 439-43. https://journals .ashs.org/horttech/view/journals/horttech/15/3/article-p439.xml.

"A study done by Portland State University researchers . . ."

Williams, Dilafruz R., Heather Brule, Sybil S. Kelley, and Ellen A. Skinner. "Science in the Learning Gardens (SciLG): A Study of Students' Motivation, Achievement, and Science Identity in Low-Income Middle Schools." *International Journal of STEM Education* 5, article no. 8 (March 26, 2018). https://doi.org/10.1186/s40594-018-0104-9.

"A study by Texas A&M researchers with more than 230 second and fourth graders . . ."

Skelly, Sonja M., and Jayne M. Zajicek. "The Effect of an Interdisciplinary Garden Program on the Environmental Attitudes of Elementary School Students." *HortTechnology* 8, no. 4 (October–December 1998): 579-83. https://journals .ashs.org/horttech/view/journals/horttech/8/4/article-p579.xml.

"A Washington State University study that surveyed adults . . ."

Lohr, Virginia, and Caroline H. Pearson-Mims. "Children's Active and Passive Interactions with Plants Influence Their Attitudes and Actions Toward Trees and Gardening as Adults." *HortTechnology* 15, no. 3 (July–September 2005). https://journals.ashs.org/horttech/view/journals/horttech/15/3 /article-p472.xml.

"We can gain some insight into how those values develop from a project in Vancouver . . ."

Mayer-Smith, Jolie, Oksana Bartosh, and Linda Peterat. "Teaming Children and Elders to Grow Food and Environmental Consciousness." *Applied Environmental Education and Communication* 6, no. 1 (April 2017): 77-85. https://doi.org/10.1080/15330150701319529.

"In one study from researchers at Sam Houston State University and Texas A&M . . ."

Robinson, Carolyn W., and Jayne M. Zajicek. "Growing Minds: The Effects of a One-Year School Garden Program on Six Constructs of Life Skills of Elementary School Children." *HortTechnology* 15, no. 3 (July–September 2005): 453-57. https://journals.ashs.org/horttech/view/journals/horttech/15/3/article-p453.xml.

"An academic review looking at fourteen different studies . . ."

Savoie-Roskos, Mateja R., Heidi Wengreen, and Carrie Durward. "Increasing Fruit and Vegetable Intake Among Children and Youth Through Gardening-Based Interventions: A Systematic Review." *Journal of the Academy of Nutrition and Dietetics* 117, no. 2 (2017): 240-50. https://doi.org/10.1016/j.jand.2016.10.014.

Koch, S., T. M. Waliczek, and J. M. Zajicek. "The Effect of a Summer Garden Program on the Nutritional Knowledge, Attitudes, and Behaviors of Children." *HortTechnology* 16, no. 4 (October–December 2006): 620-25. https://journals.ashs.org/horttech/view/journals/horttech/16/4/article-p620.xml.

Lineberger, Sarah E., and J. M. Zajicek. "School Gardens: Can a Hands-On Teaching Tool Affect Students' Attitudes and Behaviors Regarding Fruit and Vegetables?" *HortTechnology* 10 no. 3 (July–September 2000): 593-97. https://journals.ashs.org/horttech/view/journals/horttech/10/3/article-p593.xml?rskey=MQBTmN.

"A study of students in southwest Detroit . . ."

Pothukuchi, Kameshwari. "Hortaliza: A Youth 'Nutrition Garden' in Southwest Detroit." *Children, Youth and Environments* 14, no. 2 (2004): 124-55. http://digitalcommons.wayne.edu/urbstud_frp/3.

"Similarly a garden project in Flint, Michigan . . ."

Allen, Julie Ober, Katherine Alaimo, Doris Elam, and Elizabeth Perry. "Growing Vegetables and Values: Benefits of Neighborhood-Based Community Gardens for Youth Development and Nutrition." *Journal of*

Hunger and Environmental Nutrition 3, no. 4 (2008): 418–39. https://doi .org/10.1080/19320240802529169.

"Walking through growing spaces . . ."
"More Than Peanuts: Revisiting the Work and Legacy of George Washington Carver." Oak Spring Garden Foundation. February 7, 2019. https://www .osgf.org/blog/george-washington-carver.

"A study of farmers markets in upstate New York . . ."
Baber, Laura M., and Edward A. Frongillo. "Family and Seller Interactions in Farmers' Markets in Upstate New York." *American Journal of Alternative Agriculture* 18, no. 2 (June 2003): 87–94. https://www.jstor.org /stable/44503253.

"Agriculture makes up 9 percent . . ."
"Sources of Greenhouse Gas Emissions." U.S. Environmental Protection Agency. September 13, 2019. https://www.epa.gov/ghgemissions/sources -greenhouse-gas-emissions#agriculture.

CHAPTER 3: WHAT DO YOU DO WITHOUT A MINIVAN?

"An international team of researchers surveyed 3,500 commuters . . ."
Avila-Palencia, Ione, Luc Int Panis, Evi Dons, Mailin Gaupp-Berghausen, Elisabeth Raser, Thomas Götschi, Regine Gerike, et al. "The Effects of Transport Mode Use on Self-Perceived Health, Mental Health, and Social Contact Measures: A Cross-Sectional and Longitudinal Study." *Environment International* 120 (2018): 199–206. https://doi.org/10.1016/j.envint .2018.08.002.

"Similarly a study in Barcelona, Spain . . ."
Avila-Palencia, I., A. de Nazelle, T. Cole-Hunter, et al. "The Relationship Between Bicycle Commuting and Perceived Stress: A Cross-Sectional Study." *BMJ Open* 7 (2017): e013542. https://bmjopen.bmj.com/content/7/6/e013542.

"Medical studies looking at the effects of physical activity on children . . ."
Raine, L. B., H. K. Lee, B. J. Saliba, L. Chaddock-Heyman, C. H. Hillman, and A. F. Kramer. "The Influence of Childhood Aerobic Fitness on Learning and Memory." *PLoS ONE* 8, no. 9 (2013): e72666. https://doi.org/10.1371 /journal.pone.0072666.

Best, John R. "Effects of Physical Activity on Children's Executive Function: Contributions of Experimental Research on Aerobic Exercise."

Developmental Review 30, no. 4 (December 2010): 331–51. https://doi
.org/10.1016/j.dr.2010.08.001.

Hill, Liam, Justin H. G. Williams, Lorna Aucott, June Milne, Jenny Thomson, Jessie
Greig, Val Munro, and Mark Mon-Williams. "Exercising Attention Within
the Classroom." *Developmental Medicine and Child Neurology* 52, no. 10
(October 2010): 929–34. https://doi.org/10.1111/j.1469-8749.2010.03661.x.

"In fact, researchers at the University of Illinois . . ."

Chaddock-Heyman, L., C. H. Hillman, N. J. Cohen, and A. F. Kramer. "The Importance of Physical Activity and Aerobic Fitness for Cognitive Control and
Memory in Children." *Monographs of the Society for Research in Child Development* 79, no. 4 (Dec. 2014): 25–50. https://doi.org/10.1111/mono.12129.

"A review paper of studies that looked at children participating in randomized
control trials . . ."

Lees, Caitlin, and Jessica Hopkins. "Effect of Aerobic Exercise on Cognition,
Academic Achievement, and Psychosocial Function in Children: A Systematic Review of Randomized Control Trials." *Preventing Chronic Disease*
10, E174 (2013). https://doi.org/10.5888/pcd10.130010.

"After a bout of moderate exercise . . ."

Pontifex, Matthew B., Brian J. Saliba, Lauren B. Raine, Daniel L. Picchietti, and
Charles H. Hillman. "Exercise Improves Behavioral, Neurocognitive, and
Scholastic Performance in Children with ADHD." *Journal of Pediatrics* 162,
no. 3 (March 2013): 543–51. https://www.ncbi.nlm.nih.gov/pmc/articles
/PMC3556380/.

"A study—albeit sponsored by the bicycle company Specialized . . ."

RTSG Neuroscience Consultants. "ADHD Bike Program Final Report." 2013.
https://static1.squarespace.com/static/596c38bf17bffc52ba57eb30
/t/5a5e6e0df9619a0fe127523f/1516138000480/The+Specialized+
Foundation+RTSG+Report.pdf.

Paynter, Ben. "Specialized Has a Plan to Use Bicycling to Help Manage ADHD
in Schools." *Fast Company*, August 7, 2017. https://www.fastcompany
.com/40449124/specialized-has-a-plan-to-use-bicycling-to-help-manage
-adhd-in-schools.

"The Dutch also credit the fact . . ."

Acosta, Rina Mae, and Michele Hutchison. *The Happiest Kids in the World: How
Dutch Parents Help Their Kids (and Themselves) by Doing Less.* New York:
Experiment, 2017.

"Forty years ago, 50 percent of children . . ."

Jenkins, Daniel. "Children's Travel to School, National Household Travel Survey." Issue brief. U.S. Department of Transportation Federal Highway Administration. March 2019. https://nhts.ornl.gov/assets/FHWA _NHTS_%20Brief_Traveltoschool_032519.pdf.

"In a study of twenty-six nine- and ten-year-olds in the San Francisco suburbs . . ."

Appleyard, Bruce. "The Meaning of Livable Streets to Schoolchildren: An Image Mapping Study of the Effects of Traffic on Children's Cognitive Development of Spatial Knowledge." *Journal of Transport and Health* 5 (June 2017): 27–41. https://doi.org/10.1016/j.jth.2016.08.002.

"A similar study in Israel also found . . ."

Moran, Mika R., Efrat Eizenberg, and Pnina Plaut. "Getting to Know a Place: Built Environment Walkability and Children's Spatial Representation of Their Home–School (H–S) Route." *International Journal of Environmental Research and Public Health* 14, no. 6 (June 2017): 607. https://doi .org/10.3390/ijerph14060607.

"In the book *Tell Me a Story* . . ."

Reese, Elaine. *Tell Me a Story: Sharing Stories to Enrich Your Child's World.* New York: Oxford University Press, 2013.

"According to one study in Chicago by researchers at the University of Illinois. . ."

Chang, Alvin. "White America Is Quietly Self-Segregating." *Vox*, July 31, 2018. https://www.vox.com/2017/1/18/14296126/white-segregated-suburb -neighborhood-cartoon.

Krysan, M., and S. Moberg. "Trends in Racial Attitudes." University of Illinois Institute of Government and Public Affairs. August 25, 2016. http://igpa .uillinois.edu/programs/racial-attitudes.

"A study from the University of Surrey in the United Kingdom . . ."

Gatersleben, Birgitta, Niamh Murtagh, and Emma White. "Hoody, Goody or Buddy? How Travel Mode Affects Social Perceptions in Urban Neighbourhoods." *Transportation Research Part F: Traffic Psychology and Behaviour* 21 (November 2013): 219–30. https://www.sciencedirect.com/science /article/abs/pii/S1369847813000806#.

"A survey of more than 20,000 commuters in Sweden . . ."

Mattisson, Kristoffer, Carita Håkansson, and Kristina Jakobsson. "Relationships Between Commuting and Social Capital Among Men and Women in

Southern Sweden." *Environment and Behavior* 47, no. 7 (Aug. 2015): 734–53. https://www.ncbi.nlm.nih.gov/pmc/articles/PMC4509867/.

"Similarly a study of nine- to eleven-year-old children in Birmingham . . ."
Alton, D., P. Adab, L. Roberts, et al. "Relationship Between Walking Levels and Perceptions of the Local Neighbourhood Environment." *Archives of Disease in Childhood* 92 (2007): 29-33. https://adc.bmj.com/content/92/1/29.

"However, it's very helpful to travel light but effectively."
Saulter, Carla. "10 Things Learned in 10 Years as a Bus Parent." *Bus Chick*, November 1, 2017. http://www.buschick.com/?p=9727.

Saulter, Carla. "The Sane Person's Guide to Bringing Kids on Public Transit." *Grist*, March 21, 2011. https://www.grist.org/family/2011-03-21-how-to -get-kids-on-transit-without-driving-everyone-involved-out/.

"According to the U.S. Department of Transportation's latest national house-hold travel survey . . ."
"Vehicle Trips Data." National Household Travel Survey. Federal Highway Administration, U.S. Department of Transportation, 2017. https://nhts .ornl.gov/vehicle-trips.

"In a study of families participating in youth soccer in Davis, California . . ."
Tal, Gil, and Susan Handy. "Children's Biking for Nonschool Purposes: Get-ting to Soccer Games in Davis, California." *Transportation Research Record* 2074, no. 1 (January 2008): 40-45. http://www.des.ucdavis.edu/faculty /handy/AYSO_TRR.pdf.

CHAPTER 4: NOT YOUR MOTHER'S HOUSEHOLD

"The average American produces about 4.5 pounds of waste per day . . ."
"National Overview: Facts and Figures on Materials, Wastes and Recy-cling." U.S. Environmental Protection Agency. October 26, 2018. https:// www.epa.gov/facts-and-figures-about-materials-waste-and-recycling /national-overview-facts-and-figures-materials.

"Households use about 38 percent of the electricity . . ."
"Electricity Consumption in the United States Was About 3.95 Trillion Kilo-watthours (KWh) in 2018." U.S. Energy Information Administration. April 29, 2019. https://www.eia.gov/energyexplained/electricity/use-of -electricity.php.

"The average household also uses more than 300 gallons of water a day . . ."
"How We Use Water." U.S. Environmental Protection Agency. February 5, 2018. https://www.epa.gov/watersense/how-we-use-water.

"In many ways, they're similar to a method of learning that psychologists . . ."
Rogoff, Barbara, Rebeca Mejía-Arauz, and Maricela Correa-Chávez. "A Cultural Paradigm—Learning by Observing and Pitching In." In *Advances in Child Development and Behavior*, edited by Maricela Correa-Chávez, Rebeca Mejía-Arauz, and Barbara Rogoff, 1-22. Waltham, MA: Academic Press, 2015. https://doi.org/10.1016/bs.acdb.2015.10.008.

"One study led by a researcher from ITESO University . . ."
Mejía-Arauz, Rebeca, Maricela Correa-Chávez, Ulrike Keyser Ohrt, Itzel Aceves-Azuara, "Collaborative Work or Individual Chores: The Role of Family Social Organization in Children's Learning to Collaborate and Develop Initiative." In *Advances in Child Development and Behavior*, edited by Maricela Correa-Chávez, Rebeca Mejía-Arauz, and Barbara Rogoff, 25-51. Waltham, MA: Academic Press, 2015. https://doi.org/10.1016/bs.acdb.2015.10.001.

"A study by University of California Los Angeles (UCLA) researchers . . ."
Telzer, Eva H., and Andrew J. Fuligni,. "Daily Family Assistance and the Psychological Well-Being of Adolescents from Latin American, Asian, and European Backgrounds." *Developmental Psychology* 45, no. 4 (2009): 1177-89. https://doi.org/10.1037/a0014728.

"An experimental study by University of Pittsburgh and University of Tennessee researchers . . ."
Waugh, Whitney, Celia Brownell, and Brianna Pollock. "Early Socialization of Prosocial Behavior: Patterns in Parents' Encouragement of Toddlers' Helping in an Everyday Household Task." *Infant Behavior and Development* 39 (May 2015): 1-10. https://www.ncbi.nlm.nih.gov/pmc/articles/PMC4417400/.

"One study by UCLA researchers compared children . . ."
Ochs, Elinor, and Carolina Izquierdo. "Responsibility in Childhood: Three Developmental Trajectories." *Ethos* 37, no. 4 (2009): 391-413. http://www.sscnet.ucla.edu/anthro/faculty/ochs/articles/A111Ochs%20Izquierdo%20ResponsibilityArticle.pdf.

"In one study, researchers from Pitzer College observed nearly 200 children . . ."

Munroe, Ruth, Robert Munroe, and Harold Shimmin. "Children's Work in Four Cultures: Determinants and Consequences." *American Anthropologist* 86 (June 1984): 369–79. https://doi.org/10.1525/aa.1984.86.2.02a00120.

"Similarly, a study of nearly 10,000 children in the U.S. . . ."

White, Elizabeth M., Mark D. DeBoer, and Rebecca J. Scharf. "Associations Between Household Chores and Childhood Self-Competency." *Journal of Developmental and Behavioral Pediatrics* 40, no. 3 (April 2019): 176–82. https://doi.org/10.1097/DBP.0000000000000637.

"On the older end, a survey of nearly 300 undergraduate . . ."

Riggio, Heidi R., Ann Marie Valenzuela, and Dana A. Weiser. "Household Responsibilities in the Family of Origin: Relations with Self-efficacy in Young Adulthood." *Personality and Individual Differences* 48 (2010): 568–73. http://parented.wdfiles.com/local--files/chores-allowances/Household%20Responsibilities%20in%20the%20Family%20of%20Origin.pdf.

"Compared to conventional models . . ."

"Energy Efficient Products: Clothes Dryers." U.S. Environmental Protection Agency. October 26, 2019. http://www.energystar.gov/products/appliances/clothes_dryers.

"Energy Efficient Products: Clothes Washers." U.S. Environmental Protection Agency. October 26, 2019. http://www.energystar.gov/products/appliances/clothes_washers.

"According to the U.S. Department of Energy . . ."

"Energy Saver: Lighting Choices to Save You Money." U.S. Department of Energy. October 26, 2019. http://www.energy.gov/energysaver/save-electricity-and-fuel/lighting-choices-save-you-money.

"About half of all households now have the option . . ."

"Energy Saver: Buying Clean Electricity." U.S. Department of Energy. October 26, 2019. https://www.energy.gov/energysaver/buying-and-making-electricity/buying-clean-electricity.

"In *Zero Waste Home* . . ."

Johnson, Bea. *Zero Waste Home: The Ultimate Guide to Simplifying Your Life by Reducing Your Waste.* New York: Scribner, 2013.

"And paying an allowance for chores . . ."

Klein, Wendy, Anthony P. Graesch, and Carolina Izquierdo. "Children and Chores: A Mixed-Methods Study of Children's Household Work in Los

Angeles Families." *Anthropology of Work Review* 30, no. 3 (December 24, 2009):98–109.http://www.celf.ucla.edu/2010_conference_articles/Klein _et_al_2009.pdf.

CHAPTER 5: BREAKING FREE OF "STUFF"

"In the U.S., children receive $28 billion worth of toys each year . . ."
The NPD Group. "Annual U.S. Sales Data." Report for The Toy Association, 2019. http://www.toyassociation.org/ta/research/data/u-s-sales-data/toys /research-and-data/data/us-sales-data.aspx.

"In a sociological study by UCLA researchers of thirty-two families . . ."
Arnold, Jeanne E., Anthony P. Graesch, Enzo Ragazzini, and Elinor Ochs. *Life at Home in the Twenty-First Century: 32 Families Open Their Doors.* Los Angeles: The Cotsen Institute of Archaeology Press, 2012.

"One company estimated that four- to twelve-year-olds . . ."
Schor, Juliet. *Born to Buy.* New York: Scribner, 2005.

"Most of these toys are made in countries with poor labor standards . . ."
Hobbes, Michael. "Why It's Impossible to Shop Ethically." *Huffington Post*, July 15, 2015. https://highline.huffingtonpost.com/articles/en/the-myth-of -the-ethical-shopper/.

"In a survey of moms and teens . . ."
Kasser, Tim. *The High Price of Materialism.* Cambridge, MA: Bradford, 2003.

"In 2014 Scott and his wife, Gabby, decided . . ."
Dannemiller, Scott. *The Year Without a Purchase: One Family's Quest to Stop Shopping and Start Connecting.* Louisville, KY: Westminster John Knox Press, 2015.

"In both a 1979 study and a similar 2018 study . . ."
Dauch, Carly, Michelle Imwalle, Brooke Ocasio, and Alexia E. Metz. "The Influence of the Number of Toys in the Environment on Toddlers' Play." *Infant Behavior and Development* 50 (2018): 78–87. https://doi.org/10.1016 /j.infbeh.2017.11.005.

"Researchers from the University of Chicago and Cornell University . . ."
Carter, Travis, and Thomas Gilovich. "I Am What I Do, Not What I Have: The Differential Centrality of Experiential and Material Purchases to the Self." *Journal of Personality and Social Psychology* 102, no. 6 (2012): 1304–17. https://doi.org/10.1037/a0027407.

"Despite the pressure to buy physical objects . . ."

Kumar, Amit, Matthew A. Killingsworth, and Thomas Gilovich. "Waiting for Merlot: Anticipatory Consumption of Experiential and Material Purchases." *Psychological Science* 25, no. 10 (2014): 1924-31. http://citeseerx .ist.psu.edu/viewdoc/download?doi=10.1.1.865.3824&rep=rep1&type=pdf.

"Through a combination of surveys and experiments . . ."

Gilovich, Thomas, Amit Kumar, and Lily Jampol. "A Wonderful Life: Experiential Consumption and the Pursuit of Happiness." *Journal of Consumer Psychology* 25, no. 1 (2015): 152-65. http://pages.stern.nyu.edu/~lbornkam /S15Seminar/gilovich_paper.pdf.

Chan, Cindy, and Cassie Mogilner. "Experiential Gifts Foster Stronger Social Relationships Than Material Gifts." *Journal of Consumer Research* 43, no. 6 (April 2017): 913-31. https://doi.org/10.1093/jcr/ucw067.

"In one study by researchers from the University of Chicago and Cornell University . . ."

Walker, Jesse, Amit Kumar, and Thomas Gilovich. "Cultivating Gratitude and Giving Through Experiential Consumption." *Emotion* 16, no. 8 (December 2016): 1126-36. https://psycnet.apa.org/doiLanding?doi=10.1037 %2Femo0000242.

"Being grateful fulfills a number of psychological needs . . ."

Polak, Emily L., and Michael E. McCullough. "Is Gratitude an Alternative to Materialism?" *Journal of Happiness Studies* 7 (September 2006): 343-60. http://local.psy.miami.edu/faculty/mmccullough/Papers/gratitude _materialism.pdf.

"In an experiment by researchers at Northeastern University . . ."

Bartlett, Monica Y., and David DeSteno. "Gratitude and Prosocial Behavior: Helping When It Costs You." *Psychological Science* 17, no. 4 (2006): 319-25. https://greatergood.berkeley.edu/images/application_uploads/Bartlett -Gratitude+ProsocialBehavior.pdf.

"A survey led by a researcher from Hofstra University . . ."

Froh, J. J., R. A. Emmons, N. A. Card, Giacomo Bono, and Jennifer A. Wilson. "Gratitude and the Reduced Costs of Materialism in Adolescents." *Journal of Happiness Studies* 12, no. 2 (2011): 289-302. https://emmons .faculty.ucdavis.edu/wp-content/uploads/sites/90/2015/08/2010_1 -materialism1.pdf.

"Between the combination of materialism . . ."

Levine, Madeline. *The Price of Privilege: How Parental Pressure and Material Advantage Are Creating a Generation of Disconnected and Unhappy Kids.* New York: Harper Perennial, 2005.

Wallace, Jennifer Breheny. "Students in High-Achieving Schools Are Now Named an 'at-Risk' Group, Study Says." *Washington Post*, September 26, 2019. https://www.washingtonpost.com/lifestylc/2019/09/26/students -high-achieving-schools-are-now-named-an-at-risk-group/.

"In a 1999 survey by rescarchers at Columbia and Yale Universities . . ."

Luthar, Suniya S., and Karen D'Avanzo. "Contextual Factors in Substance Use: A Study of Suburban and Inner-City Adolescents." *Development and Psychopathology* 11, no. 4 (1999): 845–67. https://doi.org/10.1017 /s0954579499002357.

"Developing specific skills . . ."

Burger, Brynn. *Simple Living Right Now: Ending Life's Chaos and Reclaiming Joy.* Independently published, 2019.

"The average kid above the age of two . . ."

Moses, Lucia. "A Look at Kids' Exposure to Ads." *Adweek*, March 12, 2014. https://www.adweek.com/digital/look-kids-exposure-ads-156191/.

CHAPTER 6: GETTING DIRTY WHILE DOING GOOD

"Despite anti-litter laws and enforcement . . ."

"Key Findings: Litter." Keep America Beautiful. 2010. https://hampton.gov /documentcenter/view/309/litter-factsheet-litter.

"TreePeople, a volunteer group in Los Angeles . . ."

"Let Me Tell You About the Data and the Trees." TreePeople. 2019. https://blog .treepeople.org/treepeople-news/2018/05/salesforce.

"The award is named for William Hornaday . . ."

"William T. Hornaday Awards." Boy Scouts of America. 2019. http://www .scouting.org/awards/hornaday-awards/awards/.

"Garlic mustard is a highly invasive plant species . . ."

"Garlic Mustard." New York Invasive Species Information. July 2, 2019. http:// www.nyis.info/invasive_species/garlic-mustard/.

"As a result, fewer and fewer children are familiar . . ."

Ro, Christine. "Why 'Plant Blindness' Matters—and What You Can Do About It." BBC News, April 28, 2019. http://www.bbc.com/future/story/20190425 -plant-blindness-what-we-lose-with-nature-deficit-disorder.

"Social responsibility generally develops . . ."

Wray-Lake, Laura, Amy Syvertsen, and Constance A. Flanagan. "Developmental Change in Social Responsibility During Adolescence: An Ecological Perspective." *Developmental Psychology* 52, no. 1 (January 30, 2016): 130–42. https://www.ncbi.nlm.nih.gov/pmc/articles/PMC5634966/.

"Researchers at the University of Maryland . . ."

Yagatich, William, Anya M. Galli Robertson, and Dana R. Fisher. "How Local Environmental Stewardship Diversifies Democracy." *Local Environment* 23, no. 4 (2018): 431–47. http://www.cse.umd.edu/uploads/1/7/9/4/17940149 /how_local_environmental_stewardship_diversifies_democracy.pdf.

"A related study by University of Maryland researchers looking at volunteer tree planting initiatives . . ."

Fisher, Dana R., and Anya M. Galli. "Connecting Environmentalism to Democracy Through Environmental Stewardship." *Revue des Science Sociales* 55 (2016). https://journals.openedition.org/revss/1953?lang=en.

"A study of volunteer stream monitors in Wisconsin . . ."

Overdevest, Christine, Cailin Huyck Orr, and Kristine Stepenuck. "Volunteer Stream Monitoring and Local Participation in Natural Resource Issues." *Research in Human Ecology* 11, no. 2 (2004). https://www.human ecologyreview.org/pastissues/her112/overdevestorrstepenuck.pdf.

"Interviews with families who volunteer . . ."

Littlepage, Laura, Elizabeth Obergfell, and Gina Zanin. "Family Volunteering: An Exploratory Study of the Impact on Families." Center for Urban Policy and the Environment. 2003. https://archives.iupui.edu/bitstream /handle/2450/438/31_03-C05_Family_Volunteering.pdf.

"The outdoors element only adds another layer . . ."

Erickson, Martha Farrell. "Shared Nature Experience as a Pathway to Strong Family Bonds." Children and Nature Network. n.d. Accessed December 6, 2019. https://www.childrenandnature.org/wp-content/uploads /2015/04/LWS_Vol1_01.pdf.

"In 1995 psychologist Stephen Kaplan from the University of Michigan . . ."

Kaplan, Stephen. "The Restorative Benefits of Nature: Towards an Integrative Framework." *Journal of Environmental Psychology* 15 (1995): 169–82. https://willsull.net/resources/KaplanS1995.pdf.

"One study by a researcher currently at Cornell University . . ."

Wells, Nancy. "At Home with Nature: Effects of 'Greenness' on Children's Cognitive Functioning." *Environment and Behavior* 32, no. 6 (November 2000), 775–95. https://www.ncrs.fs.fed.us/pubs/jrnl/2000/nc_2000_wells_001.pdf.

"In a similar study, University of Illinois researchers interviewed . . ."

Taylor, Andrea Faber, Frances (Ming) E. Kuo, and William C. Sullivan. "Views of Nature and Self Discipline: Evidence from Inner City Children." *Journal of Environmental Psychology* 22, no. 1-2 (2002): 49–63. https://doi.org/10.1006/jevp.2001.0241.

"A study in Barcelona, Spain, by researchers . . ."

Dadvand, Payam, Mark J. Nieuwenhuijsen, Mikel Esnaola, Joan Forns, Xavier Basagaña, Mar Alvarez-Pedrerol, Ioar Rivas, et al. "Green Spaces and Cognitive Development in Primary Schoolchildren." *PNAS* 112, no. 26 (June 30, 2015): 7937–42. https://www.ncbi.nlm.nih.gov/pmc/articles/PMC4491800/.

"A different but related study in Barcelona . . ."

Amoly, Elmira, Payam Dadvand, Joan Forns, Mónica López-Vicente, Xavier Basagaña, Jordi Julvez, Mar Alvarez-Pedrerol, et al. "Green and Blue Spaces and Behavioral Development in Barcelona Schoolchildren: The BREATHE Project." *Environmental Health Perspectives* 122, no. 12 (2014). https://www.ncbi.nlm.nih.gov/pmc/articles/PMC4256702/.

"Researchers from the University of Illinois asked more than 400 parents . . ."

Kuo, Frances (Ming), and Andrea Faber Taylor. "A Potential Natural Treatment for Attention-Deficit/Hyperactivity Disorder: Evidence from a National Study." *American Journal of Public Health* 94, no. 9 (September 2004): 1580–86. https://www.ncbi.nlm.nih.gov/pmc/articles/PMC1448497/.

"In one study researchers from Western Washington University . . ."

Burgess, Donald J., and Jolie Mayer-Smith. "Listening to Children: Perceptions of Nature." *Journal of Natural History Education and Experience* 5 (2011): 27–43. https://cedar.wwu.edu/secondaryed_facpubs/3.

CHAPTER 7: LISTEN TO THE CHILDREN

"Fridays for Future and Climate Strike were both started . . ."

Kaplan, Sarah. "Teen Girls Are Leading the Climate Strikes and Helping Change the Face of Environmentalism." *Washington Post*, September 25, 2019. https://www.washingtonpost.com/science/2019/09/24/teen-girls -are-leading-climate-strikes-helping-change-face-environmentalism/.

"These movements, which encourage . . ."

Barclay, Eliza, and Brian Resnick. "How Big Was the Global Climate Strike? 4 Million People, Activists Estimate." *Vox*, September 22, 2019. http:// www.vox.com/energy-and-environment/2019/9/20/20876143/climate -strike-2019-september-20-crowd-estimate.

"In a study of a set of marches . . ."

Wahlström, Mattias, Piotr Kocyba, Michiel De Vydt, and Joost de Moor (eds.). "Protest for a Future: Composition, Mobilization and Motives of the Participants in Fridays for Future Climate Protests on 15 March, 2019 in 13 European Cities." Report. 2019. https://doi.org/10.17605/OSF.IO/XCNZH.

"Only 100 companies are responsible for 71 percent . . ."

Riley, Tess. "Just 100 Companies Responsible for 71% of Global Emissions, Study Says." *Guardian*, July 10, 2017. https://www.theguardian.com /sustainable-business/2017/jul/10/100-fossil-fuel-companies-investors -responsible-71-global-emissions-cdp-study-climate-change.

"It was a perfect illustration of three major skill sets . . ."

Christens, Brian D., Kymberly Byrd, N. Andrew Peterson, and David T. Lardier Jr. "Critical Hopefulness Among Urban High School Students." *Journal of Youth and Adolescence* 47, no. 8 (2018): 1649–62. https://doi.org/10.1007 /s10964-018-0889-3.

"Researchers from the University of Colorado Boulder . . ."

Kirshner, Ben, and Shawn Ginwright. "Youth Organizing as a Developmental Context for African American and Latino Adolescents." *Child Development Perspectives* 6, no. 3 (May 2012): 288–94. https://doi .org/10.1111/j.1750-8606.2012.00243.x.

"A study on youth organizing in a Midwestern city . . ."

Kirshner, Ben. "Power in Numbers: Youth Organizing as a Context for Exploring Civic Identity." *Journal of Research on Adolescence* 19, no. 3 (2009): 414–40. https://doi.org/10.1111/j.1532-7795.2009.00601.x.

"One study by Brown University researchers of 124 teenagers . . ."
Mediratta, Kavitha, Seema Shah, Sara McAlister, Norm Fruchter, Christina Mokhtar, and Dana Lockwood. "Organized Communities, Stronger Schools: A Preview of Research Findings." Annenberg Institute for School Reform at Brown University. March 2008. https://www.issuelab.org/resource/organized-communities-stronger-schools-a-preview-of-research-findings.html.

"Early environmentalists who focused on wildlife . . ."
NoiseCat, Julian Brave. "The Environmental Movement Needs to Reckon with Its Racist History." *Vice*, September 13, 2019. https://www.vice.com/en_us/article/bjwvn8/the-environmental-movement-needs-to-reckon-with-its-racist-history.

"In a study led by a researcher from the University of Wisconsin–Madison . . ."
Christens, Brian D., and Tom Dolan. "Interweaving Youth Development, Community Development, and Social Change Through Youth Organizing." *Youth and Society* 43, no. 2 (June 2011): 528–48. https://doi.org/10.1177/0044118X10383647.

"Tying one's identity to activism may cause stress . . ."
Ballard, Parissa J., and Emily J. Ozer. "The Implications of Youth Activism for Health and Well-Being." In *Contemporary Youth Activism: Advancing Social Justice in the United States*, edited by Jerusha Connor and Sonia M. Rosen, 223–44. Santa Barbara, CA: Praeger, 2016.

"A deep-dive case study written by researchers from Stanford and Villanova Universities . . ."
Strobel, Karen, Jerusha Osberg, and Milbrey McLaughlin. "Participation in Social Change: Shifting Adolescents' Developmental Pathways." In *Beyond Resistance! Youth Activism and Community Change: New Democratic Possibilities for Practice and Policy for America's Youth*, edited by Pedro Noguera, Shawn A. Ginwright, and Julio Cammarota, 197–214. New York: Routledge, 2006. http://citeseerx.ist.psu.edu/viewdoc/download?doi=10.1.1.390.5396&rep=rep1&type=pdf.

"In studies of youth organizing . . ."
Larson, R., and D. Hansen. "The Development of Strategic Thinking: Learning to Impact Human Systems in a Youth Activism Program." *Human Development* 48 (2005): 327–49. https://doi.org/10.1159/000088251.

"Unlike almost every other activity in this book . . ."

Ballard, P. J., L. T. Hoyt, and M. C. Pachucki. "Impacts of Adolescent and Young Adult Civic Engagement on Health and Socioeconomic Status in Adulthood." *Child Development* 90, no. 4 (July 2019): 1138–1154. https://doi.org/10.1111/cdev.12998.

CHAPTER 8: ENVISIONING A SUSTAINABLE FUTURE

"In a 2019 poll supported by the *Washington Post* . . ."

Kaplan, Sarah, and Emily Guskin. "Most American Teens Are Frightened by Climate Change, Poll Finds, and About 1 in 4 Are Taking Action." *Washington Post*, September 16, 2019. https://www.washingtonpost.com/science/most-american-teens-are-frightened-by-climate-change-poll-finds-and-about-1-in-4-are-taking-action/2019/09/15/1936da1c-d639-11e9-9610-fb56c5522e1c_story.html.

Kaiser Family Foundation. "Washington Post–Kaiser Family Foundation Climate Change Survey, July 9–Aug. 5, 2019." *Washington Post*, September 16, 2019. https://www.washingtonpost.com/context/washington-post-kaiser-family-foundation-climate-change-survey-july-9-aug-5-2019/601ed8ff-a7c6-4839-b57e-3f5eaa8ed09f/.

"A study by researchers at Uppsala University in Sweden . . ."

Ojala, Maria. "Coping with Climate Change among Adolescents: Implications for Subjective Well-Being and Environmental Engagement." *Sustainability* 5, no. 5 (2013): 2191–2209. https://doi.org/10.3390/su5052191.

"This approach is very similar to the definition of resilience . . ."

Krasny, Marianne E., and Justin Dillon. *Trading Zones in Environmental Education: Creating Transdisciplinary Dialogue*. New York: Peter Lang, 2013.

"While reading books is essential . . ."

Reese, Elaine. *Tell Me a Story: Sharing Stories to Enrich Your Child's World*. New York: Oxford University Press, 2013.

"Researchers from the University of East Anglia in the United Kingdom . . ."

O'Neill, Saffron, and Sophie Nicholson-Cole. "'Fear Won't Do It': Promoting Positive Engagement with Climate Change Through Visual and Iconic Representations." *Science Communication* 30, no. 3 (March 2009): 355–79. https://doi.org/10.1177/1075547008329201.

ACKNOWLEDGMENTS

Thank you first and foremost to my family. To my children, Dylan and Ethan, who inspired this book and so much of my writing over the past six years. You have given me a depth of love and a sense of urgency that I never thought possible. To my husband, Chris, who provided the encouragement, moral support, and practical assistance I needed to write this book. You reminded me that I could do this even when I wasn't sure I could. To my parents, Sherri and Richard Brescher, who have always supported my writing and environmentalism. I wouldn't be here without you introducing me to manatees and the power of editing.

Thank you to everyone I interviewed and observed for this book. I never wanted this book to be about what I personally knew—I always wanted it to draw on the wisdom and knowledge of the larger community. Lending me your expertise made this possible. Thank you to the researchers whose work I quote in this book. Your scientific knowledge is an essential complement to the lived experience I describe.

Thank you to everyone who has taught me what I know about community building and activism. So much of the information in this book about privilege, social justice, and practical skills is because of you. In particular, the good folks from the Rockville Bicycle Advisory Committee and the late, great Ecolocity Transition Towns group have taught me so much.

Thank you to my writing community, which has done so much to support me. I particularly appreciate the many writing groups on Facebook who understand the hilarity and frustrations of writing as a parent. Many thanks to the writers who provided me guidance and feedback as I went through the book proposal process. And of course, thanks to all of the editors I have worked with over the years, especially Dave Nelson and Rick Borchelt, my mentors in science and environmental writing.

Thank you to my book editor, Shayna Keyles, for being willing to take a chance on a book based on a tweet—I still can't believe it either.

Thank you to the many readers of my blog and, of course, this book. It wouldn't make much of a difference without you!

Thank you to the climate change, social justice, and environmental communities who have done so much to move forward on sustainability, especially the Indigenous and Black activists who have made it intersectional. Your work is invaluable.

INDEX

ABOUT THE AUTHOR

Shannon Brescher Shea is devoted to telling authentic, gloriously messy stories about the space where parenting, sustainability, and social justice meet. Her writing appears on her blog, *We'll Eat You Up, We Love You So*, as well as in the *Washington Post*, *Sierra* magazine, *Scary Mommy*, *Ravishly*, and *Romper*. She's performed the story of how she became a third-grade environmentalist at the Story Collider live show and was previously a staff writer for the New York State *Conservationist*. In her day job, she's a science writer for the federal government.

She's been participating in environmental activism in some form or another since she was about ten. Since then, she's participated in more marches against climate change than she can remember (including one when she was five months pregnant), biked 300 miles to raise money for climate change groups, organized community bike rides for families, and helped launch community garden projects.

She lives in the Maryland suburbs of Washington, DC, which she's working to make more environmentally and socially sustainable for all families. To read more of her writing, check out her website (www.welleatyouupweloveyouso.com), like her page on Facebook (@welleatyouupweloveyouso), or follow her on Twitter (@storiteller).

About North Atlantic Books

North Atlantic Books (NAB) is an independent, nonprofit publisher committed to a bold exploration of the relationships between mind, body, spirit, and nature. Founded in 1974, NAB aims to nurture a holistic view of the arts, sciences, humanities, and healing. To make a donation or to learn more about our books, authors, events, and newsletter, please visit www.northatlanticbooks.com.

North Atlantic Books is the publishing arm of the Society for the Study of Native Arts and Sciences, a 501(c)(3) nonprofit educational organization that promotes cross-cultural perspectives linking scientific, social, and artistic fields. To learn how you can support us, please visit our website.